For my mother and my father

A Treasury of

the Sierra Nevada

Edited by
Robert Leonard Reid

WILDERNESS PRESS · BERKELEY

Map by Paul Imazumi
Design by Thomas Winnett
Cover by Larry Van Dyke and Noelle Liebrenz
Library of Congress Card Catalog Number 82-62811
International Standard Book Number 0-89997-032-X (hard cover)
0-89997-023-0 (paperback)
Printed in the United States of America
Published by Wilderness Press
2440 Bancroft Way
Berkeley, CA 94704
Write for free catalog

Acknowledgments

Compiling this collection of writings on the Sierra Nevada has been a pleasure that took me not to the wilderness of the Sierra, but instead to the rather more civilized surroundings of the Green Library at Stanford University. This being the case, I feel obliged to express my gratitude, somewhat belatedly, to Leland Stanford, for establishing in 1891 what has since grown to become one of the world's great libraries. There are few places where one could hope to find a copy of an 1896 *Appalachia* magazine, or a first edition of Jim Beckwourth's autobiography, and I'm fortunate that one such place is located just a few miles from my home.

I owe a huge debt to the authors of two books which enabled me to untangle the sometimes fiendishly interwoven threads of Sierra history. First is the peerless historian of the Sierra, the late Francis P. Farquhar. Farquhar's *History of the Sierra Nevada* (Berkeley, Los Angeles, London: University of California Press, 1965) is a comprehensive, scholarly, and highly readable history of the entire range. The second is Margaret Sanborn, whose *Yosemite* (New York: Random House, 1981) is a thorough and delightful account of the history of the Yosemite region. Besides providing extensive historical background, Ms. Sanborn's book furnished me with an exhaustive bibliography which opened my eyes to many unusual and exciting possibilities for the present work.

When the Green Library failed me, other individuals enthusiastically came to my aid to help me track down fugitive books and articles or to render assistance in other less tangible ways. For such generosity I wish to thank Julie Ahlenius, Dave Bohn, Art Calkins, Helen Chetin, Janice Enns of the Mono Lake Committee, Julia Fuerst, John Ingvoldstad, Sierra Club librarian Barbara Lekisch, Mary Millman, Mark Palmer, The Rev. William K. Reid, Franc de la Vega, Executive Secretary of the American Alpine Club, and Mary Vocelka, Research Librarian at the Yosemite National Park Research Library.

My greatest debt, now as ever, I owe to my wife, Barbara Jurin-Reid.

Robert Leonard Reid
Palo Alto, CA
October, 1982

Contents

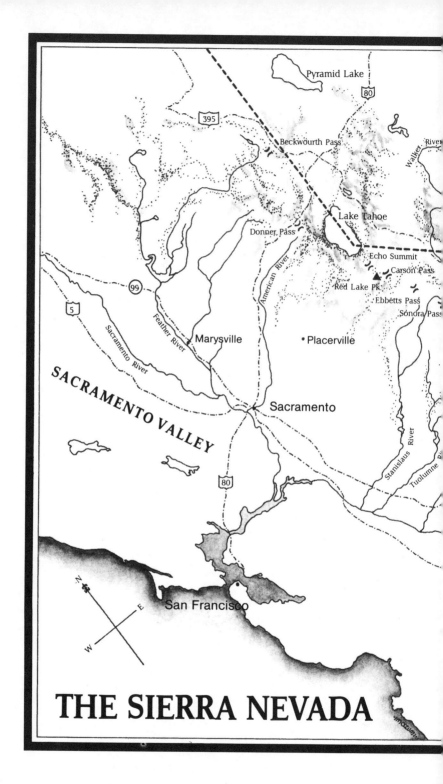

THE SIERRA NEVADA

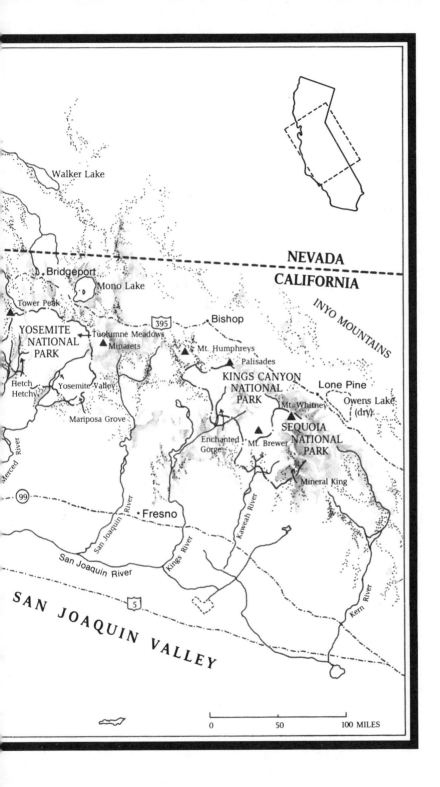

Illustration Credits

The photos by Joseph N. LeConte and Cedric Wright are from those respective collections at the Sierra Club. Prints of them for this work were made by the Bancroft Library.

Introduction

By the mid-18th Century, the practice of writing about mountains was long-established among European writers. As early as the year 1280, King Peter III of Aragon had recorded the somewhat fanciful details of his alleged ascent of the Carigou in the Pyrenees. During the Renaissance, Leonardo da Vinci wrote with his customary precision of the glaciers he observed during his travels in the Alps. And in the mid-16th Century, the Swiss Conrad Gesner set the tone for generations of later mountain writers by exalting at length the joys and the beauties to be found among the high peaks of Switzerland. These were not isolated examples but rather highlights of a continuing tradition. Few Europeans were as enraptured with mountains as Gesner. (On the contrary, most people agreed with the 17th Century English poet Andrew Marvell, who characterized mountains as "ill-designed excrescences.") But even writers who despised the high peaks were not reluctant to record their loathing in print.

In America, however, most writers still had their eyes planted firmly in front of them. A few had looked up briefly at New Hampshire's White Mountains and remarked on the pleasures they fancied were to be found there. But the mountain sense had not yet developed among the nation's men and women of letters; the important matters to be addressed in pre-Revolutionary America were social and political in nature, not Romantic.

Moreover, the great mountain ranges of North America remained almost unknown to European settlers. A handful of French fur traders and explorers had reached the Rocky Mountains. But California's Sierra Nevada had scarcely been glimpsed, let alone written about. To the few seafarers who had sailed along the west coast of North America, inland California was as much of an enigma as the fabled East had been to European explorers of Christopher Columbus's time. Not until 1769 was the first tentative step taken toward unraveling the mysteries of California's interior. In that year, Don Gaspar de Portola and Fray Junipero Serra led an expedition northward from Mexico along an inland route. In the course of their travels they discovered San Francisco Bay, a geographical feature that had been overlooked by sea-going explorers for more than two hundred years.

And what of the California mountains? In 1772 the missionary Fray Juan Crespi climbed to a viewpoint near the newly discovered bay. A grand expanse of inland California opened up before him, stretching past rivers and plains toward the distant eastern horizon. Crespi was impressed enough to record the event in his diary: "We made out that these three arms or three large rivers were formed by a very large river, a league in width at least, which descended from some high mountains to the southeast, very far distant."

It was a humble beginning, but in that moment the practice of writing about the Sierra Nevada was born. Since that day, Crespi's "high mountains to the southeast" have become the subject of a vast and fascinating body of literature. Writers great and small have waxed eloquent and wise—and sometimes embarrassingly maudlin—in their efforts to celebrate and illuminate the magnificent range of mountains which waited so long to reveal itself.

Like the literature of other mountain ranges, that of the Sierra has always reflected the human experience of the range and chosen its focus accordingly. Thus, the earliest writings are the diaries and letters of explorers relating day-to-day hardships as they attempted to cope with the unknown and dangerous peaks. One learns little about the mountain environment from these accounts; the writing necessarily centers on the writer himself and his grim task of getting from one point to the next. Only occasionally does one of these journalists look beyond himself, as when fur trader Zenas Leonard recorded two extraordinary discoveries made during his epic trans-Sierra journey of 1833: giant sequoia trees and Yosemite Valley. Even a mountain man as impassive as Leonard could not fail to be impressed by wonders such as these.

With the path opened, immigrants began to stream into California. And as familiarity with the range increased, Sierra writers could relax and concentrate on their beautiful and increasingly benign surroundings. There were still personal hardships to be recorded, like those one reads of with mounting horror in Patrick Breen's first-person account of the Donner tragedy. But more and more the subject was the Sierra itself. Scientists published detailed records of their observations of Sierra geology, botany and biology. Anthropologists documented the Indian history of the range. Vacationers traveled to Yosemite and by the hundreds were transformed into inept poets; so awed were they by what they saw—and so lacking in self-restraint— that they left behind one of the gooiest collections of poetry extant. A few examples are included herein as illustrations of the perils that can befall the bedazzled tourist who confronts Half Dome or El Capitan for the first time.

Fortunately, these ponderous efforts were the exceptions. By the turn of the century the Sierra had attracted the attention of some of the finest writers of the day. Mark Twain, Walt Whitman, Robert Louis Stevenson and John Muir all had written about the range; Bret Harte had turned out short stories set in the west slope gold fields and Clarence King had enthralled readers of the *Atlantic Monthly* with hair-raising accounts of exploration and mountaineering in the High Sierra.

Although the range had been tamed, Americans still had a soft spot in their hearts for the good old days, when any trip to the high country was an invitation to disaster. The theme of man-against-the-mountains remained as popular as ever, finding new expression in the works of such frontier revivalists as Jack London and Stewart Edward White and in the climbing accounts of the Sierra's growing legions of mountaineers. Simultaneously, John Muir was addressing a second and more alarming theme: man, the destroyer of mountains. Muir combined the sensibility of Conrad Gesner with the zeal of an evangelist and almost singlehandedly invented a new form: the crusading nature essay. He became the foremost practitioner of the form and the model for untold numbers of imitators.

During this century the Sierra has come to be regarded by most people as a place where one goes to experience intimately some aspect of the mountain environment. So it is that the important Sierra writers of our day are the conservationists, the naturalists and the mountain climbers—people like Edwin Way Teale, Kenneth Rexroth, Yvon

Chouinard and William O. Douglas, who see the Sierra as something to enjoy and to learn from, and who understand that mountains have an integrity of their own that demands our respect. At a time when a small but powerful coalition of business interests is promoting the banal notion that mountains are little more than storehouses of petroleum, timber and mineral wealth, it is important that we have such writers to keep the record straight.

The selections that follow in this, the first anthology of writings on the Sierra, provide a generous sampling of the works that have been devoted to the range, from the earliest explorer's account to a modern tale of derring-do on a vertical wall in Yosemite Valley. It is a highly personal collection, chosen to reflect my own crotchety tastes and interests rather than those of a brainstorming committee of Sierra literati. The essential writers are all here—Muir, Harte, Hutchings, King—along with a fair number of surprises. It is this latter group which in many ways is the most interesting. Everyone knows that John Muir wrote exhaustively on the Sierra; so familiar are we with his point of view that we can almost predict what he's going to say before he says it.

But what of Robert Louis Stevenson, Ralph Waldo Emerson, Gary Snyder, and John McPhee? What brought them to the Range of Light, and what did they have to say about it? Both the expected and the unexpected are here to enhance the meaning and the experience of the Sierra for all who know the range well, and for all others who would like to know it. Whether read in the comfort of one's home or by the light of a Sierra campfire, these writings provide compelling evidence that no less than a war, a country, or a king, a mountain range can inspire the creation of an important body of literature.

SECTION I:
THE EXPLORERS

During the first half of the 19th Century, a succession of missionaries, fur traders, soldiers and immigrants penetrated the wilds of the Sierra Nevada, and began to reveal its secrets for the first time to the outside world. What these explorers found in this vast mountain wilderness was news to everyone but the Indians who inhabited the lowlands surrounding the range.

California's native peoples left no written records of their ramblings through the mountains. But we can be sure that they knew the Sierra well. They traded and traveled across the range along routes well-known to backpackers today: up Bloody Canyon and through Mono Pass in the north, over Kearsarge and Taboose passes farther south. They vacationed at high mountain lakes and even climbed some of the peaks. Geologist François Matthes found a bow near the summit of 12,000-foot Parsons Peak, and arrowheads have been discovered on peaks as remote as Tower Peak and as high as Mount Whitney.

But while the truth of the Indians' experience with the Sierra is lost to us, the same is not true of the myth. We know the stories of Py-wi-ack and Tis-sa-ack, the legend of Lost Arrow and many others. Whatever the merits of these tales as history, they form an engaging foundation for the literature of the range.

The recorded history of Sierra exploration began in 1827, when Jed Smith and two companions accomplished the first crossing of the range by white men. Smith was in a sense an unwitting explorer. He was a professional wanderer, and discoveries came with the territory. Half a century later a band of wide-eyed amateurs was roaming the range searching for virgin territory for the pure thrill of it, and

5

exploration-by-vocation had evolved into exploration-for-fun. John Muir began his exultant wanderings in 1869. Mount Whitney, the highest peak in the land, was climbed for the first time in 1873 by a trio of fishermen off on a lark. Lil Winchell and Frank Dusy ranged over the wilds of the North and Middle forks of the Kings River for no better reason than that they wondered what was there.

With the formation of the Sierra Club in 1892, amateur exploration became a religion. No issue of the Sierra Club *Bulletin* was complete without several solemn accounts of sublime passes traversed, of Gothic spires ascended. Maps, the documents that officially domesticate wild country, began to disclose the final secrets—the tarns, the pocket glaciers, the seasonal streams. When Thunderbolt Peak, the last unclimbed 14,000-foot peak in the range, was finally ascended in 1931, the century-long Age of Exploration that began with Jed Smith came to an end.

The task of tying up the loose ends fell to the rock climbers and the backpackers. Like the Indians, they recorded their discoveries primarily in campfire tales and memories (and, unlike the Indians, in albums-full of cherished photographs). They too left only inferential signs of their passing, not arrowheads but rusting tin cans and piton scars. The last significant summits, couloirs, and cirques were visited during the Thirties and Forties. (Remarkably, a fine 12,000-foot peak near Mount Ritter remained unclimbed until 1964.)

Perhaps a saddle or a pile of rocks remains yet to be trod upon for the first time. Many cross-country travelers allow themselves to believe so. Few, however, have not had the crushing experience of wandering in exhilaration through some Sierra Eden seemingly glistening in primeval dew, only to come upon the imprint of a Vibram sole outlined derisively on the ground before them. The only certainly unvisited spots that remain are on some of the vertical walls and buttresses of Yosemite Valley and the High Sierra, where today's rock climbers seek out the final inches of unexplored terrain.

Stephen Powers

The Origin of the Mountains

The first person to undertake a serious anthropological study of California's Indians was not an anthropologist at all but rather a journalist, Stephen Powers. In 1869 Powers performed the extraordinary feat of walking from Raleigh, North Carolina, to San Francisco, a 3,700-mile journey that occupied him for 10 months. Soon after his arrival in California, he began his study of the state's Indians. During the next several years he lived and traveled among several dozen northern California tribes, learning their languages and documenting their customs and legends. Although Powers was an amateur ethnologist, his pioneering study of the native people, Tribes of California, *is still regarded as the best introduction to the subject.*

During Powers's sojourn among the Yokuts, the tribe that inhabited the region west of the southern Sierra, he learned the Yokut legend of the creation of the Sierra.

Once there was a time when there was nothing in the world but water. About the place where Tulare Lake is now, there was a pole standing far up out of the water, and on this pole perched a hawk and a crow. First one of them would sit on the pole awhile, then the other would knock him off and sit on it himself. Thus they sat on top of the pole above the waters for many ages. At length they wearied of the lonesomeness, and they created the birds which prey on fish such as the kingfisher, eagle, pelican, and others. Among them was a very small duck, which dived down to the bottom of the water, picked its beak full of mud, came up, died, and lay floating on the water. The hawk and the crow then fell to work and gathered from the duck's beak the earth which it had brought up, and commenced making the mountains. They began at the place now known as Ta-hi'-cha-pa Pass, and the hawk made the east range, while the crow made the west one.

Little by little, as they dropped in the earth, these great mountains grew athwart the face of the waters, pushing north. It was a work of many years, but finally they met together at Mount Shasta, and their labors were ended. But, behold, when they compared their mountains, it was found that the crow's was a great deal the larger. Then the hawk said to the crow, "How did this happen, you rascal? I warrant you have been stealing some of the earth from my bill, and that is why your mountains are the biggest." It was a fact, and the crow laughed in his claws. Then the hawk went and got some Indian tobacco and chewed it, and it made him exceedingly wise. So he took hold of the mountains and turned them round in a circle, putting his range in place of the crow's; and that is why the Sierra Nevada is larger than the Coast Range.

Bertha H. Smith

Hum-Moo, the Lost Arrow

As Powers's stolid reading of the previous legend makes clear, he disapproved of the practice of embellishing Indian myths in order to entertain an audience. He complained that popular accounts of the legend of Tis-sa-ack depicted her as a goddess rather than the "prosaic and commonplace" woman he knew her to be.

Nevertheless, entertainment won out, and romanticized versions of the Indian myths rapidly became part of the lore of the Sierra. Perhaps the most famous is the legend of Yosemite Valley's Lost Arrow, a tale Powers labeled a complete fabrication. (An Indian of his acquaintance, he claimed, dismissed the story with the contemptuous remark, "White man too much lie.") The following version, published in 1904, features a fair maiden with laughing eyes the color of acorns and a voice like the patter of rain on green leaves. Powers doubtless would have disapproved.

Tee-Hee-Neh was the fairest of the daughters of Ah-wah-nee, and the happiest, for she was the chosen bride of the brave Kos-soo-kah.

When she went forth from her father's lodge to bathe in the depths of Ke-koo-too-yem, the Sleeping Water, her step was light as the touch of a wind-swept leaf upon the rocks. When she stooped to lave her cheeks in the cool spray, her dark hair fell about her shoulders like a silken web, and the water mirror showed her a pair of laughing eyes of the color of ripened acorns, and in them the soft light of an Indian summer day. The sound of her voice was as the patter of rain on green leaves, and her heart was fearless and full of love.

No other woman of the tribe could weave such baskets as grew by the magic skill of her fingers, and she alone knew the secret of interweaving the bright feathers of the redheaded woodpecker and the topknots of mountain quail. Her acorn bread was always sweetest, the berries she gathered ripest, the deerskin she tanned softer than any

9

other; and all because of the love in her heart, for she knew that Kos-soo-kah would eat of her bread and fruit, would drink from the baskets she wove, would wear upon his feet the moccasins she made.

Kos-soo-kah was a hunter, fearless and bold, sure with bow and spear, always fortunate in the chase. In his veins ran the blood that surges hot when there are daring deeds to do, and of all the young chiefs of Ah-wah-nee he had the greatest power among his people. Like the wooing of the evening star by the crescent moon was the mating of Tee-hee-neh with Kos-soo-kah; and when the young chief gathered together robes of squirrel and deerskin and of the skins of water-fowl, arrows and spear-heads, strings of coral and bear teeth, and gave them as a marriage token to Tee-hee-neh's father, the old chief looked upon him with favor.

This was their marriage. But before Tee-hee-neh should go with Kos-soo-kah to his lodge there must be a great feast, and all day long Ah-wah-nee was astir with signs of preparation.

From many shady places came a sound like the tap-tap-tapping of woodpeckers, where the older women sat upon smooth, flat rocks pounding dried acorns into meal to make the acorn bread; and the younger women went with their baskets to the meadows and woods for grass seeds, herbs and wild honey.

Early in the morning Kos-soo-kah left his lodge and gathered about him the strongest of the young braves to go forth into the forest and net the grouse, and seek the bear and deer in their haunts, for this was the man's share of the marriage feast. While his hunters strung their bows and fastened arrow-heads to the feathered shafts, Kos-soo-kah stole away for a last word with Tee-hee-neh, his bride; and when they parted it was with the promise that at the end of the day's hunt Kos-soo-kah should drop an arrow from the cliff between Cho-look, the High Fall, and Le-ham-i-te, the Cañon of the Arrow-wood. By the number of feathers it bore, Tee-hee-neh could tell what the kill had been.

The morning mists were still tangled in the pines when Kos-soo-kah and his hunters began to climb the trail that cut into the heart of the forest. From a covert spot Tee-hee-neh watched her lover disappear through the cleft in the northern wall, where the arrow-wood grows thick; then she joined the other women and worked with a light heart until long shadows stretched across the meadow and warned her of the hour when she was to be near the foot of Cho-look to receive the message from Kos-soo-kah.

Far over the mountains Kos-soo-kah laughed loud with a hunter's pride as he bound to his swiftest arrow all the feathers of a grouse's wing. Sped by a hunter's pride and a lover's pride he leaped along the rocky trail, far in advance of the youthful braves of his band who bore among them the best of the kill. Eagerly he watched the western sky, fearful lest the sun's last kiss should tinge the brow of Tis-sa-ack[1] before he reached the cliff whence his bow should let fly the message to the waiting one below.

The frightened quail fluttered in his path unseen. A belated vulture, skimming the fading sky, seemed not to be in motion. So swiftly Kos-soo-kah ran, the wind stood still to let him pass.

He reached the valley wall at last, his strength well spent but still enough to pull his bow to a full half-circle. Poised for an instant, the feathered shaft caught on its tip a sun ray, then flew downward; but though mighty and sure the force that sent it, no message came to the faithful Tee-hee-neh.

Hour after hour she waited, the joy in her heart changing to a nameless fear as the blue sky faded gray, and the gray went purple in the thickening dusk, and yet no sign, no sound of the returning hunters.

"Kos-soo-kah! Kos-soo-kah!" trembled her voice in the stillness. Only a weird echo answered, "Kos-soo-kah."

Perhaps they had wandered far, and Kos-soo-kah could not reach the cliff till the night shadows had crept out of the valley, and over the tops of the mountains. Perhaps even now he was returning down the Cañon of the Arrow-wood. This she whispered to a heart that gave no answering hope.

She would go forward to meet him, and hear from his lips the message which the arrow failed to bring. As she hurried along the narrow trail, clinging to the slanting ledges, pushing aside the overhanging branches, she called and called, "Kos-soo-kah!"

---

[1] Half Dome

Now and again she stopped to listen for the sound of voices or of footsteps, but only the cry of a night bird or the crackling of dry twigs stirred the still air.

Trembling with uncertainty and fear, she reached the top of the sharp ascent. There by the light of the stars she saw fresh footprints in the loose, moist earth. Her heart told her they were his; her quick eye told her they went toward the cliff, but did not return. Crouching there beside them, she called again, "Kos-soo-kah!" Not even an echo answered the despairing cry.

Slowly she crept forward, following the fresh trail to the edge of the wall. She leaned far over, and there on a mound of fallen rock lay her lover, motionless, nor answering her call. Tight in his grasp was the spent bow, the sign of a promise kept.

As she looked, there came again to Tee-hee-neh's mind the dull roar of rending rock, the low moan of falling earth, that ran through the valley at the sunset hour. Now she knew that as Kos-soo-kah drew his bow to speed the messenger of love, the ground beneath his feet had given way, carrying him with the fatal avalanche.

The girl's heart no longer beat fast with fear. It seemed not to beat at all. But there was no time for grief,—perhaps Kos-soo-kah had not ceased to breathe. On the topmost point of rock she lighted a signal fire, and forced its flames high into the dark, flashing a call for help. It would be long, she knew, before any one could come; but this was the only chance to save Kos-soo-kah.

Hours passed. With feverish energy she piled dry branches high upon the signal fire, nor let its wild beckonings rest a moment. At last old men came from the valley, and the young braves from the mountains bearing with them the carcasses of deer and bear.

With their hunting-knives they cut lengths of tamarack, and lashed them together with thongs of hide from the deer killed for the marriage feast. By means of this pole they would have lowered over the edge of the cliff a strong young brave but that Tee-hee-neh pushed him aside and took his place. Hers must be the voice to whisper in Kos-soo-kah's ear the first word of hope; hers the hand to push aside the rocks that pinioned his body; hers the face his slowly opening eyes should see.

They lowered her to his side; and, loosing the cords that bound

The Lost Arrow

her, she knelt beside him, whispering in his ear, "Kos-soo-kah!" No
sound came from the cold, set lips. The wide-open eyes stared
unseeing at the sky. Tee-hee-neh knew that he was dead.

She did not cry aloud after the manner of Indian women in their
grief, but gently bound the helpless form with the deerskin cords and
raised it as high as her arms could reach when the pole was drawn
upward; then waited in silence until she was lifted by the willing
hands above.

When she found herself again at Kos-soo-kah's side, she stood for
an instant with eyes fixed upon the loved form, there in the cold,
starless dawn of her marriage day; then with his name upon her lips
she fell forward upon his breast. They drew her away, but the spirit of
Tee-hee-neh had followed the spirit of Kos-soo-kah.

The two were placed together upon the funeral pyre, and with
them was burned all that had been theirs. In Kos-soo-kah's hand was
the bow, but the arrow could not be found. The lovers had spirited
it away. In its stead they left a pointed rock lodged in the cliff between
Cho-look, the High Fall, and Le-ham-i-te, the Cañon of the Arrow-
wood, in token of Kos-soo-kah's fulfilled pledge. This rock is known
to the children of Ah-wah-nee as Hum-moo, the Lost Arrow.

Hum-Moo, the Lost Arrow, from *Yosemite Legends* by Bertha H. Smith. Paul
Elder & Co., 1904.

Jedediah Smith

Crossing Mount Joseph[1]

The decline of the Sierra's Indian population may be said to have begun with the arrival of white men in the range. Jedediah Smith, who was to die with an arrow in his side, was the first of these. Smith was one of the greatest of the mountain men, opening Wyoming's South Pass to the fur trade in 1824 and completing the first journey from the Mississippi River to California in 1826.

On the latter journey, Smith and his party bypassed the Sierra completely on the way west, entering the state by a southern route through the Mojave Desert and Cajon Pass. But on his return to the Great Salt Lake in the spring of 1827, Smith chose a route farther to the north. Twice he attempted to cross the Sierra, once on the Kings River, once on the American; both times he was turned back by snow and high water.

Finally he struck the Stanislaus and with Silas Gobel and Robert Evans succeeded in breaching the range near today's Ebbetts Pass. Smith's diary of the adventure has never turned up. But he later described the crossing of Mount Joseph—Smith's name for the Sierra—in a letter to General William Clark.

On my arrival in the province of Upper California, I was looked upon with suspicion, and was compelled to appear in presence of the governor of the Californias residing at San Diego, where, by the assistance of some American gentlemen (especially Capt. W. H. Cunningham, of the ship Courier from Boston) I was enabled to obtain permission to return with my men the route I came, and purchased such supplies as I stood in want of. The governor would

---

[1]Crossing Mount Joseph, reprinted by permission of the Publishers, The Arthur H. Clark Company, from *The Ashley-Smith Explorations and the Discovery of a Central Route to the Pacific, 1822-1829* by Harrison Dale. Copyright 1941, The Arthur H. Clark Company.

not allow me to trade up the sea coast towards Bodaga. I returned to my party and purchased such articles as were necessary, and went eastward of the Spanish settlements on the route I had come in. I then steered my course N.W. keeping from 150 miles to 200 miles from the sea coast. A very high range of mountains lay on the east. After travelling three hundred miles in that direction through a country somewhat fertile, in which there was a great many Indians, mostly naked and destitute of arms, with the exception of a few bows and arrows and what is very singular amongst Indians, they cut their hair to the length of three inches; they proved to be friendly; their manner of living is on fish, roots, acorns and grass.

On my arrival at the river which I named the *Wim-mul-che* (named after a tribe of Indians which resides on it, of that name) I found a few beaver, and elk, deer, and antelope in abundance. I here made a small hunt, and attempted to take my party across the [mountain] which I before mentioned, and which I called *Mount Joseph*, to come on and join my partners at the Great Salt lake. I found the snow so deep on Mount Joseph that I could not cross my horses, five of which starved to death; I was compelled therefore to return to the valley which I had left, and there, leaving my party, I started with two men, seven horses and two mules, which I loaded with hay for the horses and provisions for ourselves, and started on the 20th of may, and succeeded in crossing it in eight days, having lost only two horses and one mule. I found the snow on the top of this mountain from 4 to 8 feet deep, but it was so consolidated by the heat of the sun that my horses only sunk from half a foot to one foot deep.

After travelling twenty days from the east side of Mount Joseph, I struck the s.w. corner of the Great Salt lake, travelling over a country completely barren and destitute of game. We frequently travelled without water sometimes for two days over sandy deserts, where there was no sign of vegetation and when we found water in some of the rocky hills, we most generally found some Indians who appeared the most miserable of the human race having nothing to subsist on (nor any clothing) except grass seed, grass-hoppers, etc. When we arrived at the Salt lake, we had but one horse and one mule remaining, which were so feeble and poor that they could scarce carry the little camp equipage which I had along; the balance of my horses I was compelled to eat as they gave out.

The company are now staring, and therefore must close my communication. Yours respectfully,

> (signed) JEDEDIAH S. SMITH, of the firm of Smith, Jackson and Sublette.

Zenas Leonard

Across the Giddy Heights

Six years later another party traversed the Sierra farther south and left a considerably more detailed account of its journey. In 1833 a contingent of fur trappers under the leadership of an iron-hard mountain man named Joe Walker set out from the Great Salt Lake in search of beaver. Across Utah and Nevada they encountered plenty of hostile Indians but no beaver and no game of any consequence. Several months later they arrived on the east side of the Sierra nearly destitute of food.

It was now October and early winter storms awaited the party in the mountains ahead. Attempting to cross an unknown range under such conditions was hardly prudent, but the trappers had little choice: to return across the Nevada badlands was out of the question. Besides, they were convinced that the pleasures of fabled California lay only a few days ahead. Somewhere near today's settlement of Bridgeport, California, on a branch of the East Walker River, they headed upward into the High Sierra. Expedition clerk Zenas Leonard recorded the grim events of the days that followed, and the two extraordinary discoveries the party made which have earned it a place in history.

In the evening the balance of our scouting parties returned, but none of them had killed any game. One of them had found an Indian path, which they thought led over the mountain—whereupon it was resolved that in the morning we would take this path, as it seemed to be our only prospect of preservation. Accordingly, at an early hour the next morning we started on our journey along the foot of the mountain in search of the path discovered in the previous day, and found it. On examination we found that horses travelled it, and must of course come from the west. This gave us great encouragement, as we were very fearful we would not be able to get our horses over at all.

18

Here we encamped for the night. In the morning we started on our toilsome journey. Ascending the mountain we found to be very diffi-cult from the rocks and its steepness. This day we made but poor speed, and encamped on the side of the mountain.

Oct. 16. Continued our course until in the afternoon, when we arrived at what we took for the top, where we again encamped, but without any thing to eat for our horses, as the ground was covered with a deep snow, which from appearance, lays on the North side of the peaks, the whole year around. These peaks are generally covered with rocks and sand,—totally incapable of vegetation; except on the South side, where grows a kind of Juniper or Gin shrub, bearing a berry tasting similar to gin. Here we passed the night without anything to eat except these gin berries, and some of the insects from the lake described above, which our men had got from the Indians. We had not suffered much from cold for several months previous to this; but this night, surrounded as we were with the everlasting snows on the summit of this mountain, the cold was felt with three fold severity. . . .

The next morning it was with no cheerful prospect that each man prepared himself for travelling, as we had nothing to eat worth mentioning. As we advanced, in the hollows sometimes we would encounter prodigious quantities of snow. When we would come to such places, a certain portion of the men would be appointed alternately to go forward and break the road, to enable our horses to get through; and if any of the horses would get swamped, these same men were to get them out. In this tedious and tiresome manner we spent the whole day without going more than 8 or 10 miles. In some of these ravines where the snow is drifted from the peaks, it never entirely melts, and may be found at this season of the year, from ten to one hundred feet deep. From appearance it never melts on the top, but in warm weather the heap sinks by that part melting which lays next the ground. This day's travel was very severe on our horses, as they had not a particle to eat. They began to grow stupid and stiff, and we began to despair of getting them over the mountain. We encamped this night on the south side of one of these peaks or ridges without any thing to eat, and almost without fire. To add to the troubles and fatigues which we encountered in the day time, in getting over the rocks and through the snow, we had the mortification this evening to find that some of our men had become almost unmanageable, and were desirous of turning back and retracing our steps to the buffaloe country! The voice of the majority, which always directs the movements of such a company, would not pacify them; nor had the earnest appeals of our captain any effect. The distance was too great for them to undertake without being well provided, and the only way they could be prevented, was by not letting them have any of the horses or ammunition. Two of our horses were so much reduced that it was thought they would not be able to travel in the morning at all, whereupon it was agreed that they should be butchered for the use of the men. This gave our men fresh courage, and we went to bed this night in better spirits than we had done for a long time. Some of the men had fasted so long, and were so much in want of nourishment, that they did not know when they had satisfied the demands of nature, and eat as much and as eagerly of this black, tough, lean, horse flesh, as if it had been the choicest piece of beef steak.

In the morning, after freely partaking of the horse meat, and sharing the remainder to each man, we renewed our journey, now and then coming onto an Indian path, but as they did not lead in the direction we were going, we did not follow them—but the most of the distance we this day travelled, we had to encounter hills, rocks and deep snows. The snow in most of the hollows we this day passed through, looks as if it had remained here all summer, as eight or ten inches from the top it was packed close and firm—the top being loose and light, having fell only a day or two previous. About the middle of the afternoon we arrived at a small Lake or pond where we concluded to encamp, as at this pond we found a small quantity of very indifferent grass, but which our horses cropped off with great eagerness. Here we spent the night, having yet seen nothing to create a hope that we had arrived near the opposite side of the mountain— and what was equally as melancholy, having yet discovered no signs of game.

The next morning we resumed our labour, fortunately finding less snow and more timber, besides a number of small lakes, and some prospect of getting into a country that produced some kind of vegetation. The timber is principally pine, cedar and red wood, mostly of a scrubby and knotty quality. After travelling a few miles, further however, than any other day since we had reached the top of the mountain, we again encamped on the margin of another small lake, where we also had the good fortune to find some pasture for our horses. This evening it was again decided to kill three more of our horses which had grown entirely worthless from severe travelling and little food. The next morning several parties were despatched on search of a pass over the mountain, and to make search for game; but they all returned in the evening without finding either. The prospect at this time began to grow somewhat gloomy and threaten us with hard times again. We were at a complete stand. No one was acquainted with the country, nor no person knew how wide the summit of this mountain was.—We had travelled for five days since we arrived at what we supposed to be the summit—were now still surrounded with snow and rugged peaks—the vigour of every man almost exhausted—nothing to give our poor horses, which were no longer any assistance to us in travelling, but a burthen, for we had to help the most of them along as we would an old and feeble man. . . .

We travelled a few miles every day, still on the top of the mountain, and our course continually obstructed with snow hills and rocks. Here we began to encounter in our path, many small streams which would shoot out from under these high snow-banks, and after running a short distance in deep chasms which they have through ages cut in the rocks, precipitate themselves from one lofty precipice to another, until they are exhausted in rain below.—Some of these precipices appeared to us to be more than a mile high. Some of the men thought that if we could succeed in descending one of these precipices to the bottom, we might thus work our way into the valley below—but on making several attempts we found it utterly impossible for a man to descend, to say nothing of our horses.

One of the men found some acorns, which "caused no little rejoicing in our camp, not only on account of their value as food, but because they gave us the gratifying evidence that a country mild and salubrious enough to produce acorns was not far distant. . . ." Several days passed and the way now began to grow easier.

In two or three days we arrived at the brink of the mountain. This at first was a happy sight, but when we approached close, it seemed to be so near perpendicular that it would be folly to attempt a descent. In looking on the plain below with the naked eye, you have one of the most singular prospects in nature; from the great height of the mountain the plain presents a dim yellow appearance;—but on taking a view with the spy glass we found it to be a beautiful plain stretched out towards the west until the horizon presents a barrier to the sight. From the spot where we stood to the plain beneath, must at least be a distance of three miles, as it is almost perpendicular, a person cannot look down without feeling as if he was wafted to and fro in the air, from the giddy height. A great many were the surmises as to the distance and direction to the nearest point of the Pacific. Captain Walker, who was a man well acquainted with geography, was of the opinion that it was not much further than we could see with the aid of our glass, as the plain had the appearance of a sea shore. Here we encamped for the night, and sent men out to discover some convenient passage down towards the plain—who returned after an absence of a few hours and reported that they had discoverd a pass or Indian trail which they thought would answer our purpose,and also some signs of deer and bear, which was equally as joyful news—as we longed to have a taste of some palatable food. The next morning after pursuing our course a few miles along the edge of the mountain top we arrived at the path discovered by our men, and immediately commenced the descent, gladly leaving the cold and famished region of the snow behind. The mountain was extremely steep and difficult to descend, and the only way we could come any speed was by taking a zigzag direction, first climbing along one side and then turning to the other, until we arrived at a ledge or precipice of rocks, of great height, and extending eight or ten miles along the mountain—where we halted and sent men in each direction to ascertain if there was any possibilty of getting over this obstruction. In the afternoon of the same day our men returned without finding any safe passage thro' the rocks—but one man had succeeded in killing a small deer, which he carried all the way to camp on his back—this was dressed,cooked and eat in less time than a hungry wolf would devour a lamb.

    This was the first game larger than a rabbit we had killed since the 4th of August when we killed the last buffaloe near the Great Salt Lake, and the first we had eat since our dried meat was exhausted, (being 14 days,) during which time we lived on stale and forbidden horse flesh. I was conscious that it was not such meat as a dog would feast on, but we were driven to extremes and had either to do this or die. It was the most unwholesome as well as the most unpleasant food I ever eat or ever expect to eat—and I hope that no other person will ever be compelled to go through the same. It seemed to be the greatest cruelty to take your rifle, when your horse sinks to the ground from starvation, but still manifests a desire and willingness to follow you, to shoot him in the head and then cut him up & take such parts of their flesh as extreme hunger alone will render it possible for a human being to eat. This we done several times, and it was the only thing that saved us from death. 24 of our horses died since we arrived on top of the mountain—17 of which we eat the best parts.

When our men returned without finding any passage over the rocks, we searched for a place that was as smooth and gradual in the descent as possible, and after finding one we brought our horses, and by fastening ropes round them let them down one at a time without doing them any injury. After we got our horses and baggage all over the rocks we continued our course down the mountain, which still continued very steep and difficult. The circumstance of one of our men killing a deer greatly cheered the languid spirits of our hunters, and after we got safely over the rocks several of the men started out on search of game, although it was then near night. The main body continued on down until we arrived at some green oak bushes, where we encamped for the night, to wait for out hunters,—who returned soon after dark well paid for their labour, having killed two large black tailed deer and a black bear, and all very fat and in good eating order. This night we passed more cheerful and in better heart than any we had spent for a long time. Our meat was dressed and well cooked, and every man felt in good order to partake of it.

In descending the mountain this far we have found but little snow, and began to emerge into a country which had some signs of vegetation—having passed thro' several groves of green oak bushes, &c. The principal timber which we came across, is Red-Wood, White Cedar and the Balsom tree. We continued down the side of the mountain at our leisure, finding the timber much larger and better, game more abundant and the soil more fertile. Here we found plenty of oak timber, bearing a large quantity of acorns though of a different kind from those taken from the Indian on the mountain top. In the evening of the 30th we arrived at the foot or base of this mountain— having spent almost a month in crossing over. Along the base of this mountain it is quite romantic—the soil is very productive—the timber is immensely large and plenty, and game, such as deer, elk, grizzly bear and antelopes are remarkably plenty.—From the mountain out to the plain, a distance varying from 10 to 20 miles, the timber stands as thick as it could grow, and the land is well watered by a number of small streams rising here and there along the mountain. In the last two days travelling we have found some trees of the Red-wood species, incredibly large—some of which would measure from 16 to 18 fathoms round the trunk at the height of a man's head from the ground.

On the 31st we pursued our course towards the plain in a western direction.

Across the Giddy Heights, from *Narrative of the Adventures of Zenas Leonard,* by Zenas Leonard. R.R. Donnelley & Sons Co., 1934. Reprinted by permission of R.R. Donnelley & Sons Co.

John Charles Frémont

Crossing Carson Pass

Thus ended the first east-to-west crossing of the Sierra, a journey notable not only for the appalling conditions under which it was accomplished, but also for two important discoveries made during the final days of the ordeal. The valley flanked by lofty precipices that Leonard mentioned was almost certainly Yosemite Valley; the huge trees were sequoias. To the members of the Walker party goes the distinction of being the first white men to view these wonders of nature.

Walker crested the range in the vicinity of Virginia Pass. Farther north lies Carson Pass, first crossed during another perilous journey a decade later. In the depths of the winter of 1844, Lieutenant John Charles Frémont led a U.S. Army survey party from northwestern Nevada into the Carson Valley east of the Sierra. The party, an exceptionally strong one, included the famous scouts Kit Carson and Thomas Fitzpatrick.

Frémont had hoped now to head east across the Great Basin to the Rocky Mountains. But his provisions were low and his stock unfit for the eastward journey. He decided instead to cross the Sierra and resupply in the Sacramento Valley. Frémont's decision could not have been an easy one to reach, for the month was February and he was committing his party to an unknown route and to the first Sierra crossing ever attempted in the winter.

In the morning I acquainted the men with my decision, and explained to them that necessity required us to make a great effort to clear the mountains. I reminded them of the beautiful valley of the Sacramento, with which they were familiar from the descriptions of Carson, who had been there some fifteen year ago, and who, in our late privations, had delighted us in speaking of its rich pastures and abounding game, and drew a vivid contrast between its summer climate, less than a hundred miles distant, and the falling snow around us. I informed them (and long experience had given them confidence in my observations and good instruments) that almost directly west, and only about 70 miles distant, was the great farming establishment of Captain Sutter—a gentleman who had formerly lived in Missouri, and, emigrating to this country, had become the possessor of a principality. I assured them that, from the heights of the mountain before us, we should doubtless see the valley of the Sacramento river, and with one effort place ourselves again in the midst of plenty. The people received this decision with the cheerful obedience which had always characterized them; and the day was immediately devoted to the preparations necessary to enable us to carry it into effect. Leggings, moccasins, clothing—all were put into the best state to resist the cold. Our guide was not neglected. Extremity of suffering might make him desert; we therefore did the best we could for him. Leggings, moccasins, some articles of clothing, and a large green blanket, in addition to the blue and scarlet cloth, were lavished upon him, and to his great and evident contentment. He arrayed himself in all his colors; and, clad in green, blue, and scarlet, he made a gay-looking Indian; and, with his various presents, was probably richer and better clothed than any of his tribe had ever been before.

I have already said that our provisions were very low; we had neither tallow nor grease of any kind remaining, and the want of salt became one of our greatest privations. The poor dog which had been found in the Bear river valley, and which had been a *compagnon de voyage* ever since, had now become fat, and the mess to which it belonged requested permission to kill it. Leave was granted. Spread out on the snow, the meat looked very good; and it made a strengthening meal for the greater part of the camp. Indians brought in two or three rabbits during the day, which were purchased from them. . . .

February 2.—It had ceased snowing, and this morning the lower air was clear and frosty; and six or seven thousand feet above, the peaks of the Sierra now and then appeared among the rolling clouds, which were rapidly disappearing before the sun. Our Indian shook his head as he pointed to the icy pinnacles, shooting high up into the sky, and seeming almost immediately above us. Crossing the river on the ice, and leaving it immediately, we commenced the ascent of the mountain along the valley of a tributary stream. The people were unusually silent; for every man knew that our enterprise was hazardous, and the issue doubtful.

The snow deepened rapidly, and it soon became necessary to break a road. For this service, a party of ten was formed, mounted on the strongest horses; each man in succession opening the road on foot, or on horseback, until himself and his horse became fatigued, when he stepped aside; and the remaining number passing ahead, he took his station in the rear. Leaving this stream, and pursuing a very direct course, we passed over an intervening ridge to the river we had left. On the way we passed two low huts entirely covered with snow, which might very easily have escaped observation. A family was living in each; and the only trail I saw in the neighborhood was from the door hole to a nut-pine tree near, which supplied them with food and fuel. We found two similar huts on the creek where we next arrived; and, travelling a little higher up, encamped on its banks in about four feet depth of snow. Carson found near, an open hill side, where the wind and the sun had melted the snow, leaving exposed sufficient bunch grass for the animals to-night. . . .

February 4. — I went ahead early with two or three men, each with a led horse, to break the road. We were obliged to abandon the hollow entirely, and work along the mountain side, which was very steep and the snow covered with an icy crust. We cut a footing as we advanced, and trampled a road through for the animals; but occasionally one plunged outside the trail, and slided along the field to the bottom, a hundred yards below. Late in the day we reached another bench in the hollow, where in summer, the stream passed over a small precipice. Here was a short distance of dividing ground between the two ridges, and beyond an open basin, some ten miles across, whose bottom presented a field of snow. At the further or western side rose the middle crest of the mountain, a dark-looking ridge of volcanic rock.

The summit line presented a range of naked peaks, apparently destitute of snow and vegetation; but below, the face of the whole country was covered with timber of extraordinary size. Annexed [as a sketch in the book] you are presented with a view of this ridge from a camp on the western side of the basin.

Towards a pass which the guide indicated here, we attempted in the afternoon to force a road; but after a laborious plunging through two or three hundred yards, our best horses gave out, entirely refusing to make any further effort; and, for the time, we were brought to a stand. The guide informed us that we were entering the deep snow, and here began the difficulties of the mountain; and to him, and almost to all our enterprise seemed hopeless. . . .

To-night we had no shelter, but we made a large fire around the trunk of one of the huge pines; and covering the snow with small boughs, on which we spread our blankets, soon made ourselves comfortable. The night was very bright and clear, though the thermometer was only at 10°. A strong wind, which sprang up at sundown, made it intensely cold; and this was one of the bitterest nights during the journey.

Two Indians joined our party here; and one of them, an old man, immediately began to harangue us, saying that ourselves and animals would perish in the snow; and that if we would go back he would show us another and a better way across the mountain. He spoke in a very loud voice, and there was a singular repetition of phrases and arrangement of words, which rendered his speech striking, and not unmusical.

We had now begun to understand some words, and, with the aid of signs, easily comprehended the old man's simple ideas. "Rock upon rock—rock upon rock—snow upon snow—snow upon snow," said he; "even if you get over the snow, you will not be able to get down from the mountains." He made us the sign of precipices, and showed us how the feet of the horses would slip, and throw them off from the narrow trails which led along their sides. Our Chinook, who comprehended even more readily than ourselves and believed our situation hopeless, covered his head with his blanket, and began to weep and lament. "I wanted to see the whites," said he; "I came away from my own people to see the whites, and I wouldn't care to die among them; but here"—and he looked around into the cold night and gloomy forest, and, drawing his blanket over his head, began again to lament.

Seated around the tree, the fire illuminating the rocks and the tall bolls of the pines round about, and the old Indian haranguing, we presented a group of very serious faces. . . .

February 6.—Accompanied by Mr. Fitzpatrick, I sat out to-day with a reconnoitring party, on snow shoes. We marched all in a single file, tramping the snow as heavily as we could. Crossing the open basin, in a march of about ten miles we reached the top of one of the peaks, to the left of the pass indicated by our guide. Far below us, dimmed by the distance, was a large snowless valley, bounded on the western side, at the distance of about a hundred miles, by a low range of mountains, which Carson recognised with delight as the mountains bordering the coast. "There," said he, "is the little mountain—it is 15 years ago since I saw it; but I am just as sure as if I had seen it yesterday." Between us, then, and this low coast range, was the valley of the Sacramento; and no one who had not accompanied us through the incidents of our life for the last few months could realize the delight with which at last we looked down upon it. At the distance of apparently 30 miles beyond us were distinguished spots of prairie; and a dark line, which could be traced with the glass, was imagined to be the course of the river; but we were evidently at a great height above the valley, and between us and the plains extended miles of snowy fields and broken ridges of pine-covered mountains.

It was late in the day when we turned towards the camp; and it grew rapidly cold as it drew towards night. One of the men became fatigued, and his feet began to freeze, and, building a fire in the trunk of a dry old cedar, Mr. Fitzpatrick remained with him until his clothes could be dried, and he was in a condition to come on. After a day's march of 20 miles, we straggled into camp, one after another, at night fall; the greater number excessively fatigued, only two of the party having ever travelled on snow shoes before. . . .

February 10. . . . The elevation of the camp, by the boiling point, is 8,050 feet. We are now 1,000 feet above the level of the South Pass in the Rocky mountains; and still we are not done ascending. The top of a flat ridge near was bare of snow, and very well sprinkled with bunch grass, sufficient to pasture the animals two or three days; and this was to be their main point of support. This ridge is composed of a compact trap, or basalt, of a columnar structure; over the surface are scattered large boulders of porous trap. The hills are in many places entirely covered with small fragments of volcanic rock.

Putting on our snow shoes, we spent the afternoon in exploring a road ahead. The glare of the snow, combined with great fatigue, had rendered many of the people nearly blind; but we were fortunate in having some black silk handkerchiefs, which, worn as veils, very much relieved the eye. . . .

February 13.—We continued to labor on the road; and in the course of the day had the satisfaction to see the people working down the face of the opposite hill, about three miles distant. During the morning we had the pleasure of a visit from Mr. Fitzpatrick, with the information that all was going on well. A party of Indians had passed on snow shoes, who said they were going to the western side of the mountain after fish. This was an indication that the salmon were coming up the streams; and we could hardly restrain our impatience as we thought of them, and worked with increased vigor.

The meat train did not arrive this evening, and I gave Godey leave to kill our little dog, (Tlamath,) which he prepared in Indian fashion; scorching off the hair, and washing the skin with soap and snow, and then cutting it up into pieces, which were laid on the snow. Shortly afterwards, the sleigh arrived with a supply of horse meat; and we had to-night an extraordinary dinner—pea soup, mule, and dog.

February 14.—Annexed is a view of the dividing ridge of the Sierra, taken from this encampment. With Mr. Preuss, I ascended to-day the highest peak to the right; from which we had a beautiful view of a mountain lake at our feet, about fifteen miles in length, and so entirely surrounded by mountains that we could not discover an outlet.[1] We had taken with us a glass; but, though we enjoyed an extended view, the valley was half hidden in mist, as when we had seen it before. Snow could be distinguished on the higher parts of the coast mountains; eastward, as far as the eye could extend, it ranged over a terrible mass of broken snowy mountains, fading off blue in the distance. The rock composing the summit consists of a very coarse dark volcanic conglomerate; the lower parts appeared to be of a slaty structure. The highest trees were a few scattering cedars and aspens. From the immediate foot of the peak, we were two hours in reaching the summit, and one hour and a quarter in descending. The day had

---

[1]According to historian Francis P. Farquhar, the mountain that Frémont and Preuss ascended was Red Lake Peak. The lake they saw from the summit was Lake Tahoe, here receiving its first recorded mention.

been very bright, still, and clear, and spring seems to be advancing rapidly. While the sun is in the sky, the snow melts rapidly, and gushing springs cover the face of the mountain in all the exposed places; but their surface freezes instantly with the disappearance of the sun. . . .

February 16.—We had succeeded in getting our animals safely to the first grassy hill; and this morning I started with Jacob on a reconnoitring expedition beyond the mountain. We travelled along the crests of narrow ridges, extending down from the mountain in the direction of the valley, from which the snow was fast melting away. On the open spots was tolerably good grass; and I judged we should succeed in getting the camp down by way of these. Towards sundown we discovered some icy spots in a deep hollow and, descending the mountain, we encamped on the head water of a little creek, where at last the water found its way to the Pacific.

The night was clear and very long. We heard the cries of some wild animals, which had been attracted by our fire, and a flock of geese passed over during the night. Even these strange sounds had something pleasant to our senses in this region of silence and desolation.

We started again early in the morning. The creek acquired a regular breadth of about 20 feet, and we soon began to hear the rushing of the water below the ice surface, over which we travelled to avoid the snow; a few miles below we broke through, where the water was several feet deep, and halted to make a fire and dry our clothes. We continued a few miles farther, walking being very laborious without snow shoes.

I was now perfectly satisfied that we had struck the stream on which Mr. Sutter lived; and, turning about, made a hard push, and reached the camp at dark. Here we had the pleasure to find all the remaining animals, 57 in number, safely arrived at the grassy hill near the camp; and here, also, we were agreeably surprised with the sight of an abundance of salt. Some of the horse guard had gone to a neighboring hut for pine nuts, and discovered unexpectedly a large cake of very white fine-grained salt, which the Indians told them they had brought from the other side of the mountain; they used it to eat with their pine nuts, and readily sold it for goods.

On the 19th, the people were occupied in making a road and bringing up the baggage; and, on the afternoon of the next day,

February 20, 1844, we encamped with the animals and all the *materiel* of the camp, on the summit of the PASS in the dividing ridge, 1,000 miles by our travelled road from the Dalles of the Columbia. . . .

Frémont's troubles were hardly over. Three days later, he experienced his most trying day of the journey.

February 23. —This was our most difficult day: we were forced off the ridges by the quantity of snow among the timber, and obliged to take to the mountain sides, where, occasionally, rocks and a southern exposure afforded us a chance to scramble along. But these were steep, and slippery with snow and ice; and the tough evergreens of the mountain impeded our way, tore our skins, and exhausted our patience. Some of us had the misfortune to wear moccasins with *parflêche* soles, so slippery that we could not keep our feet, and generally crawled across the snow beds. Axes and mauls were necessary to-day, to make a road through the snow. Going ahead with Carson to reconnoitre the road, we reached in the afternoon the river which made the outlet of the lake. Carson sprang over, clear across a place where the stream was compressed among rocks, but the *parflêche* sole of my moccasin glanced from the icy rock, and precipitated me into the river. It was some few seconds before I could recover myself in the current, and Carson, thinking me hurt, jumped in after me, and we both had an icy bath. We tried to search a while for my gun, which had been lost in the fall, but the cold drove us out; and making a large fire on the bank, after we had partially dried ourselves we went back to meet the camp. We afterwards found that the gun had been slung under the ice which lined the banks of the creek.

Using our old plan of breaking the road with alternate horses, we reached the creek in the evening, and encamped on a dry open place in the ravine.

Another branch, which we had followed, here comes in on the left; and from this point the mountain wall, on which we had travelled to-day, faces to the south along the right bank of the river, where the sun appears to have melted the snow; but the opposite ridge is entirely covered. Here, among the pines, the hill side produces but little grass—barely sufficient to keep life in the animals. We had the pleasure to be rained upon this afternoon; and grass was now our greatest solicitude. Many of the men looked badly; and some this evening were giving out.

Crossing Carson Pass, from *Report of the Exploring Expedition to the Rocky Mountains, and to Oregon and California in the Years 1843-'44* by John C. Frémont. Gales & Seaton, Printers, 1845.

Kit Carson

With Frémont in the Sierra

But none in fact gave out. With the worst behind them, the party pushed on, and by March 8, 1844, all had arrived safely at Sutter's Fort in New Helvetia. Kit Carson dictated his memoirs some 12 years later. A man of far fewer words than Lieutenant Frémont, Carson had this to say about the journey across the Sierra pass that now bears his name.

Our course was through a barren, desolate, and unexplored country till we reached the Sierra Nevada, which we found covered with snow from one end to the other. We were nearly out of provisions and cross the mountain we must, let the consequences be what they may. We went as far in the snow as we possibly could with animals, then was compelled to send them back. Then we commenced making a road through the snow. We beat it down with mallets. The snow was six feet on the level for three leagues. We made snow shoes and passed over the snow to find how far we would have to make a road. Found it to be the distance afore stated.

After we reached the extremity of the snow, we could see in the distance the green valley of the Sacramento and the Coast Range. I knew the place well, had been there seventeen years before. Our feelings can be imagined when we saw such beautiful country. Having nothing to eat but mule meat, we returned to the place from which we had sent back our animals and commenced the work of making the road. In fifteen days our task was accomplished. Sent back for the animals. They had, through hunger eaten one another's tails and the leather of the pack saddles, in fact, everything they could lay hold of. They were in a deplorable condition and we would frequently kill one to keep it from dying, then use the meat for food.

We continued our march and by perseverance in making the

road, for the wind had drifted the snow and, in many places, filled up the path which we had made, we finally got across, and then commenced descending the mountain. Then we left Fitzpatrick in charge of the main party. Frémont, myself, and five or six men went ahead to Sutter's Fort for provisions.

The second day after leaving Fitzpatrick, Mr. Preus, Frémont's assistant, got lost. We made search for him, travelled slowly, fired guns so that he could know where we were. We could not find him. In four days the old man returned. Had his pockets full of acorns, having had no other food since he left [us]. We were all rejoiced at his return, for the old man was much respected by the party.

We arrived safely at Sutter's Fort, three days after the return to camp of Mr. Preus. When we arrived at the fort we were naked and in as poor a condition as men possibly could be. We were well received by Mr. Sutter and furnished in a princely manner, everything we required by him.

With Frémont in the Sierra, from *Dear Old Kit: The Historical Christopher Carson* by Harvey Lewis Carter. Copyright 1968 by the University of Oklahoma Press. Reprinted by permission of the University of Oklahoma Press.

Lafayette Bunnell

Discovery of the Yosemite

Although Joe Walker in all likelihood peered down into Yosemite Valley in 1833, he did not publicize his discovery, and the valley remained unknown to white settlers for nearly two decades afterward. With the discovery of gold in the western foothills, however, and the swarms of prospectors that followed, Yosemite Valley could not remain a secret for long.

By 1850 the "Indian problem" near the gold camps was extreme. Bloody clashes between whites and the inconvenient Indians were occurring regularly. When James Savage's trading post near Coarse Gold was raided and his employees murdered, it appeared that war might erupt.

Somehow, most of the rebellious Indians were persuaded to cease hostilities and to settle on reservations. But a few refused, taking refuge in an unknown valley on the Merced River. Savage was appointed to lead a volunteer militia, called the Mariposa Battalion, on a search for the rebels. In March 1851 the battalion set out to find the "Yosemites" and bring them to justice. A friendly Indian named Pon-wat-chee acted as the party's guide. A second Indian was sent ahead to urge the chief of the rebels to lay down his arms.

Lafayette Bunnell, a member of Savage's party, later recalled what happened when the chief showed up unexpectedly one day at the Mariposa Battalion's camp.

He came alone, and stood in dignified silence before one of the guard, until motioned to enter camp. He was immediately recognized by Pon-wat-chee as Ten-ie-ya, the old chief of the Yosemites, and was kindly cared for—being well supplied with food—after which, with the aid of the other Indians, the Major informed him of the wishes of the commissioners. The old sachem was very suspicious of Savage, and feared he was taking this method of getting the Yosemites into his power for the purpose of revenging his personal wrongs. Savage told him that if he would go to the commissioners and make a treaty of

peace with them, as the other Indians were going to do, there would
be no more war. Ten-ie-ya cautiously inquired as to the object of
taking all the Indians to the plains of the San Joaquin valley, and said:
"My people do not want anything from the 'Great Father' you tell me
about. The Great Spirit is our father, and he has always supplied us
with all we need. We do not want anything from white men. Our
women are able to do our work. Go, then; let us remain in the mountains where we were born; where the ashes of our fathers have been
given to the winds. I have said enough!"

This was abruptly answered by Savage, in Indian dialect and
gestures: "If you and your people have all you desire, why do you steal
our horses and mules? Why do you rob the miners' camps? Why do
you murder the white men, and plunder and burn their houses?"

Ten-ie-ya sat silent for some time; it was evident he understood
what Savage had said, for he replied: "My young men have sometimes
taken horses and mules from the whites. It was wrong for them to do
so. It is not wrong to take the property of enemies, who have wronged
my people. My young men believed the white gold-diggers were our
enemies; we now know they are not, and we will be glad to live in
peace with them. We will stay here and be friends. My people do not
want to go to the plains. The tribes who go there are some of them very
bad. They will make war on my people. We cannot live on the plains
with them. Here we can defend ourselves against them."

In reply to this Savage very deliberately and firmly said: "Your
people must go to the Commissioners and make terms with them. If
they do not, your young men will again steal our horses, your people
will again kill and plunder the whites. It was your people who robbed
my stores, burned my houses, and murdered my men. If they do not
make a treaty, your whole tribe will be destroyed, not one of them will
be left alive." At this vigorous ending of the Major's speech, the old
chief replied: "It is useless to talk to you about who destroyed your
property and killed your people. If the Chow-chillas do not boast of it,
they are cowards, for they led us on. I am old and you can kill me if
you will, but what use to lie to you who know more than all the
Indians, and can beat them in their big hunts of deer and bear.
Therefore I will not lie to you, but promise that if allowed to return to
my people I will bring them in."

Ten-ie-ya was allowed to go. The next day he returned to the camp and convinced Savage that his people would soon follow. But when several days passed and none of Ten-ie-ya's followers showed up, Savage decided to go after them. The old chief agreed to accompany the battalion to the Indians' hiding place.

While ascending to the divide between the South Fork and the main Merced we found but little snow, but at the divide, and beyond, it was from three to five feet in depth, and in places much deeper. The sight of this somewhat cooled our ardor, but none asked for a *"furlough."*

To somewhat equalize the laborious duties of making a trail, each man was required to take his turn in front. The leader of the column was frequently changed; no horse or mule could long endure the fatigue without relief. To effect this, the tired leader dropped out of line, resigning his position to his followers, taking a place in the rear, on the beaten trail, exemplifying, that "the first shall be last, and the last shall be first." The snow packed readily, so that a very comfortable trail was left in the rear of our column.

Old Ten-ie-ya relaxed the rigidity of his bronze features, in admiration of our method of making a trail, and assured us, that, notwithstanding the depth of snow, we would soon reach his village. We had in our imaginations pictured it as in some deep rocky canon in the mountains.

While in camp the frantic efforts of the old chief to describe the location to Major Savage, had resulted in the unanimous verdict among the "boys," who were observing him, that "it must be a devil of a place." Feeling encouraged by the hope that we should soon arrive at the residence of his Satanic majesty's subjects, we wallowed on, alternately becoming the object of a joke, as we in turn were extricated from the drifts. When we had traversed a little more than half the distance, as was afterwards proved, we met the Yosemites on their way to our rendezvous on the South Fork.

Seventy-two Indians gave up without a fight. Ten-ie-ya insisted that none of his braves were left in the valley, but Savage was unconvinced. Ten-ie-ya now joined his people on the march out from the mountains, while Savage and his men pressed on.

We found the traveling much less laborious than before, and it seemed but a short time after we left the Indians before we suddenly came in full view of the valley in which was the village, or rather the encampments of the Yosemites. The immensity of rock I had seen in my vision on the Old Bear Valley trail from Ridley's Ferry was here presented to my astonished gaze. The mystery of that scene was here disclosed. My awe was increased by this nearer view. The face of the immense cliff was shadowed by the declining sun; its outlines only had been seen at a distance. . . .

That stupendous cliff is now known as "El Capitan" (the Captain), and the plateau from which we had our first view of the valley, as Mount Beatitude.

It has been said that "it is not easy to describe in words the precise impressions which great objects make upon us." I cannot describe how completely I realized this truth. None but those who have visited this most wonderful valley, can even imagine the feelings with which I looked upon the view that was there presented. The grandeur of the scene was but softened by the haze that hung over the valley,—light as gossamer—and by the clouds which partially dimmed the higher cliffs and mountains. This obscurity of vision but increased the awe with which I beheld it, and as I looked, a peculiar exalted sensation seemed to fill my whole being, and I found my eyes in tears with emotion. . . .

To obtain a more distinct and *quiet* view, I had left the trail and my horse and wallowed through the snow alone to a projecting granite rock. So interested was I in the scene before me, that I did not observe that my comrades had all moved on, and that I would soon be left indeed alone. My situation attracted the attention of Major Savage,—who was riding in rear of column,—who hailed me from the trail below with, "you had better wake up from that dream up there, or you may lose your hair; I have no faith in Ten-ie-ya's statement that there are no Indians about here. We had better be moving; some of the murdering devils may be lurking along this trail to pick off stragglers." I hurriedly joined the Major on the descent, and as other views presented themselves, I said with some enthusiasm, "If my hair is now required, I can depart in peace, for I have here seen the power and glory of a Supreme being; the majesty of His handy-work is in that

'Testimony of the Rocks.' That mute appeal—pointing to El Capitan—illustrates it, with more convincing eloquence than can the most powerful arguments of surpliced priests." "Hold up, Doc! you are soaring too high for me; and perhaps for yourself. This is rough riding; we had better mind this devilish trail, or we shall go *soaring* over some of these slippery rocks." We, however, made the descent in safety. When we overtook the others, we found blazing fires started, and preparations commenced to provide supper for the hungry command; while the light-hearted "boys" were indulging their tired horses with the abundant grass found on the meadow near by, which was but lightly covered with snow.

Discovery of the Yosemite, from *Discovery of the Yosemite and the Indian War of 1851 Which Led to that Event* by Lafayette H. Bunnell, M.D. Fleming H. Revell Co., 1880.

William Brewer

A Scientist in the Sierra

The fame of the miraculous valley on the Merced spread quickly. But wonders of nature held little sway with California's growing legions of boosters, whose economic hopes lay in minerals, not picturesque valleys. By 1860 notable gold, silver, tin and coal strikes had convinced most sensible people that California was a vast treasure trove just waiting to be tapped. Sober minds now saw the need for a comprehensive survey of the state's resources so that California's economic future could be plotted with accuracy. The legislature responded in 1860 by ordering a statewide geological survey under the direction of Professor Josiah Dwight Whitney.

Whitney chose William Brewer to lead the field parties. The extraordinary assignment given Brewer was nothing less than to explore and map a practically unexplored, unmapped state, and to ascertain all geological, botanical, and zoological resources along the way. For the next four years, Brewer and his men checked in at some of the wildest spots in California—the Siskiyous, Mount Shasta, and the Yosemite and Kings Canyon backcountries. In large part they failed to satisfy the legislature's charge. But given the enormity of their task, it is remarkable that they accomplished as much as they did.

Brewer exemplified that uniquely 19th Century phenomenon, the gentleman of universal learning, unflagging confidence and boundless energy. Despite the weight of his official responsibilities, his journal makes clear that he had a wonderful time wandering through wild, unexplored country with his men. No passage better illustrates this than his account of a sojourn on the Roaring River (which he called the South Fork of the Kings), culminating in his ascent of the mountain now named for him. His companions on this trip were Clarence King, Dick Cotter, Charles Hoffmann and James Gardner.

41

In camp on the south fork of Kings River
July 7. [1864]

It is a pleasant, clear day. For three days the sky has been of the intensest blue, not a cloud in sight day or night. I am alone in a beautiful camp and I will write.

We have come down into a deep valley, where it is warmer and there is good grass. We are still camped high, however—about 7,500 feet. A fine breeze plays up the valley, very pleasant, but it makes it hard to write—it flutters the paper and gives much trouble. The desolate granite peaks lie in sight—bare granite and glistening snow. It freezes every night.

Tuesday, June 28, we had a fine clear morning, and four of us started to visit a peak a few miles distant. We had a rough trail, over sharp ridges, and finally up a very steep pile of granite rocks, perhaps a thousand feet high, to the peak, which is over eleven thousand feet high, and which we called Mount Silliman, in honor of Professor Silliman, Junior.

In crossing a ridge we came on fresh bear tracks, and soon saw the animal himself, a fine black bear. We all shouted, and he went galloping away over the rocks and into a canyon. We had gone but a short distance farther when we saw a very large female grizzly with two cubs. She was enormous—would weigh as much as a small ox. After we looked at her a few minutes we all set up a shout. She rose on her hind legs, but did not see us, as we sat perfectly still. We continued to shout. She became frightened at the unseen noise, which echoed from the cliffs so that she could not tell where it came from, so she galloped away with the cubs. These would weigh perhaps 150 pounds each; she would weigh perhaps 900 pounds or more. We also saw a fine buck during the trip.

We reached the summit after a hard climb, and had a grand view of the rough landscape. Great rocky amphitheaters surrounded by rocky ridges, very sharp, their upper parts bare or streaked with snow, constituted a wild, rough, and desolate landscape. Clouds suddenly came on, and a snowstorm, which was a heavy rain in camp. We got back tired enough.

The next day King, Gardner, and I took some sketches. Dick went

Members of the California State Geological Survey, 1864.
Left to right: James Gardner, Dick Cotter, William Brewer, Clarence King

after a deer, but saw only a bear. The animals strolled off, and several hours were consumed in getting them, during which the boys saw more bear and deer.

June 30 we were up early and left. We changed our route and came on about ten miles, by such a terrible way that it was a hard day's work—over rocks, through canyons and brush. We sank into a canyon and camped about two thousand feet below our last camp. We had some trouble with our fire—it got into some dead logs and we feared a general burn. We fought it, and Gardner came near being bitten by a rattlesnake that was driven out. He was an enormous fellow, but had lost most of his rattles.

July 1 we came on by a still rougher way, about eleven miles. We crossed the south fork of Kings River, down over tremendous rocks and up again by as rough a way. We struck a ridge which is a gigantic moraine left by a former glacier, the largest I have ever seen or heard of. It is several miles long and a thousand feet high.

We were working back toward high peaks, where we hoped to discover the sources of Kings, Kaweah, and Kern rivers, geographical problems of some considerable interest and importance. We got back as far as we could and camped at an altitude of 9,750 feet, by a rushing stream, but with poor feed. Wood was plenty, dry, from trees broken by avalanches in winter. A beautiful little lake was near us.[1] About five miles east lay the high granite cone we hoped to reach—high and sharp, its sides bristling with sharp pinnacles.[2]

Saturday, July 2, we were up at dawn and Hoffmann and I climbed this cone, which I had believed to be the highest of this part of the Sierra. We had a rough time, made two unsuccessful attempts to reach the summit, climbing up terribly steep rocks, and at last, after eight hours of very hard climbing, reached the top. The view was yet wilder than we have ever seen before. We were not on the highest peak, although we were a thousand feet higher than we anticipated any peaks were. We had not supposed there were any over 12,000 or 12,500 feet, while we were actually up over 13,600, and there were a dozen peaks in sight beyond as high or higher!

---

[1] The source of Brewer Creek
[2] Mount Brewer

Such a landscape! A hundred peaks in sight over thirteen thousand feet—many very sharp—deep canyons, cliffs in every direction almost rivaling Yosemite, sharp ridges almost inaccessible to man, on which human foot has never trod—all combined to produce a view the sublimity of which is rarely equaled, one which few are privileged to behold.

There is not so much snow as in the mountains farther north, not so much falls in winter, the whole region is drier, but all the higher points, above 12,000 feet are streaked with it, and patches occur as low as 10,500 feet. The last trees disappear at 11,500—above this desolate bare rocks and snow. Several small lakes were in sight, some of them frozen over.

The view extended north eighty to ninety miles, south nearly as far—east we caught glimpses of the desert mountains east of Owens Valley—west to the Coast Range, 130 or more miles distant.

On our return we slid down a slope of snow perhaps eight hundred feet. We came down in two minutes the height that we had been over

Mt. Brewer summit register with Brewer's and Gardner's signatures

three hours in climbing. We got back very tired, but a cup of good tea and a fine venison soup restored us.

Sunday, July 3, we lay until late. On calculating the height of the peak, finding it so much higher than we expected, and knowing there were still higher peaks back, we were, of course, excited. Here there is the highest and grandest group of the Sierra—in fact, the grandest in the United States—not so high as Mount Shasta, but a great assemblage of high peaks.

King is enthusiastic, is wonderfully tough, has the greatest endurance I have ever seen, and is withal very muscular. He is a most perfect specimen of health. He begged me to let him and Dick try to reach them on foot. I feared them inaccessible, but at last gave in to their importunities and gave my consent. They made their preparations that day, anxious for a trip fraught with so much interest, hardship, and danger.

July 4 all were up at dawn. We got breakfast, and King and Dick packed their packs—six days' provisions, blankets, and instruments made packs of thirty-five or forty pounds each, to be packed into such a region! Gardner and I resolved to climb the cone again, as I had left instruments on the top, expecting someone would go up. Our way lay together for five miles, and up to thirteen thousand feet. I packed Dick's heavy pack to that point to give him a good start. I could never pack it as far as they hope to. Here we left them, and as we scaled the peak they disappeared over a steep granite ridge, the last seen of them.[1]

Gardner and I reached the summit much easier than Hoffmann and I had two days before. The sky was cloudy and the air cold, 25°. We were on top about two hours. We planted the American flag on top, and left a paper in a bottle with our names, the height, etc. It is not at all probable that any man was ever on the top before, or that any one will be again—for a long time at least. There is nothing but love of adventure to prompt it after we have the geography of the region described.

We were back before sundown; a hearty dinner and pleasant camp fire closed the day. We sang "Old John Brown" around the camp fire that night—we three, alone in these solitudes. Thus was spent Independence Day. The last was with Hoffmann alone, in the Sierra farther north. We heard not a gun. Would that we might know the war news—we are over a month behind.

The next morning we lay in our blankets very late, after the fatigue of the previous day—in fact were in bed eleven hours. We stayed in camp and took latitude observations. It was a most lovely day.

A Scientist in the Sierra, from *Up and Down California in 1860-1864,* edited by Francis P. Farquhar. © 1966 by The Regents of the University of California, reprinted by permission of the University of California Press.

---

[1]King's account of his famous attempt to reach and climb the nation's highest peak appears in the section "The Climbers."

Elisha Winchell

The Amateur Explorer

Until now, those who wandered through the unexplored Sierra did so because they were searching for riches or a place to graze their sheep or because, like William Brewer and Jed Smith, wandering was their job. In the years following the Civil War, however, a few adventurers began to explore the Sierra simply out of curiosity over what might be there.

Judge Elisha Cotton Winchell was one of these. In September, 1868, Winchell set out on horseback with Captain John Appleton and William Haines to explore the Kings River Canyon. True, Winchell had a calculating eye on both the timber and copper ore he thought he might find in the canyon; but he was equally intrigued, he wrote, with "exploring so unfrequented and interesting a district." Arriving above the South Fork of the Kings River on the south canyon wall above today's Cedar Grove, Winchell spotted the mountain now called Lookout Peak.

As we came down the slope just mentioned, our attention had been drawn to a remarkable peak of broken granite crags that rose, like a misshapen pyramid, or cone, high out of the forest before us; and when it was found that our night halt was made within half a mile of its southwestern base, I set out, while my comrades were arranging camp affairs for the night, to climb to the summit before the sun should set. On reaching the apex—a smooth block of granite—I found that it commanded an outlook to the west over all the woods, streams and mountains we had passed, and that the San Joaquin plain would also have been visible but for the strange, misty veil, which, as thousands will remember, ominously hung over California for a month prior to the earthquake of October 20th, of that year. But the view to the north, to the east, to the southeast, and downward, was undimmed, for this peak rose abreast the lower end of the King's River Cañon, and looked down into its awful depths.

I regret that I cannot measure the grandeur of this scene by the features of Yosemite, which I have never visited; but no paintings of that gorge and its surroundings as seen from "Inspiration Point" or "Cloud's Rest," convey to my mind the idea of so sublime a landscape as that which, without warning, burst upon my vision as I looked over the granite block into a deep, dread, silent, stupendous amphitheatre, twenty miles across, crowded with adamant mountains, pinnacled crests, thunder-scarred cliffs, green lines of forests, snows in eternal sleep, horrid gorges and yawning gulfs. Eastward, the sharply serrated contour of the main ridge of the Sierras tore the twilight sky; northward rose the huge, massive barrier that fills the space between the middle fork and south fork; southward, the great, gashed Kaweah Divide bore to heaven its balmy forests; while *more than a vertical mile down,* in the midst of this vast arena, lay a granite trough ten miles long, half a mile wide, bordered by perpendicular cliffs rising thousands of feet. A *green mound of forests* hid the floor of the gorge, and a thread-like streak of water faintly gleamed out of it.

Awe-struck, I gazed till the misty veil of the plain drew nearer, and the weird gloom deepened. Silence the most profound brooded over the stony depths. Not a wave of air touched the sprays of the dark green forest which far below me enveloped our camp, nor swayed the straight column of light blue smoke that stole up higher than the trees from the deep-red star of the camp-fire. As the sun set I offered, with due reverence, from this exalted altar-stone the improvised incense of flame and smoke from both barrels of my gun, and before the myriad-echoed thunders had ceased their clamorings over the startled abyss I was descending the peak to rejoin my comrades.

The next morning Winchell reascended the peak with his compaions. They christened it "Winchell's Peak"—in honor of one of his cousins, Winchell was quick to add. Then they descended to the South Fork of the Kings. Apparently unaware that the Brewer party had passed this way four years before, they exercised the explorer's prerogative of naming everything in sight. It is a measure of the obscurity to which Winchell's expedition has been consigned that not one of his appellations took.

In this primeval paradise, all day long we lingered mingling our sordid speculations in regard to the practicability of floating rafts of saw-logs down the river to the San Joaquin plain, with our feelings of wonder at the scenes around us. With our guns and fishing-tackle we rambled through the woods and by the stream in search of mountain grouse and mountain trout. Two miles below we found that the valley, which was three-quarters of a mile wide at the camp, contracted to a V-shaped cañon, only wide enough for the egress of the narrow river. No perpendicular cliffs border this western section, though the walls rise at a steep angle. Looking up the valley, we could see great cliffs that drew near each other, from opposite sides; but having no way of measuring altitudes, we could only guess at the elevations. Early the next morning, we pursued our way up the valley, on the south side of the river, which we crossed at a deep, swift ford, two miles above our camp. The cañon grew narrower—its sides more precipitous. A mile above the ford we passed the mouth of "Kettle

Building a suspension bridge, South Fork Kings River

Brook," which leaps into the gorge from the southeast, down a slope of 45 degrees, through an impassable ravine. From here, onward, there was an unending succession of naked, perpendicular battlements, of various heights and forms, severed by breaks and gorges, out of which rushed foaming torrents. We were lost in amazement. There was a resistless fascination in those mural heights which impelled us to gaze fixedly at each new form, till it had passed and its successor rose to receive the like homage. We made many attempts to estimate the altitudes; but there were no data to guide us, and all our calculations failed. We believed the walls to reach thousands of feet above the valley, but whether 3,000 or 6,000, I have never dared to say. Opposite Kettle Brook are the "Pillars of Hercules," towering at the portals of the stony realm beyond; and next, on the same side, is "Appleton's Peak"—a sheer, blank wall near whose top the great pines that plume it seem but a span long. "Leach's Peak," on the south side, fills the angle made by the Brook. The cañon here is but one-fourth of a mile wide, but rapidly widens again and contracts in elliptic form, making a rude oval, half a mile wide, and thrice as long, named "The Coliseum." Its lofty, fringing cliffs are yet nameless. At the eastern end a furious torrent darts out of a steep gully on the north side, with deafening roar, and gave us trouble in crossing, for which we repaid it with the title, "Thunder Creek." Further in is a second, irregular ellipse, a mile long, its northern wall a broad, angular peak, the "Pyramid of Cheops." On the south "Three Sisters" correspond in form to the "Three Brothers" of Yosemite. Another stream emerges from a glen east of the Pyramid, to which, because of its proximity to the copper mine alluded to in the early part of this sketch, we applied the name "Malachite Creek." The deposit of ore crops out 400 feet above the valley on the east side of this rivulet, and appears to be of rich quality. A third swell in the cañon seemed so nearly circular, being only three-quarters of a mile long and of almost equal width, that we called it "The Rotunda." Its enclosing heights are yet unchristened. Finally, beyond, is the noblest apartment of the series. The great cañon of King's River is here abruptly terminated by a magnificent granite tablet which stands across the valley and faces the west. Two similar tablets uplift from the green floor, at right angles with the former, on opposite sides of the river, thus constituting the three inner walls of a vast Titanic

temple, open to the setting sun. But through the enclosed, inner corners leap into this enchanted, and enchanting arena, two bold and
glassy torrents from the north and the south—new-born of the snows—
which, rushing together, instantaneously coalesce, forming the jubi-
lant south fork, and sweep in matchless beauty and wedded gladness
down through the embowered and rock-walled valley.

Here ended our advance; and here, at 11 o'clock A.M. of Tuesday,
September 29th, we drew rein, and alighted in a delightful spot,
where graceful pines and cottonwoods shadowed the green sward
and the awful trio of cliffs seemed to bend over our heads. Words
avail not to picture a scene like this. The Yosemite towers may, or may
not, exceed these in height; it is immaterial. I cannot divest myself of
the belief that no spot has yet been found on American soil where so
much of grandeur concentrates in so small a space. The insatiate eye
seeks again and again that trio of templed cliffs, and never tires of
their supernal majesty. They seem to form Nature's own chosen
cathedral, where deep organ-tones from sounding streams ever
repeat the anthems taught by Deity.

The Amateur Explorer, from "Kings River Canyon in 1868" by E.C. Winchell.
Sierra Club Bulletin, 1926. Reprinted by permission of The Sierra Club.

John Muir

The Discovery of Glaciers

No special skills were required to stand on an overlook and be awed, as Elisha Winchell was, by a grand array of Sierra peaks sweeping toward the horizon. But to see and understand subtle features and inconspicuous details, and then place them in context, required the eye of a different kind of explorer, one not yet common in the Sierra. William Brewer introduced such patient, thoughtful exploration to the range, and John Muir transformed it into an art.

Muir roamed over the Sierra as widely as anyone, and was unsurpassed in his ability to be staggered by a panorama of mountain peaks. But it is his exposition of detail that one remembers in his writings—his sense of how the pieces fit and what they mean. His discovery of living glaciers in the Sierra illustrates this patient, thoughtful brand of exploration perfectly.

When Muir arrived in Yosemite in 1869, official wisdom had it that there were no active glaciers in the Sierra. This was the view of no less an authority than Professor Whitney, director of the State Geological Survey, and no serious scientist disagreed with him.

Muir soon reached a different conclusion, however. When he published his findings, he was ridiculed by the professionals. But he stuck to his guns and gradually his view came to supersede Whitney's. Today we know that scores of glaciers dot the Sierra.

It was one of Muir's endearing qualities that, solemn though he may have been about his mission, he was never one to pass up a hair-raising adventure. One of the highlights of his account of his discovery of Sierra glaciation, under the north face of Merced Peak, is his recollection of several exciting minutes spent crawling about in a bergschrund like an enraptured ice worm.

The first Sierra glacier was discovered in October, 1871, in a wide, shadowy amphitheatre, comprehended by the bases of Red and Black mountains, two of the dominating summits of the Merced group.

This group consists of the highest portion of a long crooked spur that straggles out from the main axis of the range in the direction of Yosemite Valley. At the time of my discovery I was engaged in exploring its *névé* amphitheatres, and in tracing the channels of the ancient glaciers which they poured down into the basin of Illilouette. Beginning on the northwestern extremity of the group with Mount Clark, I examined the chief tributaries in succession, their moraines, *roches moutonnées*, and shining glacial pavements, taking them as they came in regular course without any reference to the time consumed in their study.

The monuments of the tributary that poured its ice from between Red and Black mountains I found to be far the grandest of them all; and when I beheld its magnificent moraines ascending in majestic curves to the dark, mysterious solitudes at its head, I was exhilarated with the work that lay before me, as if on the verge of some great discovery. It was one of the golden days of Indian summer, when the sun melts all the roughness from the rockiest alpine landscapes. The path of the dead glacier shone as if washed with silver, the pines stood transfigured in the living light, poplar groves were masses of orange and yellow, and solidagoes were in full bloom, adding gold to gold.

Pushing on over my glacial highway, I passed lake after lake set in solid basins of granite, and many a thicket and meadow watered by the stream; now clanking over naked rock where not a leaf tries to grow, now wading through plush bogs knee-deep in yellow and purple sphagnum, or brushing through luxuriant garden patches among larkspurs eight feet high and lilies with thirty flowers on a single stalk. The main lateral moraines bounded the view on either side like artificial embankments, covered with a superb growth of silver-fir and pine, many specimens attaining a height of two hundred feet or more. But all this garden and forest luxuriance was speedily left behind. The trees were dwarfed. The gardens became exclusively alpine. Patches of the heathy bryanthus and cassiope began to appear, and arctic willows, pressed into flat close carpets with the weight of winter snow. The lakelets, which a few miles down the valley were so richly broidered with meadows, had here, at an elevation of about 10,000 feet above the sea, only small mats of carex, leaving bare glaciated rocks around more than half their shores. Yet amidst all this

RUSH CREEK GLACIER, ON THE EASTERN SLOPE OF THE SIERRA, NORTH OF MOUNT RITTER.

alpine suppression the sturdy brown-barked mountain pine tossed his storm-beaten branches in ledges and buttresses of Red Mountain; some specimens over a hundred feet high and twenty-four feet in circumference, seemingly as fresh and vigorous as if made wholly of sunlight and snow.

Evening came on just as I got fairly within the portal of the grand fountain amphitheatre. I found it to be about a mile wide in the middle, and a little less than two miles long. Crumbling spurs and battlements of Red Mountain inclose it on the north, the sombre, rudely sculptured precipices of Black Mountain on the south, and a hacked and splintery *col* curves around from mountain to mountain at the head, shutting it in on the east.

I chose a camping ground for the night down on the brink of a glacier lake, where a thicket of Williamson spruce sheltered me from the night wind. After making a tin-cupful of tea, I sat by my camp fire, reflecting on the grandeur and significance of the glacial records I had seen, and speculating on the developments of the morrow. As the night advanced, the mighty rocks of my mountain mansion seemed to come nearer. The starry sky stretched across from wall to wall like a ceiling, and fitted closely down into all the spiky irregularities of the summits. After a long fireside rest and a glance at my field-notes, I cut a few pine tassels for a bed, and fell into the clear death-like sleep that always comes to the tired mountaineer.

Early next morning I set out to trace the ancient ice current back to its farthest recesses, filled with that inexpressible joy experienced by every explorer in nature's untrodden wilds. The mountain voices were still as in the hush of evening; the wind scarce stirred the branches of the mountain pine; the sun was up, but it was yet too cold for the birds and marmots—only the stream, cascading from pool to pool, seemed wholly awake and doing. Yet the spirit of the opening, blooming day called to action. The sunbeams came streaming gloriously through jagged openings of the *col*, glancing on ice-burnished pavements, and lighting the mirror surface of the lake, while every sunward rock and pinnacle burned white on the edges, like melting iron in a furnace. I passed round the north shore of the lake, and then followed the guidance of the stream back into the recesses of the amphitheatre. It led me past a chain of small lakelets set on bare granite benches, and connected by cascades and falls. The scenery became more rigidly arctic. The last dwarf pine was left far below, and the stream was bordered with icicles. As the sun advanced, rocks were loosened on shattered portions of the walls, and came bounding down gullies and *coulairs* in smokey, spattering avalanches, echoing wildly from crag to crag.

The main lateral moraines, that stretch so formally from the huge jaws of the amphitheatre out into the middle of the Illilouette basin, are continued upward in straggled masses along the amphitheatre walls, while separate stones, thousands of tons in weight, are left stranded here and there out in the middle of the main channel. Here, also, I observed a series of small, well-characterized, frontal moraines, ranged in regular order along the south wall of the amphitheatre, the shape and size of each moraine corresponding with the shapes and sizes of the daily shadows cast by different portions of the walls. This correspondence between moraines and shadows afterward became plain.

Tracing the stream back to the last of its chain of lakelets, I noted a fine gray mud covering the stones on the bottom, excepting where the force of the entering and outflowing currents prevented its settling. On examination it proved to be wholly mineral in composition, and resembled the mud worn from a fine-grit grindstone. I at once suspected its glacial origin, for the stream which carried it came gurgling out of the base of a raw, fresh-looking moraine, which seemed to be in process of formation at that very moment. Not a plant, lichen, or weather-stain was any where visible upon its rough, unsettled surface. It is from sixty to over a hundred feet in height, and comes plunging down in front at an angle of thirty-eight degrees, which is the very steepest at which this moraine material will lie. Climbing the moraine in front was, therefore, no easy undertaking. The slightest touch loosened ponderous blocks, that went rumbling to the bottom, followed by a train of smaller stones and sand. Picking my way with the utmost caution, I at length gained the top, and beheld a small but well-characterized glacier swooping down from the sombre precipices of Black Mountain to the terminal moraine in a finely graduated curve. The solid ice appeared on all the lower portions of the glacier, though it was gray with dirt and stones imbedded in its surface. Farther up, the ice disappeared beneath coarsely granulated snow.

The surface of the glacier was still further characterized by dirt bands and the outcropping edges of blue veins that swept across from side to side in beautiful concentric curves, showing the laminated structure of the mass of the glacier ice. At the head of the glacier, where the *névé* joined the mountain, it was traversed by a huge yawing *Bergschrund,* in some places twelve or fourteen feet wide, and bridged at intervals by the remains of snow avalanches. Creeping along the edge of the *Schrund,* holding on with benumbed fingers, I discovered clear sections where the bedded and ribbon structure was beautifully illustrated. The surface snow, though every where sprinkled with stones shot down from the cliffs above, was in some places almost pure white, gradually becoming crystalline, and changing to porous whitish ice of different shades, and this again changing at a depth of twenty or thirty feet to bluer ice, some of the ribbon-like bands of which were nearly pure and solid, and blended with the paler bands in the most gradual and exquisite manner imaginable, reminding one of the way that color bands come together in a rainbow.

A series of rugged zigzags enabled me to make my way down into the weird ice world of the *Schrund.* Its chambered hollows were hung with a multitude of clustered icicles, amidst which thin subdued light pulsed and shimmered with indescribably loveliness. Water dripped and tinkled overhead, and from far below there came strange solemn murmurs from currents that were feeling their way among veins and fissures on the bottom.

Ice creations of this kind are perfectly enchanting, notwithstanding one feels so entirely out of place in their pure fountain beauty. I was soon uncomfortably cold in my shirt sleeves, and the leaning wall of the *Schrund* seemed ready to ingulph me. Yet it was hard to leave the delicious music of the water, and still more the intense loveliness of the light.

Coming again to the surface of the glacier, I noticed blocks of every size setting out on their downward journey to be built into the terminal moraine.

The noon sun gave birth to a multitude of sweet-voiced rills that ran gracefully down the glacier, curling and swirling in their shining channels, and cutting clear sections in which the structure of the ice was beautifully revealed.

The series of frontal moraines I had observed in the morning extending along the base of the south wall of the amphitheatre corresponds in every particular with the moraines of this active glacier; and the causes of all that is special in their forms and order of distribution with reference to shadows now plainly unfolded themselves. When those climatic changes came on that broke upon the main glacier that once filled the amphitheatre from wall to wall, a series of residual glaciers was left in the cliff shadows, under whose protection they lingered until they formed the frontal moraines we are studying. But as the seasons became warm, or the snow supply became less abundant, they died in succession, all excepting the one we have just examined, and the causes of its longer life are sufficiently apparent in the greater extent of snow basin it drains and in its more perfect shelter from the sun. How much longer this little glacier will live will, of course, depend upon climate and the changes slowly effected in the form and exposure of its basin.

The Discovery of Glaciers, from "Living Glaciers of California" by John Muir. *Harper's New Monthly Magazine,* November, 1875.

Theodore Solomons

The Enchanted Gorge

One of the most peripatetic of Sierra explorers was Theodore Solomons, a charter member of the Sierra Club. It was Solomons who conceived the idea of a Yosemite-to-Mount Whitney trail along the crest of the range, an idea that later was realized in the John Muir Trail.

In the mid-1890s, Solomons made several extended trips into the High Sierra in search of a possible route for his trail. On the third of these, he and Ernest Bonner explored and named Evolution Valley and the surrounding peaks— Darwin, Huxley, Wallace, Spencer and Haeckel. They climbed Mount Goddard, then dropped down into the narrow valley that is still regarded as the most inaccessible spot in the Sierra: the Enchanted Gorge. The name of the gorge alone has fired the imaginations of countless hikers since Solomons passed through, but few have repeated his journey.

We were caught in a storm while on Mt. Goddard, and were glad to camp at the highest clump of tamarack shrubbery we could find. This happened to be considerably above the big frozen lake, and ice and snow lay all about us. I have never passed a night in a higher altitude than this, nor do I care to, for we must have been nearly 13,500 feet high. We had no sooner built a fire than the snow began to fall, and though for a time it was nip and tuck between the two elements, our pitch-saturated logs conquered at last. In the morning we climbed round the southern base of the mountain, and made our way along the divide in a blinding storm, which becoming monotonous after six or eight hours, we determined to descend a deep gorge that had captured our admiration and aroused our curiosity when on the summit of Goddard. At half-past one this gorge lay directly south of us, and in an hour we had descended to its head, which we found was guarded by a nearly frozen lake, whose sheer, ice-smoothed walls

arose on either side, up and up, seemingly into the very sky, their
crowns two sharp black peaks of most majestic form. A Scylla and a
Charybdis they seemed to us, as we stood at the margin of the lake
and wondered how we might pass the dangerous portal. By a little
careful climbing we got around the lake, and stood at the head of the
gorge. Instead of the precipice we had feared to find, the narrow
bottom was filled with snow, furnishing us a kind of turnpike, down
which we fairly flew. Down, down, by sinuous curves, our road
conducted us, as though into the bowels of the earth; for the walls,
black, glinting, weird, rose a thousand and two thousand feet almost
perpendicularly over our heads, and were lost in the storm-clouds
that were discharging upon us a copious rain. For at least three miles
we sped over the snow, when of a sudden the gorge widened into a
kind of rotunda, the snow disappeared, and the stream which I
expected to emerge from under it was conspicuous by its absence, nor
could the roar of its subterranean flow be even faintly heard. Imagine
a well a thousand feet wide and nearly twice as deep, its somewhat
narrow bottom piled with fragments of rock, from the size of pebbles
to that of buildings, the walls and floor of every hue that lends itself
readily to a general effect of blackness, and the rotunda is pictured.
Several torrents fell over the perpendicular western wall into a lake
that had no visible outlet.

After an hour's struggle over the gorge floor, the roughness of
which defies description, we reached the lower end of the rotunda
and the beginning of another shorter stretch of snow. The walls had
now taken on the metallic lustre of many shades of bronze, the
brilliancy of which was heightened by the polish imparted by the
glacier which had formerly filled this deep gorge. The snow floor
again giving place to monster rock fragments, again we struggled over
the uneven surface; when, without warning, below a little moraine-
like embankment, out gushed a great torrent of water, which, on
reaching a part of the gorge so narrow that the snow yet filled it,
burrowed underneath, darted out a hundred yards beyond, soon met
another drift of snow under which it burrowed, as before, and in the
middle of which it formed a lake with perpendicular banks of snow
fully thirty feet in height, only to plunge again under the snow, this
time leaving a roof so thin that my companion's feet pierced the crust,

and he fell in up to his waist. With great coolness and dexterity, however, he extricated himself before I had more than grasped the situation. And so, till the fast-gathering gloom warned us to seek a camping-spot, we worked our way among the manifold wonders of that marvellous gorge. When finally we found trees on a kind of shelf, high above the stream, and, wearied with our day's toil, prepared to camp, the barometer registered a drop of nearly six thousand feet from the Goddard divide.

Next day we continued the descent of the gorge to its confluence with Goddard Creek, which from Mt. Goddard we had identified as heading in a number of lakes on the southeastern base of the mountain. Five miles below the confluence of the stream draining the Enchanted Gorge, Goddard Creek empties into the main Middle Fork of the King's River, twenty miles above Tehipitee Valley, the deepest "Yosemite" in the range. We explored and photographed this Middle Fork country and the Tehipitee, securing a number of excellent negatives, and then took the Granite Basin trail to our destination, the King's River Cañon, which we reached on July 28th, hungry and tattered, but in superb physical condition.

So accustomed had we become to our packs during the latter week of our trip, that it is no exaggeration to say that we had not felt the weight of the knapsacks, though when we reached our journey's end they weighed not less than twenty pounds apiece. The little expedition had been an entire success. In sixteen days we had covered fully three times as much territory as we could have hoped to explore had we travelled with a mule or burro. Yet my eyes had constantly been on the alert for passages practicable for animals; and to such good purpose had the quest been pursued that the Sierra Club will shortly place on file in its Club Rooms maps and descriptions which will enable the enterprising mountaineer to leave the Yosemite Valley with loaded animals, and to thread his way to the King's River Cañon through the very heart of the High Sierra.

The Enchanted Gorge, from "Mount Goddard and its Vicinity" by Theodore S. Solomons. *Appalachia,* January, 1896.

With the Enchanted Gorge named and tamed, most of the principal features of the Sierra were now known. The unvisited spots that remained were the summits, walls, and airy ridges of the High Sierra, the province of the mountain climbers. Their story will be told in a later section.

ON THE WAY TO THE SUMMIT.

Members of the Donner Party struggle to reach Donner Pass

SECTION II:
THE IMMIGRANTS

The men and women who traveled overland to California to make a new home for themselves were not, as we sometimes imagine, wily frontiersmen practiced in the ways of the wild. They were hardy, that much is certain: No one could survive that harrowing trip across the unforgiving Nevada desert and up over the Sierra who was not tough as buckskin. But the majority were flatland farmers and city folk with no more experience turning away hostile Indians or driving wagons through mountain passes than you or I might have. What sustained them was not wilderness cunning but rather an obsession with the promised land—a conviction that in California was to be found the realization of their dreams.

At first the dream was pure and simple: prolific farmland, blessed weather, a generous home for one's family. Such were the virtues that captivated schoolmaster John Bidwell and led him to organize the first overland party to California in 1841. Seven years later Sam Brannan rode through the streets of San Francisco shouting "Gold! Gold! Gold from the American River!" and the dream, though still simple, was no longer quite so pure. The trickle of immigrants that began with the Bidwell party swelled overnight to a tide. Within a year the non-Indian population of California soared from 2,000 to well over 50,000 people. One by one the passes were opened up: Donner Pass in 1844, Carson Pass in 1848, Echo Summit in 1852. A network of trans-Sierra routes soon crisscrossed the once-impenetrable range. When the transcontinental railroad was completed in 1869, neither a dream nor a strong constitution was needed to get to California, merely the price of a train ticket.

The hold that California exercised on the restless masses of the last century remains as strong today as ever. Twenty-four million people now make their homes in the state, and still they come: annually California's population increases eight times as much as it did in that banner year 1849. The methods of travel have changed considerably since the first wagons pointed west, but for many of today's immigrants, the points of entry into California remain the same: Donner Pass, Carson Pass, Echo Summit, and the other mountain passes to the east. For these contemporary immigrants as for their forebears, life in the Golden State still begins with a tradition-bound rite of passage over the arching crest of the Sierra.

John Bidwell

The First Immigrant Party

The tradition was founded in the spring of 1841 when John Bidwell set out from the Missouri River with 68 rather-too-optimistic companions. Their goal was to reach and settle in California. For the first part of the journey they followed the Oregon Trail, hardly a superhighway but nevertheless a well-traveled route to the Northwest for nearly 30 years. In southeastern Idaho the bulk of the party decided to continue on to Oregon; Bidwell and the rest gritted their teeth and headed southwest into uncharted country.

It was an audacious decision and for a time one that appeared foredoomed to failure. To deduce the route to California party members had little choice but to follow their noses, which did not always point in the same direction. During the torturous crossing of the Humboldt Sink supplies began to run short. The party abandoned its wagons altogether and packed its supplies onto horses and oxen. Independent-minded John Bartleson took seven men and headed south in search of a better route. The others, demoralized and disenchanted, pushed on toward the Sierra, arriving there in mid-October, 1841.

Forty-nine years later, John Bidwell recalled the remainder of the journey in an article in Century Magazine.

We were now camped on Walker River, at the very eastern base of the Sierra Nevada, and had only two oxen left. We sent men ahead to see if it would be possible to scale the mountains, while we killed the better of the two oxen and dried the meat in preparation for the ascent. The men returned towards evening and reported that they thought it would be possible to ascend the mountains, though very difficult. We had eaten our supper, and were ready for the climb in the morning. Looking back on the plains we saw something coming, which we decided to be Indians. They traveled very slowly, and it was difficult to understand their movements. To make a long story short, it was the eight men that had left us nine days before. They had gone farther south than we and had come to a lake, probably Carson Lake, and there had found Indians who supplied them plentifully with fish and pine nuts. Fish caught in such water are not fit to eat at any time, much less in the fall of the year. The men had all eaten heartily of fish and pine nuts, and had got something akin to cholera morbus. We were glad to see them although they had deserted us. We ran out to meet them and shook hands, and put our frying-pans on and gave them the best supper we could. Captain Bartleson, who when we started from Missouri was a portly man, was reduced to half his former girth. He said: "Boys, if ever I get back to Missouri I will never leave that country. I would gladly eat out of the troughs with my dogs." He seemed to be heartily sick of his late experience, but that did not prevent him from leaving us twice after that.

We were now in what is at present Nevada, and probably within forty miles of the present boundary of California. We ascended the mountains on the north side of Walker River to the summit, and then struck a stream running west which proved to be the extreme source of the Stanislaus River. We followed it down for several days and finally came to where a branch ran into it, each forming a cañon. The main river flowed in a precipitous gorge in places apparently a mile deep, and the gorge that came into it was but little less formidable. At night we found ourselves on the extreme point of the promontory between the two, very tired, and with neither grass nor water. We had to stay there that night. Early the next morning two men went down to see if it would be possible to get through down the smaller cañon. I was one of them, Jimmy John the other. Benjamin Kelsey, who had shown himself expert in finding the way, was now, without any election, still recognized as leader, as he had been during the absence of Bartleson. A party also went back to see how far we should have to go around before we could pass over the tributary cañon. The understanding was, that when we went down the cañon if it was practicable to get through we were to fire a gun so that all could follow; but if not, we were not to fire, even if we saw game. When Jimmy and I got down about three-quarters of a mile I came to the conclusion that it was impossible to get through, and said to him, "Jimmy, we might as well go back; we can't go here." "Yes, we can," said he; and insisting that we could, he pulled out a pistol and fired. It was an old dragoon pistol, and reverberated like a cannon. I hurried back to tell the company not to come down, but before I reached them the captain and his party had started. I explained, and warned them that they could not get down; but they went on as far as they could go, and then were obliged to stay all day and night to rest the animals, and had to go about among the rocks and pick a little grass for them, and go down to the stream through a terrible place in the cañon to bring water up in cups and camp-kettles, and some of the men in their boots, to pour down the animals' throats in order to keep them from perishing. Finally, four of them pulling and four of them pushing a mule, they managed to get them up one by one, and then carried all the things up again on their backs—not an easy job for exhausted men.

In some way, nobody knows how, Jimmy got through that cañon and into the Sacramento Valley. He had a horse with him—an Indian horse that was bought in the Rocky Mountains, and which could come as near climbing a tree as any horse I ever knew. Jimmy was a character. Of all men I have ever known I think he was the most fearless; he had the bravery of a bulldog. He was not seen for two months—until he was found at Sutter's, afterwards known as Sutter's Fort, now Sacramento City. . . .

We were now on the edge of the San Joaquin Valley, but we did not even know that we were in California. We could see a range of mountains lying to the west,—the Coast Range,—but we could see no valley. The evening of the day we started down into the valley we were very tired, and when night came our party was strung along for three or four miles, and every man slept right where darkness overtook him. He would take off his saddle for a pillow and turn his horse or mule loose, if he had one. His animal would be too poor to walk away, and in the morning he would find him, usually within fifty feet. The jaded horses nearly perished with hunger and fatigue. When we overtook the foremost of the party the next morning we found they had come to a pond of water, and one of them had killed a fat coyote; when I came up it was all eaten except the lights and the windpipe, on which I made my breakfast. From that camp we saw timber to the north of us, evidently bordering a stream running west. It turned out to be the stream that we had followed down in the mountains—the Stanislaus River. As soon as we came in sight of the bottom land of the stream we saw an abundance of antelopes and sandhill cranes. We killed two of each the first evening. Wild grapes also abounded. The next day we killed thirteen deer and antelopes, jerked the meat and got ready to go on, all except the captain's mess of seven or eight, who decided to stay there and lay in meat enough to last them into California! We were really almost down to tidewater, but did not know it. Some thought it was five hundred miles yet to California. But all thought we had to cross at least that range of mountains in sight to the west before entering the promised land, and how many more beyond no one could tell. Nearly all thought it best to press on lest the snows might overtake us in the mountains before us, as they had already nearly done on the mountains behind us (the Sierra Nevada). It was now about the first of November. Our party set forth bearing northwest, aiming for a seeming gap north of a high mountain in the chain to the west of us. That mountain we found to be Mount Diablo. At night the Indians attacked the captain's camp and stole all their animals, which were the best in the company, and the next day the men had to overtake us with just what they could carry in their hands.

The next day, judging by the timber we saw, we concluded there was a river to the west. So two men went ahead to see if they could find a trail or a crossing. The timber seen proved to be along what is now known as the San Joaquin River. We sent two men on ahead to spy out the country. At night one of them returned, saying they had come across an Indian on horseback without a saddle who wore a cloth jacket but no other clothing. From what they could understand the Indian knew Dr. Marsh and had offered to guide them to his place. . . . One man went with the Indian to Marsh's ranch and the other came back to tell us what he had done, with the suggestion that we should go on and cross the river (San Joaquin) at the place to which the trail was leading. In that way we found ourselves two days later at Dr. Marsh's ranch, and there we learned that we were really in California and our journey at an end. After six months we had now arrived at the first settlement in California, November 4, 1841.

The First Immigrant Party, from "The First Emigrant Train to California" by John Bidwell. *The Century Illustrated Magazine,* November 1890. Reprinted by permission of *Current History.*

Moses Schallenberger

A Winter Alone

Despite Bidwell's success in crossing the Sierra, he had failed to discover a practicable route that could be followed by other immigrants. That problem was solved in 1844 when Elisha Stevens led a party over the range by a route that would become the gateway to California. Somewhere in western Nevada the Stevens party met an Indian whose name they translated as "Truckee." Truckee convinced them that they should head due west rather than continue south as Bidwell had done. Following this advice, the group soon struck a river issuing from the Sierra; not long after, on November 25, 1844, they manhandled their wagons through the snow at what we now know as Donner Pass. These were the first wagons driven over the range into California.

The Stevens party is remembered for discovering Donner Pass, though of course the credit belongs to Truckee. In any event, the greater drama of that winter of 1844 took place not at the pass but a few miles to the east, at the edge of Donner Lake. Several wagons were left at the lake until members of the party could return for them with fresh animals. Three men— Moses Schallenberger, Joseph Foster, and Allen Montgomery—volunteered to winter at the lake to protect the abandoned wagons.

The plan was short-lived. The weather soon turned brutal. Ten feet of snow fell. With rawhide and bows from the wagons, the three men fashioned snowshoes, but the contraptions were too heavy to use. Early in December food supplies began to run short. Realizing that they must escape from their snowbound prison, the three decided to set out across the Sierra on foot, in hope of finding the rest of the party.

As they prepared for their dangerous journey, Schallenberger little realized that he would not be up to the Sierra crossing. Ahead of him lay one of the most trying ordeals in the history of the range: a winter alone in the heart of the mountains. A remarkable enough accomplishment for any person . . . and all the more so for a young man only seventeen years old.

Death, the fearful, agonizing death by starvation, literally stared us in the face. At last, after due consideration, we determined to start for California on foot. Accordingly we dried some of our beef, and each of us carrying ten pounds of meat, a pair of blankets, a rifle and ammunition, we set out on our perilous journey. Not knowing how to fasten snow-shoes to our feet made it very fatiguing to walk with them. We fastened them to heel and toe, and thus had to lift the whole weight of the shoe at every step, and as the shoe would necessarily sink down somewhat, the snow would crumble in on top of it, and in a short time each shoe weighed about ten pounds.

Foster and Montgomery were matured men, and could consequently stand a greater amount of hardship than I, who was still a growing boy with weak muscles and a huge appetite, both of which were being used in exactly the reverse order designed by nature. Consequently, when we reached the summit of the mountain about sunset that night, having traveled a distance of about fifteen miles, I was scarcely able to drag one foot after the other. The day had been a hard one for us all, but particularly painful to me. The awkward manner in which our snow-shoes were fastened to our feet made the mere act of walking the hardest kind of work. In addition to this, about the middle of the afternoon I was seized with cramps. I fell down with them several times, and my companions had to wait for me, for it was impossible for me to move until the paroxysm had passed off. After each attack I would summon all my will power and press on, trying to keep up with the others. Toward evening, however, the attacks became more frequent and painful, and I could not walk more than fifty yards without stopping to rest.

When night came on we cut down a tree and with it built a fire on top of the snow. We then spread some pine brush for our beds, and after eating a little jerky and standing around our fire in a vain attempt to get warm, we laid down and tried to sleep. Although we were thoroughly exhausted, sleep would not come. Anxiety as to what might have been the fate of those that had preceded us, as well as uncertainty as to our fate, kept us awake all night. Every now and then one of us would rise to replenish the fire, which, though it kept us from freezing, could not make us comfortable. When daylight came we found that our fire had melted the snow in a circle of about fifteen feet in diameter and had sunk to the ground, a distance also of about fifteen feet. The fire was so far down that we could not get to it but as we had nothing to cook, it made but little difference. We ate our jerky while we deliberated as to what we should do next. I was so stiff that I could hardly move, and my companions had grave doubts as to whether I could stand the journey. If I should give out they could afford me no assistance, and I would necessarily be left to perish in the snow. I fully realized the situation, and told them that I would return to the cabin and live as long as possible on the quarter of beef that was still there, and when it was all gone I would start out again alone for California. They reluctantly assented to my plan, and promised that if they ever got to California and it was possible to get back, they would return to my assistance.

We did not say much at parting; our hearts were too full for that. There was simply a warm clasp of the hand accompanied by the familiar word, "Good-by," which we all felt might be the last words we should ever speak to each other. The feeling of loneliness that came over me as the two men turned away I cannot express, though it will never be forgotten, while the "Good-by, Mose," so sadly and reluctantly spoken, rings in my ears today. I desire to say here that both Foster and Montgomery were brave, warm-hearted men, and it was by no fault of theirs that I was thus left alone. It would only have made matters worse for either of them to remain with me, for the quarter of beef at the cabin would last me longer alone, and thus increase my chances of escape. While our decision was a sad one, it was the only one that could be made.

My companions had not been long out of sight before my spirits began to revive, and I began to think, like Micawber, that something might "turn up." So I strapped on my blankets and dried beef, shouldered my gun, and began to retrace my steps to the cabin. It had frozen during the night and this enabled me to walk on our trail without the snow-shoes. This was a great relief, but the exertion and sickness of the day before had so weakened me that I think I was never so tired in my life as when, just a little before dark, I came in sight if the cabin. The door-sill was only nine inches high, but I could not step over it without taking my hands to raise my leg. As soon as I was able to crawl around the next morning I put on my snow-shoes, and, taking my rifle, scoured the country thoroughly for foxes. The result was as I had expected—just as it had always been—plenty of tracks but no fox.

Discouraged and sick at heart, I came in from my fruitless search and prepared to pass another night of agony. As I put my gun in the corner, my eyes fell upon some steel traps that Captain Stevens had brought with him and left behind in his wagon. In an instant the thought flashed across my mind, "If I can't shoot a coyote or fox, why not trap one." There was inspiration in the thought, and my spirits began to rise immediately. The heads of the two cows I cut to pieces for bait, and, having raked the snow from some fallen trees, and found other sheltered places, I set my traps. That night I went to bed with a lighter heart and was able to get some sleep.

As soon as daylight came I was out to inspect the traps. I was anxious to see them and still I dreaded to look. After some hesitation I commenced the examination, and to my delight I found in one of them a starved coyote. I soon had his hide off and his flesh roasted in a Dutch oven. I ate this meat, but it was horrible. I next tried boiling him, but it did not improve the flavor. I cooked him in every possible manner my imagination, spurred by hunger, could suggest, but could not get him into a condition where he could be eaten without revolting my stomach. But for three days this was all I had to eat. On the third night I caught two foxes. I roasted one of them, and the meat, though entirely devoid of fat, was delicious. I was so hungry that I could easily have eaten a fox at two meals, but I made one last me two days.

I often took my gun and tried to find something to shoot, but in vain. Once I shot a crow that seemed to have got out of his latitude and stopped on a tree near the cabin. I stewed the crow, but it was difficult for me to decide which I liked best, crow or coyote. I now gave my whole attention to trapping, having found how useless it was to hunt for game. I caught, on an average, a fox in two days, and every now and then a coyote. These last-named animals I carefully hung up under the brush shed on the north side of the cabin, but I never got hungry enough to eat one of them again. There was eleven hanging there when I came away. I never really suffered for something to eat, but was in almost continual anxiety for fear the supply would give out. For instance, as soon as one meal was finished I began to be distressed for fear I could not get another one. My only hope was that the supply of foxes would not become exhausted.

One morning two of my traps contained foxes. Having killed one, I started for the other, but, before I could reach it, the fox had left his foot in the traps and started to run. I went as fast as I could to the cabin for my gun, and then followed him. He made for a creek about a hundred yards from the house, into which he plunged and swam across. He was scrambling up the opposite bank when I reached the creek. In my anxiety at the prospect of losing my breakfast, I had forgotten to remove a greasy wad that I usually kept in the muzzle of my gun to prevent it from rusting, and when I fired, the ball struck the snow about a foot above reynard's back. I reloaded as rapidly as possible, and as the gun was one of the old-fashioned flint-locks that primed itself, it did not require much time. But, short as the time was, the fox had gone about forty yards when I shot him. Now the problem was to get him to camp. The water in the stream was about two and a half feet deep and icy cold. But I plunged in, and, on reaching the other side, waded for forty yards through the snow, into which I sank to my arms, secured my game, and returned the way I came. I relate this incident to illustrate how much affection I had for the fox. It is strange that I never craved anything to eat but good fat meat. For bread or vegetables I had no desire. Salt I had in plenty, but never used. I had just coffee enough for one cup, and that I saved for Christmas.

My life was more miserable than I can describe. The daily struggle for life and the uncertainty under which I labored were very wearing. I was always worried and anxious, not about myself alone, but in regard to the fate of those who had gone forward. I would lie awake nights and think of these things, and revolve in my mind what I would do when the supply of foxes became exhausted. The quarter of beef I had not touched and I resolved to dry it, and, when the foxes were all gone, to take my gun, blankets, and dried beef and follow in the footsteps of my former companions.

Fortunately, I had a plenty of books, Dr. Townsend having brought out quite a library. I used often to read aloud, for I longed for some sound to break the oppressive stillness. For the same reason, I would talk aloud to myself. At night I built large fires and read by the light of the pine knots as late as possible, in order that I might sleep late the next morning, and thus cause the days to seem shorter. What I wanted most was enough to eat, and next the thing I tried hardest to do was to kill time. I thought the snow would never leave the ground, and the few months I had been living here seemed years.

One evening, a little before sunset, about the last of February, as I was standing a short distance from my cabin I thought I could distinguish the form of a man moving towards me. I first thought it was an Indian, but very soon I could recognize the familiar face of Dennis Martin. My feelings can be better imagined than described. He relieved my anxiety about those of our party, who had gone forward with the wagons. They had all arrived safety in California and were then in Yuba. They were all safe, although some of them had suffered much from hunger. Mrs. Patterson and her children had eaten nothing for fourteen days but rawhides. Mr. Martin had brought a small amount of provisions on his back, which were shared among them. All the male portion of the party, except Foster and Montgomery, had joined Captain Sutter and gone to the Micheltorena war. Dr. Townsend was surgeon of the corps. My sister Mrs. Townsend, hearing that Mr. Martin was about to return to pilot the emigrants out of the wilderness, begged him to extend his journey a little farther and lend a helping hand to her brother Moses. He consented to do so, and here he was.

A Winter Alone, from "Robinson Crusoe in the Sierra Nevada" by Erwin G. Gudde. *Sierra Club Bulletin,* May, 1951. Reprinted by permission of the Sierra Club.

Patrick Breen

May God Send Us Help

Schallenberger's miraculous rescue was completed shortly thereafter when he and Martin, traveling on an improved design of snowshoe, caught up with the main section of the Stevens party camping on the Yuba River. The way was now open for other immigrants to cross the Sierra into California, and many were quick to accept the challenge. The following autumn several parties traversed the Sierra without incident by way of Donner Pass. Then in 1846, two years after Schallenberger wintered at the lake, a tragedy was played out in that forlorn spot that is unparalleled in the history of the westward migration.

Winter arrived early that year, and the Donner party late. When the 82 members of the party reached the foot of the pass, they found they were unable to get through. Several members pushed on alone, but most decided to remain at the lake. Schallenberger's cabin was still standing and it quickly became home for part of the party; makeshift accommodations served for the rest.

It is impossible to comprehend fully the calamity that ensued as blizzards raged and the food ran out and family and friends died of starvation one after another. If the horror of those days can be glimpsed anywhere, it is in the stoic words of Patrick Breen, who kept a journal of the events of that winter, and was one of the lucky ones who survived.

As the new year of 1847 began, Breen noted that an unusual spell of fair weather had set in. . . .

Satd 9th   Continues fine   freezeing hard at night   this a beatiful morning   wind about S.S.E.   Mrs. Reid here Virginias toes frozen   a little snow settleing none to be perceivd.

Sund. 10   Began to snow last night still continues   wind W N W.

Mond. 11th   Still continues to snow fast, looks gloomy   Mrs Reid at Keysburgs   Virg. with us   wood scarce difficult to get any more   wind W.

ARRIVAL OF RELIEF PARTY,
FEB. 18TH 1847.

Tuesd 12th   Snows fast yet   new snow about 3 feet deep   wind S:W no sign of clearing off.

Wens. 13th   Snowing fast   wind N.W   snow higher than the shanty must be 13 feet deep   dont know how to get wood this morning   it is dredful to look at. . . .

Sund. 17th   Fine morning   sun shineing clear   wind S.S.E   Eliza came here this morning, sent her back again to Graves   Lanthrom crazy last night so Bill says, Keyburg sent Bill to get hides off his shanty & carry thim home this morning,   provisions scarce hides are the only article we depend on, we have a little meat yet, may God send us help. . . .

Thursd. 21   Fine morning   wind W   did not freze quite so hard last night as it has done,   John Battice & Denton came this morning with Eliza she wont eat hides Mrs Reid sent her back to live or die on them.   Milt. got his toes froze   the Donoghs are all well. . . .

Weds 27th   Began to snow yesterday & still continues to sleet thawing a little   wind W   Mrs. Keyber here this morning   Lewis Suitor she says died three days ago   Keysburg sick & Lanthrom lying in bed the whole of his time   dont have fire enough to cook their hides. Bill & Murphy sick. . . .

Satd. 30th   Fine pleasant morning   wind W   begining to thaw in the sun   John & Edwd. went to Graves this morning   the Graves seized on Mrs Reids goods untill they would be paid also took the hides that she & family had to live on, she got two peices of hides from there & the ballance they have taken   you may know from these proceedings what our fare is in camp   there is nothing to be got by hunting yet perhaps there soon will.   God send it   Amen. . . .

Mond. February the 1st   Froze very hard last night cold to day & cloudy   wind N W.   sun shines dimly   the snow has not settled much John is unwell to day   with the help of God & he will be well by night Amen.

Tuesday 2nd   Began to snow this morning & continued to snow untill night   now clear   wind during the storm S. W.

Wend. 3rd   Cloudy   looks like more snow   not cold, froze a little last night   wind S.S W.   it was clear all last night   sun shines out at times.

Thurd. 4th   Snowd. hard all night & still continues with a strong S:
W. wind untill now abated   looks as if it would snow all day   snowd.
about 2 feet deep now.

Frid. 5th   Snowd. hard all until 12 o'clock at night   wind still
continud to blow hard from the S. W: to day pretty clear a few clouds
only   Peggy very uneasy for fear we shall all perrish with hunger   we
have but a little meat left & only part of 3 hides   has to support Mrs.
Reid she has nothing left but one hide & it is on Graves shanty   Milt is
living there & likely will keep that hide   Eddys child died last night.

Satd. 6th   It snowd. faster last night & day to day than it has done
this winter & still continues without an intermission   wind S. W
Murphys folks or Keysburgs say they cant eat hides I wish we had
enough of them   Mrs Eddy very weak.

Sund. 7th   Ceasd. to snow last after one of the most severe storms
we experienced this winter the snow fell about 4 feet deep. I had to
shovel the snow off our shanty this morning it thawd so fast & thawd.
during the whole storm.   to day it is quite pleasant   wind S. W.   Milt
here to day says Mrs Reid has to get a hide from Mrs. Murphy &
McCutchins child died 2nd of this month.

Mond. 8th   Fine clear morning   wind S. W.   froze hard last.
Spitzer died last night about 3 o clock to we will bury him in the snow
Mrs Eddy died on the night of the 7th.

Tuesd. 9th   Mrs. Murphy here this morning   Pikes child all but
dead   Milt at Murphys not able to get out of bed   Keyburg never gets
up says he is not able.   John went down to day to bury Mrs Eddy &
child   heard nothing from Graves for 2 or 3 days Mrs Murphy just now
going to Graves   fine morning   wind S. E. froze hard last night   begins
to thaw in the sun.

Wednsd. 10th   Beautiful morning   wind W: froze hard last night,
to day thawing in the sun   Milt Elliot died las night at Murphys
shanty about 9 o'clock P: M: Mrs Reid went there this morning to see
after his effects.   J Denton trying to borrow meat for Graves had none
to give they have nothing but hides   all are entirely out of meat but a
little we have   our hides are nearly all eat up but with Gods help spring
will soon smile upon us. . . .

*Fair weather set in again, with freezing temperatures at night but thawing
during the day. On February 18 Breen was able to report "all in good health."
The same day a rescue party arrived at last from Sutter's Fort in the
Sacramento Valley. Breen was so enervated by now that he reported this glad
occasion with no more enthusiasm than he noted the morning wind direction. On
February 22, 24 of his companions left for Sutter's Fort with the rescuers. Breen
and the rest stayed behind to await a second relief party, and to confront a new
horror, one that has since come to be inextricably linked to the name Donner.*

Tuesd. 23   Froze hard last night   to day fine & thawey has the
appearance of spring all but the deep snow   wind S:S.E.   shot Towser
to day & dressed his flesh   Mrs Graves came here this morning to
borrow meat dog or ox they think I have meat to spare but I know to
the contrary they have plenty hides I live principally on the same.

Wend. 24th   Froze hard last night   to day cloudy looks like a
storm   wind blows hard from the W.   Commenced thawing   there
has not any more returned from those who started to cross the mts.

Thursd. 25th   Froze hard last night   fine & sunshiny to day
wind W.   Mrs Murphy says the wolves are about to dig up the dead
bodies at her shanty, the nights are too cold to watch them, we hear
them howl.

Frid 26th   Froze hard last night   today clear & warm   Wind S: E:
blowing briskly   Marthas jaw swelled with the toothache;   hungry
times in camp, plenty hides but the folks will not eat them we eat them
with a tolerable good apetite.   Thanks be to Almighty God.   Amen
Mrs Murphy said here yesterday that thought she would commence
on Milt. & eat him.   I dont that she has done so yet, it is distressing
The Donnos told the California folks that they commence to eat the
dead people 4 days ago, if they did not succeed that day or next in
finding their cattle then under ten or twelve feet of snow & did not
know the spot or near it, I suppose they have done so ere this time.

Satd. 27th   Beautiful morning sun shineing brilliantly,   wind
about S.W.   the snow has fell in debth about 5 feet but no thaw but
the sun in day time it freezeing hard every night,   heard some geese
fly over last night saw none.

Sund. 28th   Froze hard last night to day fair & sunshine wind S.E.
1 solitary Indian passed by yesterday come from the lake had a heavy

pack on his back gave me 5 or 6 roots resembleing onions in shape taste some like a sweet potatoe, all full of little tough fibres.

    Mond. March the 1st   So fine & pleasant froze hard last night there has 10 men arrived this morning from Bear Valley with provisions   we are to start in two or three days & cash our goods here there is amongst them some old they say the snow will be here untill June.

May God Send Us Help, from *Diary of Patrick Breen,* edited by Frederick J. Teggart. *Publications of the Academy of Pacific Coast History,* July 1910.

Virginia Reed Murphy

Too Full of the Beautiful

So ends the diary of one who survived. Another was Virginia Reed, who was 12 years old at the time. More than 40 years later, married and the mother of six children, she finally recorded her memories of the ordeal. Her recollection of detail quite naturally had faded during the intervening years. But her sense of the drama of those days had, if anything, heightened from years of reflection. Her thoughtful words contrast sharply with the tortured diary entries Patrick Breen set down during the days at Donner Lake.

This excerpt from Virginia Reed Murphy's account begins with the joyful and long-dreamed-of arrival of the first rescue party from Sutter's Fort.

On the evening of February 19th, 1847, they reached our cabins, where all were starving. They shouted to attract attention. Mr. Breen, clambered up icy steps from our cabin, and soon we heard the blessed words, "Relief, thank God, relief!" There was joy at Donner Lake that night, for we did not know the fate of the Forlorn Hope[1] and we were told that relief parties would come and go until all were across the mountains. But with the joy sorrow was strangely blended. There were tears in other eyes than those of children; strong men sat down and wept. For the dead were lying about on the snow, some even unburied, since the living had not had strength to bury their dead. When Milt Elliott died,—our faithful friend, who seemed so like a brother,—my mother and I dragged him up out of the cabin and covered him with snow. Commencing at his feet, I patted the pure white snow down softly until I reached his face. Poor Milt! it was hard to cover that face from sight forever, for with his death our best friend was gone.

---

[1]"Forlorn Hope" was the name given to fifteen members of the Donner party who earlier had tried to escape to Sutter's Fort. Eight perished during the attempt.

On the 22nd of February the first relief started with a party of twenty-three—men, women and children. My mother and her family were among the number. It was a bright sunny morning and we felt happy, but we had not gone far when Patty and Tommy gave out. They were not able to stand the fatigue and it was not thought safe to allow them to proceed, so Mr. Glover informed mama that they would have to be sent back to the cabins to await the next expedition. What language can express our feelings? My mother said that she would go back with her children—that we would all go back together. This the relief party would not permit, and Mr. Glover promised mama that as soon as they reached Bear Valley he himself would return for her children. Finally my mother, turning to Mr. Glover said, "Are you a Mason?" He replied that he was. "Will you promise me on the word of a Mason that if we do not meet their father you will return and save my children?" He pledged himself that he would. My father was a member of the Mystic Tie and mama had great faith in the word of a Mason. It was a sad parting—a fearful struggle. The men turned aside, not being able to hide their tears. Patty said, "I want to see papa, but I will take good care of Tommy and I do not want you to come back." Mr. Glover returned with the children and, providing them with food, left them in the care of Mr. Breen.

With sorrowful hearts we traveled on, walking through snow in single file. The men wearing snow-shoes broke the way and we followed in their tracks. At night we lay down on the snow to sleep, to awake to find our clothing all frozen, even to our shoe-strings. At break of day we were again on the road, owing to the fact that we could make better time over the frozen snow. The sunshine, which it would seem would have been welcome, only added to our misery. The dazzling reflection of the snow was very trying to the eyes, while its heat melted our frozen clothing, making them cling to our bodies. My brother was too small to step in the tracks made by the men, and in order to travel he had to place his knee on the little hill of snow after each step and climb over. Mother coaxed him along, telling him that every step he took he was getting nearer papa and nearer something to eat. He was the youngest child that walked over the Sierra Nevada. On our second day's journey John Denton gave out and declared it would be impossible for him to travel, but he begged his companions to continue their journey. A fire was built and he was left lying on a bed of freshly cut pine boughs, peacefully smoking. He looked so comfortable that my little brother wanted to stay with him; but when the second relief party reached him poor Denton was past waking. His last thoughts seemed to have gone back to his childhood's home, as a little poem was found by his side, the pencil apparently just dropped from his hand.

Captain Tucker's party on their way to the cabins had lightened their packs of a sufficient quantity of provisions to supply the sufferers on their way out. But when we reached the place where the cache had been made by hanging the food on a tree, we were horrified to find that wild animals had destroyed it, and again starvation stared us in the face. But my father was hurrying over the mountains, and met us in our hour of need with his hands full of bread. He had expected to meet us on this day, and had stayed up all night baking bread to give us. He brought with him fourteen men. Some of his party were ahead, and when they saw us coming they called out, "Is Mrs. Reed with you? If she is, tell her Mr. Reed is here." We heard the call; mother knelt on the snow, while I tried to run to meet papa.

When my father learned that two of his children were still at the cabins, he hurried on, so fearful was he that they might perish before he reached them. He seemed to fly over the snow, and made in two days the distance we had been five in traveling, and was overjoyed to find Patty and Tom alive. He reached Donner Lake on the first of March, and what a sight met his gaze! The famished little children and the death-like look of all made his heart ache. He filled Patty's apron with biscuits, which she carried around, giving one to each person. He had soup made for the infirm, and rendered every assistance possible to the sufferers. Leaving them with about seven days' provisions, he started out with a party of seventeen, all that were able to travel. Three of his men were left at the cabins to procure wood and assist the helpless. My father's party (the second relief) had not traveled many miles when a storm broke upon them. With the snow came a perfect hurricane. The crying of half-frozen children, the lamenting of the mothers, and the suffering of the whole party was heart-rending; and above all could be heard the shrieking of the storm King. One who has never witnessed a blizzard in the Sierra can form no idea of the situation. All night my father and his men worked unceasingly through the raging storm, trying to erect shelter for the dying women and children. At times the hurricane would burst forth with such violence that he felt alarmed on account of the tall timber surrounding the camp. The party were destitute of food, all supplies that could be spared having been left with those at the cabins. The relief party had cached provisions on their way over to the cabins, and my father had sent three of the men forward for food before the storm set in; but they could not return. Thus, again, death stared all in the face. At one time the fire was nearly gone; had it been lost, all would have perished. Three days and nights they were exposed to the fury of the elements. Finally my father became snow-blind and could do no more, and he would have died but for the exertions of William McClutchen and Hiram Miller, who worked over him all night. From this time forward, the toil and responsibility rested upon McClutchen and Miller.

The storm at last ceased, and these two determined to set out over the snow and send back relief to those not able to travel. Hiram Miller picked up Tommy and started. Patty thought she could walk, but gradually everything faded from her sight, and she too seemed to be dying. All other sufferings were now forgotten, and everything was done to revive the child. My father found some crumbs in the thumb of his woolen mitten; warming and moistening them between his own lips, he gave them to her and thus saved her life, and afterward she was carried along by different ones in the company. Patty was not alone in her travels. Hidden away in her bosom was a tiny doll, which she had carried day and night through all of our trials. Sitting before a nice, bright fire at Woodworth's Camp, she took dolly out to have a talk, and told her of all her new happiness.

There was untold suffering at that "Starved Camp," as the place has since been called. When my father reached Woodworth's Camp, a third relief started in at once and rescued the living. A fourth relief went on to Donner Lake, as many were still there—and many remain there still, including George Donner and wife, Jacob Donner and wife and four of their children. George Donner had met with an accident which rendered him unable to travel; and his wife would not leave him to die alone. It would take pages to tell of the heroic acts and noble deeds of those who lie sleeping about Donner Lake.

Most of the survivors, when brought in from the mountains, were taken by the different relief parties to Sutter's Fort, and the generous hearted captain did everything possible for the sufferers. Out of the eighty-three persons who were snowed in at Donner Lake, forty-two perished, and of the thirty-one emigrants who left Springfield, Illinois, that spring morning, only eighteen lived to reach California. Alcalde Sinclair took my mother and her family to his own home, and we were surrounded with every comfort. Mrs. Sinclair was the dearest of women. Never can I forget their kindness. But our anxiety was not over, for we knew that my father's party had been caught in the storm. I can see my mother now, as she stood leaning against the door for hours at a time, looking towards the mountains. At last my father arrived at Mr. Sinclair's with the little ones, and our family were again united. That day's happiness repaid us for much that we had suffered; and it was spring in California.

Words cannot tell how beautiful the spring appeared to us coming out of the mountains from that long winter at Donner Lake in our little dark cabins under the snow. Before us now lay, in all its beauty, the broad valley of the Sacramento. I remember one day, when traveling down Napa Valley, we stopped at noon to have lunch under the shade of an oak; but I was not hungry; I was too full of the beautiful around me to think of eating. So I wandered off by myself to a lovely little knoll and stood there in a bed of wild flowers, looking up and down the green valley, all dotted with trees. The birds were singing with very joy in the branches over my head, and the blessed sun was smiling down upon all as though in benediction. I drank it in for a moment, and then began kissing my hand and wafting kisses to Heaven in thanksgiving to the Almighty for creating a world so beautiful. I felt so near God at that moment that it seemed to me I could feel His breath warm on my cheek. By and by I heard papa calling, "Daughter, where are you? Come, child, we are ready to start, and you have had no lunch," I ran and caught him by the hand, saying, "Buy this place, please, and let us make our home here." He stood looking around for a moment, and said, "It *is* a lovely spot," and then we passed on.

Too Full of the Beautiful, from "Across the Plains in the Donner Party" by Virginia Reed Murphy. *The Century Illustrated Magazine,* July 1891. Reprinted by permission of *Current History.*

Jim Beckwourth

Destined to Disappointment

*The difficulties of the Donner Pass entrance into California were so severe
that alternate routes, once located, were far to be preferred. One such route was
discovered by veteran mountain man Jim Beckwourth. Beckwourth, by his own
account at least, led one of those larger-than-life lives, hunting beaver with
William Ashley, trading with the Mexicans at Santa Fe, stealing horses, fighting
grizzlies, and scalping Indians, to say nothing of being elected First Counselor of
the Crow Nation.*

*In 1851 Beckwourth discovered a pass near the headwaters of the Feather
River which was 2,000 feet lower and immeasurably easier than Donner Pass.
He immediately realized the economic importance of his discovery. Like the
Chamber of Commerce that diverts traffic from the main highway into the
downtown business district, Beckwourth decided to guide wagons away from the
standard route to his own pass, then down to Marysville. As he saw it, the citizens
of the towns along the way would reward him handsomely for this service.*

*Unfortunately, things turned out differently, for reasons Beckwourth outlined
grumpily in his autobiography.*

While on this excursion I discovered what is now known as
"Beckwourth's Pass" in the Sierra Nevada. From some of the elevations over which we passed I remarked a place far away to the southward that seemed lower than any other. I made no mention of it to my
companion, but thought that at some future time I would examine
into it farther. I continued on to Shasta with my fellow-traveler, and
returned after a fruitless journey of eighteen days.

After a short stay in the American Valley, I again started out with a
prospecting party of twelve men. We killed a bullock before starting
and dried the meat, in order to have provisions to last us during the
trip. We proceeded in an easterly direction, and all busied themselves

89

in searching for gold; but my errand was of a different character: I had come to discover what I suspected to be a pass.

It was the latter end of April when we entered upon an extensive valley at the northwest extremity of the Sierra range. The valley was already robed in freshest verdure, contrasting most delightfully with the huge snow-clad mass of rock we had just left. Flowers of every variety and hue spread their variegated charms before us; magpies were chattering, and gorgeously-plumaged birds were caroling in the delights of unmolested solitude. Swarms of wild geese and ducks were swimming on the surface of the cool crystal stream, which was the central fork of the Rio de las Plumas, or sailed the air in clouds over our heads. Deer and antelope filled the plains, and their boldness was conclusive that the hunters' rifle was to them unknown. Nowhere visible were any traces of the white man's approach, and it is probable that our steps were the first that ever marked the spot. We struck across this beautiful valley to the waters of the Yuba, from thence to the waters of the Truchy, which latter flowed in an easterly direction, telling us we were on the eastern slope of the mountain range. This, I at once saw, would afford the best wagon-road into the American Valley approaching from the eastward, and I imparted my views to three of my companions in whose judgment I placed the most confidence. They thought highly of the discovery, and even proposed to associate with me in the opening of the road. We also found gold, but not in sufficient quantity to warrant our working it; and, furthermore, the ground was too wet to admit of our prospecting to any advantage.

On my return to the American Valley, I made known my discovery to a Mr. Turner, proprietor of the American Ranch, who entered enthusiastically into my views; it was a thing, he said, he had never dreamed of before. If I could but carry out my plan, and divert travel into that road, he thought I should be a made man for life. Thereupon he drew up a subscription list, setting forth the merits of the project, and showing how the road could be made practicable to Bidwell's Bar, and thence to Marysville, which latter place would derive peculiar advantages from the discovery. He headed the subscription with two hundred dollars.

When I reached Bidwell's Bar and unfolded my project, the town was seized with a perfect mania for the opening of the route. The subscriptions amounted to five hundred dollars. I then proceeded to Marysville, a place which would unquestionably derive greater benefit from the newly-discovered route than any other place on the way, since this must be the entrepôt or principal starting-place for emigrants. I communicated with several of the most influential residents on the subject in hand. They also spoke very encouragingly of my undertaking, and referred me, before all others, to the mayor of the city. Accordingly, I waited upon that gentleman (a Mr. Miles), and brought the matter under his notice, representing it as being a legitimate matter for his interference, and offering substantial advantages to the commercial prosperity of the city. The mayor entered warmly into my views, and pronounced it as his opinion that the profits resulting from the speculation could not be less than from six to ten thousand dollars; and as the benefits accruing to the city would be incalculable, he would insure my expenses while engaged upon it.

I mentioned that I should prefer some guarantee before entering my labors, to secure me against loss of what money I might lay out.

"Leave that to me," said the mayor; "I will attend to the whole affair. I feel confident that a subject of so great importance to our interests will engage the earliest attention."

I thereupon left the whole proceeding in his hands, and, immediately setting men to work upon the road, went out to the Truchy to turn emigration into my newly-discovered route. While thus busily engaged I was seized with erysipelas, and abandoned all hopes of recovery; I was over one hundred miles away from medical assistance, and my only shelter was a brush tent. I made my will, and resigned myself to death. Life still lingered in me, however, and a train of wagons came up, and encamped near to where I lay. I was reduced to a very low condition, but I saw the drivers, and acquainted them with the object which had brought me out there. They offered to attempt the new road if I thought myself sufficiently strong to guide them through it. The women, God bless them! came to my assistance, and through their kind attention and excellent nursing I rapidly recovered from my lingering sickness, until I was soon able to mount my horse, and lead the first train, consisting of seventeen wagons, through "Beckwourth's Pass." We reached the American Valley without the least accident, and the emigrants expressed entire satisfaction with the route. I returned with the train through to Marysville, and on the intelligence being communicated of the practicability of the road, there was quite a public rejoicing. A northern route had been discovered, and the city had received an impetus that would advance her beyond all her sisters on the Pacific shore. I felt proud of my achievement, and was foolish enough to promise myself a substantial recognition of my labors.

I was destined to disappointment, for that same night Marysville was laid in ashes. The mayor of the ruined town congratulated me upon bringing a train through. He expressed great delight at my good fortune, but regretted that their recent calamity had placed it entirely beyond his power to obtain for me any substantial reward. With the exception of some two hundred dollars subscribed by some liberal-minded citizens of Marysville, I have received no indemnification for the money and labor I have expended upon my discovery. The city had been greatly benefited by it, as all must acknowledge, for the emigrants that now flock to Marysville would otherwise have gone to Sacramento. Sixteen hundred dollars I expended upon the road is forever gone, but those who derive advantage from this outlay and loss of time devote no thought to the discoverer; nor do I see clearly how I am to help myself, for every one knows I can not roll a mountain into the pass and shut it up. But there is one thing certain: although I recognize no superior in love of country, and feel in all its force the obligation imposed upon me to advance her interests, still, when I go out hunting in the mountains a road for every body to pass through, and expending my time and capital upon an object from which I shall derive no benefit, it will be because I have nothing better to do.

Destined to Disappointment, from *The Life and Adventures of James P. Beckwourth,* written from his own dictation by T.D. Bonner. Harper & Bros. Publishers, 1856.

Charles F. Browne (Artemus Ward)

"Keep Your Seat, Horace!"

In 1852 a new trans-Sierra route was discovered by Colonel John Calhoun "Cock Eye" Johnson. Following essentially the paths of today's highways 89 and 50, Johnson's route connected Carson Valley with Placerville by way of Luther Pass and Echo Summit. Within a few years it had become the standard route for stage coach travelers entering California from Nevada.

In 1859 an incident occurred along the Echo Summit road which was so trivial and so unremarkable it should quickly have been forgotten. Yet for some unfathomable reason it was not. Rather, the story of "Hank and Horace" prospered like none other before it, becoming ultimately perhaps the most famous anecdote in Sierra history.

How this happened is a question for students of social history and mass psychology to ponder. What is certain is that the tale spread through the western mining towns like news of a fresh strike. Every traveler heard it once if not a dozen times. Mark Twain called "Hank and Horace" a "mouldy," "odious," "pointless," but "unkillable anecdote which everybody had long ago grown weary of, weary unto death." Twain himself told the story hundreds of times.

In its bare-bones details, "Hank and Horace" is true, though few who told the tale could resist embroidering it generously. Hank Monk, one of the West's best stagecoach drivers, was hired to drive Horace Greeley, editor of the New York Tribune, to Placerville. Greeley was a celebrity from the East, a founder of the Republican Party, popularizer of the bromide "Go west, young man," and soon to be candidate for President. In the story, the great man is humiliated, dominated—tamed by Monk, a mere country bumpkin, and therein may have lain the secret of the tale's popularity.

"Hank and Horace" received its most exaggerated and probably least truthful treatment at the hands of humorist Charles F. Browne, who doctored it almost beyond recognition. Browne, better known by his pseudonym Artemus

Ward, enjoyed a reputation as Abraham Lincoln's favorite humorist. Here is his
version of the unkillable story of Hank and Horace.

When Mr. Greeley was in California ovations awaited him at every
town. He had written powerful leaders in the *Tribune* in favor of the
Pacific Railroad, which had greatly endeared him to the citizens of the
Golden State. And therefore they made much of him when he went to
see them.

At one town the enthusiastic populace tore his celebrated white
coat to pieces, and carried the pieces home to remember him by.

The citizens of Placerville prepared to fête the greate journalist,
and an extra coach, with extra relays of horses, was chartered of the
California Stage Company to carry him from Folsom to Placerville—
distance, forty miles. The extra was in some way delayed, and did not
leave Folsom until late in the afternoon. Mr. Greeley was to be fêted at
7 o'clock that evening by the citizens of Placerville, and it was
altogether necessary that he should be there by that hour. So the Stage
Company said to Henry Monk, the driver of the extra, "Henry, this
great man must be there by 7 to-night." And Henry answered, "The
great man shall be there."

The roads were in an awful state, and during the first few miles out
of Folson slow progress was made.

"Sir," said Mr. Greeley, "are you aware that I *must* be at Placerville
at 7 o'clock to-night."

"I've got my orders!" laconically returned Henry Monk.

Still the coach dragged slowly forward.

"Sir," said Mr. Greeley, "this is not a trifling matter. I *must* by
there at 7!"

Again came the answer, "I've got my orders!"

But the speed was not increased, and Mr. Greeley chafed away
another half hour; when, as he was again about to remonstrate with
the driver, the horses suddenly started into a furious run, and all sorts
of encouraging yells filled the air from the throat of Henry Monk.

"That is right, my good fellow!" cried Mr. Greeley. "I'll give you
ten dollars when we get to Placerville. Now we *are* going!"

They were indeed, and at a terrible speed.

Crack, crack! went the whip, and again "that voice" split the air. "Git up! Hi yi! G'long! Yip—yip!"

And on they tore over stones and ruts, up hill and down, at a rate of speed never before achieved by stage horses.

Mr. Greeley, who had been bouncing from one end of the coach to the other like an india-rubber ball, managed to get his head out of the window, when he said:

"Do—on't—on't—on't you—u—u think we—e—e—e shall get there by seven if we do—on't—on't go so fast?"

"I've got my orders!" That was all Henry Monk said. And on tore the coach.

It was becoming serious. Already the journalist was extremely sore from the terrible jolting, and again his head "might have been seen" at the window.

"Sir," he said, "I don't care—care—*air*, if we *don't* get there at seven!"

"I have got my orders!" Fresh horses. Forward again, faster than before. Over rocks and stumps, on one of which the coach narrowly escaped turning a summerset.

"See here!" shrieked Mr. Greeley, "I don't care if we don't get there at all!"

"I've got my orders! I work for the Californy Stage Company, *I* do. That's wot I *work* for. They said, 'git this man through by seving.' An' this man's goin' through. You bet! Gerlong! Whoo-ep!"

Another frightful jolt, and Mr. Greeley's bald head suddenly found its way through the roof of the coach, amidst the crash of small timbers and the ripping of strong canvas.

"Stop, you —— maniac!" he roared.

Again answered Henry Monk:

"I've got my orders! *Keep your seat, Horace!*"

At Mud Springs, a village a few miles from Placerville, they met a large delegation of the citizens of Placerville, who had come out to meet the celebrated editor, and escort him into town. There was a military company, a brass band, and a six-horse wagon-load of beautiful damsels in milk-white dresses, representing all the States in the Union. It was nearly dark now, but the delegation were amply provided with torches, and bonfires blazed all along the road to Placerville.

The citizens met the coach in the outskirts of Mud Springs, and Mr. Monk reined in his foam-covered steeds.

"Is Mr. Greeley on board?" asked the chairman of the committee.

"*He was, a few miles back!*" said Mr. Monk; "yes," he added, after looking down through the hole which the fearful jolting had made in the coach-roof—"yes, I can see him! He is there!"

"Mr. Greeley," said the Chairman of the Committee, presenting himself at the window of the coach, "Mr. Greeley, sir! We are come to most cordially welcome you, sir —— why, God bless me, sir, you are bleeding at the nose!"

"I've got my orders!" cried Mr. Monk. "My orders is as follers: Git him there by seving! It wants a quarter to seving. Stand out of the way!"

"But, sir," exclaimed the Committee-man, seizing the off leader by the reins—"Mr. Monk, we are come to escort him into town! Look at the procession, sir, and the brass band, and the people, and the young women, sir!"

"*I've got my orders!*" screamed Mr. Monk. 'My orders don't say nothing' about no brass bands and young women. My orders says, 'git him there by seving?' Let go them lines! Clear the way there! Whoo-ep! KEEP YOUR SEAT, HORACE!" and the coach dashed wildly through the procession, upsetting a portion of the brass band, and violently grazing the wagon which contained the beautiful young women in white.

Years hence, gray-haired men, who were little boys in this procession, will tell their granchildren how this stage tore through Mud Springs, and how Horace Greeley's bald head ever and anon showed itself, like a wild apparition, above the coach roof.

Mr. Monk was on time. There is a tradition that Mr. Greeley was very indignant for a while; then he laughed, and finally presented Mr. Monk with a bran new suit of clothes.

Mr. Monk himself is still in the employ of the California Stage Company, and is rather fond of relating a story that has made him famous all over the Pacific coast. But he says he yields to no man in his admiration for Horace Greeley.

"Keep Your Seat, Horace!" from *His Works, Complete* by Artemus Ward. G.W. Carleton & Co. Publishers, 1877.

James W. Marshall

An Unforgettable Morning

To overland travelers bound for California before 1848, the Sierra was an always trying, sometimes dangerous gamut that had to be run—to be done with!—before the promised land was reached. As a destination in itself, it held no more interest than Nebraska's Chimney Rock or Nevada's Humboldt Sink: one looked forward to it only as a landmark one hoped soon to look back upon.

With the discovery of gold at Coloma, the Sierra itself became the destination. Where earlier one found nothing more agreeable than Indians, wild animals and blizzards, one now found Rough and Ready, Fiddletown, and Poker Flat. Whether this was an improvement may be debated today but never was at the time. The Sierra was suddenly the route not simply to the promised land but, better yet, to Easy Street; this was reason enough to overrun the range with a thousand shanty towns.

Coloma lies in the western foothills near a hairpin turn in the South Fork of the American River. Before the discovery of gold, magnificent yellow-pine forests carpeted the surrounding foothills. In 1847, John Sutter chose the site for a sawmill to supply lumber for his fort 45 miles downstream. Sutter hired a millwright named James Marshall and put him in charge of the operation.

Through the fall and early winter, Marshall oversaw the construction of log houses, a dam, and the foundation for the sawmill. Then, one morning in January 1848, a morning he later recalled as clear, cold, and unforgettable. . .

. . . as I was taking my usual walk along the race after shutting off the water, my eye was caught with the glimpse of something shining in the bottom of the ditch. There was about a foot of water running then. I reached my hand down and picked it up; it made my heart thump, for I was certain it was gold. The piece was about half the size and of the shape of a pea. Then I saw another piece in the water. After taking it out I sat down and began to think right hard. I thought it was gold, and yet it did not seem to be of the right color: all the gold coin I had seen was of a reddish tinge; this looked more like brass. I recalled to mind all the metals I had ever seen or heard of, but I could find none that resembled this. Suddenly the idea flashed across my mind that it might be iron pyrites. I trembled to think of it! This question could soon be determined. Putting one of the pieces on a hard river stone, I took another and commenced hammering it. It was soft, and didn't break: it therefore must be gold, but largely mixed with some other metal, very likely silver; for pure gold, I thought, would certainly have a brighter color.

When I returned to our cabin for breakfast I showed the two pieces to my men. They were all a good deal excited, and had they not thought that the gold only existed in small quantities they would have abandoned everything and left me to finish my job alone. However, to satisfy them, I told them that as soon as we had the mill finished we would devote a week or two to gold hunting and see what we could make out of it.

While we were working in the race after this discovery we always kept a sharp lookout, and in the course of three or four days we had picked up about three ounces—our work still progressing as lively as ever, for none of us imagined at that time that the whole country was sowed with gold.

In about a week's time after the discovery I had to take another trip to the fort; and, to gain what information I could respecting the real value of the metal, took all that we had collected with me and showed it to Mr. Sutter, who at once declared it was gold, but thought with me that it was greatly mixed with some other metal. It puzzled us a good deal to hit upon the means of telling the exact quantity of gold contained in the alloy; however, we at last stumbled on an old American cyclopedia, where we saw the specific gravity of all the metals, and the rules given to find the quantity of each in a given bulk. After hunting over the whole fort and borrowing from some of the men, we got three dollars and a half in silver, and with a small pair of scales we soon ciphered it out that there was no silver nor copper in the gold but that it was entirely pure.

This fact being ascertained, we thought it our best policy to keep it as quiet as possible till we should have finished our mill. But there was a great number of disbanded Mormon soldiers in and about the fort, and when they came to hear of it, why it just spread like wildfire, and soon the whole country was in a bustle. I had scarcely arrived at the mill again till several persons appeared with pans, shovels, and hoes, and those that had not iron picks had wooden ones, all anxious to fall to work and dig up our mill; but this we would not permit. As fast as one party disappeared another would arrive, and sometimes I had the greatest kind of trouble to get rid of them. I sent them all off in different directions, telling them about such and such places, where I was certain there was plenty of gold if they would only take the trouble of looking for it. At that time I never imagined that the gold was so abundant. I told them to go to such and such places, because it appeared that they would dig nowhere but in such places as I pointed out, and I believe such was their confidence in me that they would have dug on the very top of yon mountain if I had told them to do so.

The second place where gold was discovered was in a gulch near the Mountaineer House, on the road to Sacramento. The third place was on a bar on the South Fork of the American River a little above the junction of the Middle and South forks. The diggings at Hangtown [now Placerville] were discovered next by myself, for we all went out for a while as soon as our job was finished. The Indians next discovered the diggings at Kelsey's, and thus in a very short time we discovered that the whole country was but one bed of gold. So there, stranger, is the entire history of the gold discovery in California—a discovery that hasn't as yet been of much benefit to me.

An Unforgettable Morning, from "Marshall's Narrative" by James W. Marshall, dictated to Charles B. Gillespie. *The Century Illustrated Magazine,* February, 1891. Reprinted by permission of *Current History.*

Jack London

All Gold Cañon

El Dorado was enormous, a 30-mile-wide swath in the Sierra foothills stretching some 200 miles from the Feather River to the Merced. Prospectors on their way to the gold fields dreamed of taking fortunes back to their families in the East. After confronting hardscrabble reality in California, however, most felt fortunate if they could scratch up enough gold to pay for their tickets home. Discovering a worthwhile placer required hard work as well as luck, a fact that is lost in the stereotyped tale of the shiftless prospector who stumbles onto a nugget the size of a cannonball. For a close look at the actual business of searching for gold, we can turn to a story by Jack London which illustrates how tedious—and dangerous—the task could be.

London, of course, is best known for his brutal tales of life beyond the pale of civilization in the Far North—The Call of the Wild, To Build a Fire, Love of Life, and the rest. But he wrote of other places too, particularly those where circumstances combined to bring out the worst in people. Such a place was the Sierra Nevada of All Gold Cañon. London's tale of Bill the prospector depicts in intricate detail the painstaking method that was used to locate the source of a promising speck of paydirt. But London could never have been satisfied with such a mundane plot, and before the story is finished it has become as barbarous as any of his famous tales of the North.

IT was the green heart of the canyon, where the walls swerved back from the rigid plan and relieved their harshness of line by making a little sheltered nook and filling it to the brim with sweetness and roundness and softness. Here all things rested. Even the narrow stream ceased its turbulent downrush long enough to form a quiet pool. Knee-deep in the water, with drooping head and half-shut eyes, drowsed a red-coated, many-antlered buck.

On one side, beginning at the very lip of the pool, was a tiny meadow, a cool, resilent surface of green that extended to the base of the frowning wall. Beyond the pool a gentle slope of earth ran up and up to meet the opposing wall. Fine grass covered the slope—grass that was spangled with flowers, with here and there patches of color, orange and purple and golden. Below, the canyon was shut in. There was no view. The walls leaned together abruptly and the canyon ended in a chaos of rocks, moss-covered and hidden by a green screen of vines and creepers and boughs of tree. Up the canyon rose far hills and peaks, the big foothills, pine-covered and remote. And far beyond, like clouds upon the border of the sky, towered minarets of white, where the Sierra's eternal snows flashed austerely the blazes of the sun.

There was no dust in the canyon. The leaves and flowers were clean and virginal. The grass was young velvet. Over the pool three cottonwoods sent their snowy fluffs fluttering down the quiet air. On the slope the blossoms of the wine-wooded manzanita filled the air with springtime odors, while the leaves, wise with experience, were already beginning their vertical twist against the coming aridity of summer. In the open spaces on the slope, beyond the farthest shadow-reach of the manzanita, poised the mariposa lilies, like so many flights of jeweled moths suddenly arrested and on the verge of trembling into flight again. Here and there that woods harlequin, the madroña, permitting itself to be caught in the act of changing its pea-green trunk to madder red, breathed its fragrance into the air from great clusters of waxen bells. Creamy white were these bells, shaped like lilies of the valley, with the sweetness of the perfume that is of the springtime.

There was not a sigh of wind. The air was drowsy with its weight of perfume. It was a sweetness that would have been cloying had the air been heavy and humid. But the air was sharp and thin. It was as starlight transmuted into atmosphere, shot through and warmed by sunshine, and flower-drenched with sweetness.

An occasional butterfly drifted in and out through the patches of light and shade. And from all about rose the low and sleepy hum of mountain bees—feasting sybarites that jostled one another good-naturedly at the board, nor found time for rough discourtesy. So quietly did the little stream drip and ripple its way through the canyon that it spoke only in faint and occasional gurgles. The voice of the stream was as a drowsy whisper, ever interrupted by dozings and silences, ever lifted again in the awakenings.

The motion of all things was a drifting in the heart of the canyon. Sunshine and butterflies drifted in and out among the trees. The hum of the bees and the whisper of the stream were a drifting of sound. And the drifting sound and drifting color seemed to weave together in the making of a delicate and intangible fabric which was the spirit of the place. It was a spirit of peace that was not of earth, but of smooth-pulsing life, of quietude that was not silence, of movement that was not action, of repose that was quick with existence without being violent with struggle and travail. The spirit of the place was the spirit of the peace of the living, somnolent with the easement and content of prosperity, and undisturbed by rumors of far wars.

The red-coated, many-antlered buck acknowledged the lordship of the spirit of the place and dozed knee-deep in the cool, shaded pool. There seemed no flies to vex him and he was languid with rest. Sometimes his ears moved when the stream awoke and whispered; but they moved lazily, with foreknowledge that it was merely the stream grown garrulous at discovery that it had slept.

But there came a time when the buck's ears lifted and tensed with swift eagerness for sound. His head was turned down the canyon. His sensitive, quivering nostrils scented the air. His eyes could not pierce the green screen through which the stream rippled away, but to his ears came the voice of a man. It was a steady, monotonous, singsong voice. Once the buck heard the harsh clash of metal upon rock. At the sound he snorted with a sudden start that jerked him through the air from water to meadow, and his feet sank into the young velvet, while he pricked his ears and again scented the air. Then he stole across the tiny meadow, pausing once and again to listen, and faded away out of the canyon like a wraith, soft-footed and without sound.

The clash of steel-shod soles against the rocks began to be heard, and the man's voice grew louder. It was raised in a sort of chant and became distinct with nearness, so that the words could be heard:

> *"Tu'n around an' tu'n yo' face*
> *Untoe them sweet hills of grace.*

> *(D' pow'rs of sin yo' am scornin'!)*
> *Look about an' look aroun',*
> *Fling yo' sin pack on d' groun'.*
> *(Yo' will meet wid d' Lord in d'mornin'!)"*

A sound of scrambling accompanied the song, and the spirit of the place fled away on the heels of the red-coated buck. The green screen was burst asunder, and a man peered out at the meadow and the pool and the sloping sidehill. He was a deliberate sort of man. He took in the scene with one embracing glance, then ran his eyes over the details to verify the general impression. Then, and not until then, did he open his mouth in vivid and solemn approval:

"Smoke of life an' snakes of purgatory! Will you just look at that! Wood an' water an' grass an' a sidehill! A pocket hunter's delight an' a cayuse's paradise! Cool green for tired eyes! Pink pills for pale people ain't in it. A secret pasture for prospectors and a resting place for tired burros, by damn!"

He was a sandy-complexioned man in whose face geniality and humor seemed the salient characteristics. It was a mobile face, quick-changing to inward mood and thought. Thinking was in him a visible process. Ideas chased across his face like windflaws across the surface of a lake. His hair, sparse and unkempt of growth, was as indeterminate and colorless as his complexion. It would seem that all the color of his frame had gone into his eyes, for they were startlingly blue. Also they were laughing and merry eyes, within them much of the naïveté and wonder of the child; and yet, in an unassertive way, they contained much of calm self-reliance and strength of purpose founded upon self-experience and experience of the world.

From out the screen of vines and creepers he flung ahead of him a miner's pick and shovel and gold pan. Then he crawled out himself into the open. He was clad in faded overalls and black cotton shirt, with hobnailed brogans on his feet, and on his head a hat whose shapelessness and stains advertised the rough usage of wind and rain and sun and camp smoke. He stood erect, seeing wide-eyed the secrecy of the scene and sensuously inhaling the warm, sweet breath of the canyon garden through nostrils that dilated and quivered with delight.

His eyes narrowed to laughing slits of blue, his face wreathed itself in joy, and his mouth curled in a smile as he cried aloud:

"Jumping dandelions and happy hollyhocks, but that smells good to me! Talk about your attar o' roses an' cologne factories! They ain't in it!"

He had the habit of soliloquy. His quick-changing facial expressions might tell every thought and mood, but the tongue, perforce, ran hard after, repeating, like a second Boswell.

The man lay down on the lip of the pool and drank long and deep of its water. "Tastes good to me," he murmured, lifting his head and gazing across the pool at the sidehill, while he wiped his mouth with the back of his hand. The sidehill attracted his attention. Still lying on his stomach, he studied the hill formation long and carefully. It was a practiced eye that traveled up the slope to the crumbling canyon wall and back and down again to the edge of the pool. He scrambled to his feet and favored the sidehill with a second survey.

"Looks good to me," he concluded, picking up his pick and shovel and gold pan.

He crossed the stream below the pool, stepping agilely from stone to stone. Where the sidehill touched the water he dug up a shovelful of dirt and put it into the gold pan. He squatted down, holding the pan in his two hands, and partly immersing it in the stream. Then he imparted to the pan a deft circular motion that sent the water sluicing in and out through the dirt and gravel. The larger and the lighter particles worked to the surface, and these, by a skillful dipping movement of the pan, he spilled out and over the edge. Occasionally, to expedite matters, he rested the pan and with his fingers raked out the large pebbles and pieces of rock.

The contents of the pan diminished rapidly until only fine dirt and the smallest bits of gravel remained. At this stage he began to work very deliberately and carefully. It was fine washing, and he washed fine and finer, with a keen scrutiny and delicate and fastidious touch. At the last the pan seemed empty of everything but water; but with a quick semicircular flirt that sent the water flying over the shallow rim into the stream he disclosed a layer of black sand on the bottom of the pan. So thin was this layer that it was like a streak of paint. He examined it closely. In the midst of it was a tiny golden speck. He dribbled a little water in over the depressed edge of the pan. With a quick flirt he sent the water sluicing across the bottom, turning the grains of black sand over and over. A second tiny golden speck rewarded his effort.

The washing had now become very fine—fine beyond all need of ordinary placer mining. He worked the black sand, a small portion at a time, up the shallow rim of the pan. Each small portion he examined sharply, so that his eyes saw every grain of it before he allowed it to slide over the edge and away. Jealously, bit by bit, he let the black sand slip away. A golden speck, no larger than a pin point, appeared on the rim, and by his manipulation of the water it returned to the bottom of the pan. And in such fashion another speck was disclosed, and another. Great was his care of them. Like a shepherd he herded his flock of golden specks so that not one should be lost. At last, of the pan of dirt nothing remained but his golden herd. He counted it, and then, after all his labor, sent it flying out of the pan with one final swirl of water.

But his blue eyes were shining with desire as he rose to his feet. "Seven," he muttered aloud, asserting the sum of the specks for which he had toiled so hard and which he had so wantonly thrown away. "Seven," he repeated, with the emphasis of one trying to impress a number on his memory.

He stood still a long while, surveying the hillside. In his eyes was a curiosity, new-aroused and burning. There was an exultance about his bearing and a keenness like that of a hunting animal catching the fresh scent of game.

He moved down the stream a few steps and took a second panful of dirt.

Again came the careful washing, the jealous herding of the golden specks, and the wantoness with which he sent them flying into the stream when he had counted their number.

"Five," he muttered, and repeated, "five."

He could not forbear another survey of the hill before filling the pan farther down the stream. His golden herds diminished. "Four, three, two, two, one," were his memory tabulations as he moved down the stream. When but one speck of gold rewarded his washing he stopped and built a fire of dry twigs. Into this he thrust the gold pan and burned it till it was blue-black. He held up the pan and examined it critically. Then he nodded approbation. Against such a color background he could defy the tiniest yellow speck to elude him.

Still moving down the stream, he panned again. A single speck was his reward. A third pan contained no gold at all. Not satisfied with this, he panned three times again, taking his shovels of dirt within a foot of one another. Each pan proved empty of gold, and the fact, instead of discouraging him, seemed to give him satisfaction. His elation increased with each barren washing, until he arose, exclaiming jubilantly:

"If it ain't the real thing, may God knock off my head with sour apples!"

Returning to where he had started operations, he began to pan up the stream. At first his golden herds increased—increased prodigiously. "Fourteen, eighteen, twenty-one, twenty-six," ran his memory tabulations. Just above the pool he struck his richest pan—thirty-five colors.

"Almost enough to save," he remarked regretfully as he allowed the water to sweep them away.

The sun climbed to the top of the sky. The man worked on. Pan by pan he went up the stream, the tally of results steadily decreasing.

"It's just boojul, the way it peters out," he exulted when a shovelful of dirt contained no more than a single speck of gold.

And when no specks at all were found in several pans he straightened up and favored the hillside with a confident glance.

"Aha! Mr. Pocket!" he cried out as though to an auditor hidden somewhere above him beneath the surface of the slope. "Aha! Mr. Pocket! I'm a-comin', I'm a-comin', an' I'm shorely gwine to get yer! You heah me, Mr. Pocket? I'm gwine to get yer as shore as punkins ain't cauliflowers!"

He turned and flung a measuring glance at the sun poised above him in the azure of the cloudless sky. Then he went down the canyon, following the line of shovel holes he had made in filling the pans. He crossed the stream below the pool and disappeared through the green screen. There was little opportunity for the spirit of the place to return with its quietude and repose, for the man's voice, raised in ragtime song, still dominated the canyon with possession.

After a time, with a greater clashing of steel-shod feet on rock, he returned. The green screen was tremendously agitated. It surged back and forth in the throes of a struggle. There was a loud grating and clanging of metal. The man's voice leaped to a higher pitch and was sharp with imperativeness. A large body plunged and panted. There was a snapping and ripping and rending, and amid a shower of falling leaves a horse burst through the screen. On its back was a pack, and from this trailed broken vines and torn creepers. The animal gazed with astonished eyes at the scene into which it had been precipitated, then dropped its head to the grass and began contentedly to graze. A second horse scrambled into view, slipping once on the mossy rocks and regaining equilibrium when its hoofs sank into the yielding surface of the meadow. It was riderless, though on its back was a high-horned Mexican saddle, scarred and discolored by long usage.

The man brought up the rear. He threw off pack and saddle, with an eye to camp location, and gave the animals their freedom to graze. He unpacked his food and got out frying pan and coffeepot. He gathered an armful of dry wood, and with a few stones made a place for his fire.

"My," he said, "but I've got an appetite! I could scoff iron filings an' horseshoe nails an' thank you kindly, ma'am, for a second helpin'."

He straightened up, and while he reached for matches in the pocket of his overalls his eyes traveled across the pool to the sidehill. His fingers had clutched the matchbox, but they relaxed their hold and the hand came out empty. The man wavered perceptibly. He looked at his preparations for cooking and he looked at the hill.

"Guess I'll take another whack at her," he concluded, starting to cross the stream.

"They ain't no sense in it, I know," he mumbled apologetically. "But keepin' grub back an hour ain't goin' to hurt none, I reckon."

A few feet back from his first line of test pans he started a second line. The sun dropped down the western sky, the shadows lengthened, but the man worked on. He began a third line of test pans. He was crosscutting the hillside, line by line, as he ascended. The center of each line produced the richest pans, while the ends came where no colors showed in the pan. And as he ascended the hillside the lines grew perceptibly shorter. The regularity with which their length diminished served to indicate that somewhere up the slope the last line would be so short as to have scarcely length at all, and that beyond could come only a point. The design was growing into an inverted V. The converging sides of this V marked the boundaries of the gold-bearing dirt.

The apex of the V was evidently the man's goal. Often he ran his eye along the converging sides and on up the hill, trying to divine the apex, the point where the gold-bearing dirt must cease. Here resided "Mr. Pocket"—for so the man familiarly addressed the imaginary point above him on the slope, crying out:

"Come down out o' that, Mr. Pocket! Be right smart an' agreeable an' come down!"

"All right," he would add later, in a voice resigned to determination. "All right, Mr. Pocket. It's plain to me I got to come right up an' snatch you out bald-headed. An' I'll do it! I'll do it!" he would threaten still later.

Each pan he carried down to the water to wash, and as he went higher up the hill the pans grew richer, until he began to save the gold in an empty baking-powder can which he carried carelessly in his lap pocket. So engrossed was he in his toil that he did not notice the long twilight of oncoming night. It was not until he tried vainly to see the gold colors in the bottom of the pan that he realized the passage of time. He straightened up abruptly. An expression of whimsical wonderment and awe overspread his face as he drawled:

"Gosh darn my buttons, if I didn't plumb forget dinner!"

He stumbled across the stream in the darkness and lighted his long-delayed fire. Flapjacks and bacon and warmed-over beans constituted his supper. Then he smoked a pipe by the smoldering coals, listening to the night noises and watching the moonlight stream through the canyon. After that he unrolled his bed, took off his heavy shoes, and pulled the blankets up to his chin. His face showed white in the moonlight, like the face of a corpse. But it was a corpse that knew its resurrection, for the man rose suddenly on one elbow and gazed across at his hillside.

"Good night, Mr. Pocket," he called sleepily. "Good night."

He slept through the early gray of morning until the direct rays of the sun smote his closed eyelids, when he awoke with a start and looked about him until he had established the continuity of his existence and identified his present self with the days previously lived.

To dress, he had merely to buckle on his shoes. He glanced at his fireplace and at his hillside, wavered, but fought down the temptation and started the fire.

"Keep yer shirt on, Bill; keep yer shirt on," he admonished himself. "What's the good of rushin'? No use in gettin' all het up an' sweaty. Mr. Pocket'll wait for you. He ain't a-running' away before you can get yer breakfast. Now what you want, Bill, is something fresh in yer bill o' fare. So it's up to you to go an' get it."

He cut a short pole at the water's edge and drew from one of his pockets a bit of line and a draggled fly that had once been a royal coachman.

"Mebbe they'll bite in the early morning," he muttered as he made his first cast into the pool. And a moment later he was gleefully crying: "What'd I tell you, eh? What'd I tell you?"

He had no reel nor any inclination to waste time, and by main strength, and swiftly, he drew out of the water a flashing ten-inch trout. Three more, caught in rapid succession, furnished his breakfast. When he came to the steppingstones on his way to his hillside, he was struck by a sudden thought, and paused.

"I'd just better take a hike downstream a ways," he said. "There's no tellin' what cuss may be snoopin' around."

But he crossed over on the stones, and with a "I really oughter take that hike" the need of the precaution passed out of his mind and he fell to work.

At nightfall he straightened up. The small of his back was stiff from stooping toil and as he put his hand behind him to soothe the protesting muscles he said:

"Now what d'ye think of that, by damn? I clean forgot my dinner again! If I don't watch out Ill sure be degeneratin' into a two-meal-a-day crank."

"Pockets is the damnedest things I ever see for makin' a man absent-minded," he communed that night as he crawled into his blankets. Nor did he forget to call up the hillside. "Good night, Mr. Pocket! Good night!"

Rising with the sun, and snatching a hasty breakfast, he was early at work. A fever seemed to be growing in him, nor did the increasing richness of the test pans allay this fever. There was a flush in his cheek other than that made by the heat of the sun, and he was oblivious to fatigue and the passage of time. When he filled a pan with dirt he ran down the hill to wash it; nor could he forbear running up the hill again, panting and stumbling profanely, to refill the pan.

He was now a hundred yards from the water, and the inverted V as assuming definite proportions. The width of the pay dirt steadily decreased, and the man extended in his mind's eye the sides of the V to their meeting place far up the hill. This was his goal, the apex of the V, and he panned many times to locate it.

"Just about two yards above that manzanita bush an' a yard to the right," he finally concluded.

Then the temptation seized him. "As plain as the nose on your face," he said as he abandoned his laborious crosscutting and climbed to the indicated apex. He filled a pan and carried it down the hill to wash. It contained no trace of gold. He dug deep, and he dug shallow, filling and washing a dozen pans, and was unrewarded even by the tiniest speck. He was enraged at having yielded to the temptation, and cursed himself blasphemously and pridelessly. Then he went down the hill and took up the crosscutting.

"Slow an' certain, Bill; slow an' certain," he crooned. "Short cuts to fortune ain't in your line, an' it's about time you know it. Get wise, Bill; get wise. Slow an' certain's the only hand you can play; so go to it, an' keep to it, too."

As the crosscuts decreased, showing that the sides of the V were converging, the depth of the V increased. The gold trace was dipping into the hill. It was only at thirty inches beneath the surface that he could get colors in his pan. The dirt he found at twenty-five inches from the surface, and at thirty-five inches, yielded barren pans. At the base of the V, by the water's edge, he had found the gold colors at the grass roots. The higher he went up the hill, the deeper the gold dipped. To dig a hole three feet deep in order to get one test pan was no mean magnitude; while between the man and the apex intervened an untold number of such holes to be dug. "An' there's no tellin' how much deeper it'll pitch," he sighed in a moment's pause, while his fingers soothed his aching back.

Feverish with desire, with aching back and stiffening muscles, with pick and shovel gouging and mauling the soft brown earth, the man toiled up the hill. Before him was the smooth slope, spangled with flowers and made sweet with their breath. Behind him was devastation. It looked like some terrible eruption breaking out on the smooth skin of the hill. His slow progress was like that of a slug, befouling beauty with a monstrous trail.

Though the dipping gold trace increased the man's work, he found consolation in the increasing richness of the pans. Twenty cents, thirty cents, fifty cents, sixty cents, were the values of the gold found in the pans, and at nightfall he washed his banner pan, which gave him a dollar's worth of gold dust from a shovelful of dirt.

"I'll just bet it's my luck to have some inquisitive cuss come buttin' in here on my pasture," he mumbled sleepily that night as he pulled the blankets up to his chin.

Suddenly he sat upright. "Bill!" he called sharply. "Now listen to me, Bill; d'ye hear! It's up to you, tomorrow mornin', to mosey round an' see what you can see. Understand? Tomorrow morning, an' don't you forget it!"

He yawned and glanced across at his sidehill. "Good night, Mr. Pocket," he called.

In the morning he stole a march on the sun, for he had finished breakfast when its first rays caught him, and he was climbing the wall of the canyon where it crumbled away and gave footing. From the outlook at the top he found himself in the midst of loneliness. As far as he could see, chain after chain of mountains heaved themselves into his vision. To the east his eyes, leaping the miles between range and range and between many ranges, brought up at last against the white-peaked Sierras—the main crest, where the backbone of the Western world reared itself against the sky. To the north and south he could see more distinctly the cross systems that broke through the main trend of the sea of mountains. To the west the ranges fell away, one behind the other, diminishing and fading into the gentle foothills that, in turn, descended into the great valley which he could not see.

And in all that mighty sweep of earth he saw no sign of man nor of the handiwork of man—save only the torn bosom of the hillside at his feet. The man looked long and carefully. Once, far down his own canyon, he thought he saw in the air a faint hint of smoke. He looked again and decided that it was the purple haze of the hills made dark by a convolution of the canyon wall at its back.

"Hey, you, Mr. Pocket!" he called down into the canyon. "Stand out from under! I'm a-comin', Mr. Pocket! I'm a-comin'!"

The heavy brogans on the man's feet made him appear clumsy-footed, but he swung down from the giddy height as lightly and airily as a mountain goat. A rock, turning under his foot on the edge of the precipice, did not disconcert him. He seemed to know the precise time required for the turn to culminate in disaster, and in the meantime he utilized the false flooring itself for the momentary earth contact neces-sary to carry him on into safety. Where the earth sloped so steeply that it was impossible to stand for a second upright, the man did not hesitate. His foot pressed the impossible surface for but a fraction of the fatal second and gave him the bound that carried him onward. Again, where even the fraction of a second's footing was out of the question, he would swing his body past by a moment's handgrip on a jutting knob of rock, a crevice, or a precariously rooted shrub. At last, with a wild leap and yell, he exchanged the face of the wall for an earth slide and finished the descent in the midst of several tons of sliding earth and gravel.

His first pan of the morning washed out over two dollars in coarse gold. It was from the center of the V. To either side the diminution in the values of the pans was swift. His lines of crosscutting holes were growing very short. The converging sides of the inverted V were only a few yards apart. Their meeting point was only a few yards above him. But the pay streak was dipping deeper and deeper into the earth. By early afternoon he was sinking the test holes five feet before the pans could show the gold trace.

For that matter the gold trace had become something more than a trace; it was a placer mine in itself, and the man resolved to come back after he had found the pocket and work over the ground. But the increasing richness of the pans began to worry him. By late afternoon the worth of the pans had grown to three and four dollars. The man scratched his head perplexedly and looked a few feet up the hill at the manzanita bush that marked approximately the apex of the V. He nodded his head and said oracularly:

"It's one o' two things, Bill; one o' two things. Either Mr. Pocket's spilled himself all out an' down the hill, or else Mr. Pocket's that damned rich you maybe won't be able to carry him all away with you. And that'd be hell, wouldn't it, now?" He chuckled at contemplation of so pleasant a dilemma.

Nightfall found him by the edge of the stream, his eyes wrestling with the gathering darkness over the washing of a five-dollar pan.

"Wisht I had an electric light to go on working" he said.

He found sleep difficult that night. Many times he composed himself and closed his eyes for slumber to overtake him; but his blood pounded with too strong desire, and as many times his eyes opened and he murmured wearily, "Wisht it was sunup."

Sleep came to him in the end, but his eyes were open with the first paling of the stars, and the gray of dawn caught him with breakfast finished and climbing the hillside in the direction of the secret abiding place of Mr. Pocket.

The first crosscut the man made, there was space for only three holes, so narrow had become the pay streak and so close was he to the fountainhead of the golden stream he had been following for four days.

"Be ca'm, Bill; be ca'm," he admonished himself as he broke ground for the final hole where the sides of the V had at last come together in a point.

"I've got the almighty cinch on you, Mr. Pocket, an' you can't lose me" he said many times as he sank the hole deeper and deeper.

Four feet, five feet, six feet, he dug his way down into the earth. The digging grew harder. His pick grated on broken rock. He examined the rock. "Rotten quartz," was his conclusion as, with the shovel, he cleared the bottom of the hole of loose dirt. He attacked the crumbling quartz with the pick, bursting the disintegrating rock asunder with every stroke.

He thrust his shovel into the loose mass. His eye caught a gleam of yellow. He dropped the shovel and squatted suddenly on his heels. As a farmer rubs the clinging earth from fresh-dug potatoes, so the man, a piece of rotten quartz held in both hands, rubbed the dirt away.

"Sufferin' Sardanopolis!" he cried. "Lumps an' chunks of it! Lumps an' chunks of it!"

It was only half rock he held in his hand. The other half was virgin gold. He dropped it into his pan and examined another piece. Little yellow was to be seen, but with his strong fingers he crumbled the rotten quartz away till both hands were filled with glowing yellow. He rubbed the dirt away from fragment after fragment, tossing them into the gold pan. It was a treasure hole. So much had the quartz rotted away that there was less of it than there was of gold. Now and again he found a piece that was all gold. A chunk, where the pick had laid open the heart of the gold, glittered like a handful of yellow jewels, and he cocked his head at it and slowly turned it around and over to observe the rich play of the light upon it.

"Talk about yer Too Much Gold diggin's!" the man snorted contemptuously. "Why, this diggin'd make it look like thirty cents. This diggin' is all gold. An' right here an' now I name this yere canyon 'All Gold Canyon,' b' gosh!"

Still squatting on his heels, he continued examining the fragments and tossing them into the pan. Suddenly there came to him a premonition of danger. It seemed a shadow had fallen upon him. But there was no shadow. His heart had given a great jump up into his throat and was choking him. Then his blood slowly chilled and he felt the sweat of his shirt cold against his flesh.

He did not spring up nor look around. He did not move. He was considering the nature of the premonition he had received, trying to locate the source of the mysterious force that had warned him, striving to sense the imperative presence of the unseen thing that threatened him. There is an aura of things hostile, made manifest by messengers too refined for the senses to know; and this aura he felt, but knew not how he felt it. His was the feeling as when a cloud passes over the sun. It seemed that between him and life had passed something dark and smothering and menacing; a gloom, as it were, that swallowed up life and made for death—his death.

Every force of his being impelled him to spring up and confront the unseen danger, but his soul dominated the panic, and he remained squatting on his heels, in his hands a chunk of gold. He did not dare to look around, but he knew by now that there was something behind him and above him. He made believe to be interested in the gold in his hand. He examined it critically, turned it over and over, and rubbed the dirt from it. And all the time he knew that something behind him was looking at the gold over his shoulder.

Still feigning interest in the chunk of gold in his hand, he listened intently and he heard the breathing of the thing behind him. His eyes searched the ground in front of him for a weapon, but they saw only the uprooted gold, worthless to him now in his extremity. There was his pick, a handy weapon on occasion; but this was not such an occasion. The man realized his predicament. He was in a narrow hole that was seven feet deep. His head did not come to the surface of the ground. He was in a trap.

He remained squatting on his heels. He was quite cool and collected; but his mind, considering every factor, showed him only his helplessness. He continued rubbing the dirt from the quartz fragments and throwing the gold into the pan. There was nothing else for him to do. Yet he knew that he would have to rise up, sooner or later, and face the danger that breathed at his back. The minutes passed, and with the passage of time when he must stand up or else— and his wet shirt went cold against his flesh again at the thought—or else he might receive death as he stooped there over his treasure.

Still he squatted on his heels, rubbing dirt from gold and debating in just what manner he should rise up. He might rise up with a rush and claw his way out of the hole to meet whatever threatened on the even footing above ground. Or he might rise up slowly and careless, and feign casually to discover the thing that breathed at his back. His instinct and every fighting fiber of his body favored the mad, clawing rush to the surface. His intellect, and the craft thereof, favored the slow and cautious meeting with the thing that menaced and which he could not see. And while he debated, a loud, crashing noise burst on his ear. At the same instant he received a stunning blow on the left side of the back, and from the point of impact felt a rush of flame through his flesh. He sprang up in the air, but halfway to his feet collapsed. His body crumpled in like a leaf withered in sudden heat, and he came down, his chest across his pan of gold, his face in the dirt and rock, his legs tangled and twisted because of the restricted space at the bottom of the hole. His legs twitched convulsively several times.

Drawn by Jay Hambidge.　Half-tone plate engraved by Robert Varley.

"HIS BODY CRUMPLED IN LIKE A LEAF"

His body was shaken as with a mighty ague. There was a slow expansion of the lungs, accompanied by a deep sigh. Then the air was slowly, very slowly, exhaled, and his body as slowly flattened itself down into inertness.

Above, revolver in hand, a man was peering down over the edge of the hole. He peered for a long time at the prone and motionless body beneath him. After a while the stranger sat down on the edge of the hole so that he could see into it, and rested the revolver on his knee. Reaching his hand into a pocket, he drew out a wisp of brown paper. Into this he dropped a few crumbs of tobacco. The combination became a cigarette, brown and squat, with the ends turned in. Not once did he take his eyes from the body at the bottom of the hole. He lighted the cigarette and drew its smoke into his lungs with a caressing intake of the breath. He smoked slowly. Once the cigarette went out and he relighted it. And all the while he studied the body beneath him.

In the end he tossed the cigarette stub away and rose to his feet. He moved to the edge of the hole. Spanning it, a hand resting on each edge, and with the revolver still in the right hand, he muscled his body down into the hole. While his feet were yet a yard from the bottom he released his hands and dropped down.

At the instant his feet struck bottom he saw the pocket miner's arm leap out, and his own legs knew a swift, jerking grip that overthrew him. In the nature of the jump his revolver hand was above his head. Swiftly as the grip had flashed about his legs, just as swiftly he brought the revolver down. He was still in the air, his fall in process of completion, when he pulled the trigger. The explosion was deafening in the confined space. The smoke filled the hole so that he could see nothing. He struck the bottom on his back, and like a cat's the pocket miner's body was on top of him. Even as the miner's body passed on top, the stranger crooked in his right arm to fire; and even in that instant the miner with a quick thrust of elbow, struck his wrist. The muzzle was thrown up and the bullet thudded into the dirt of the side of the hole.

The next instant the stranger felt the miner's hand grip his wrist. The struggle was now for the revolver. Each man strove to turn it against the other's body. The smoke in the hole was clearing. The stranger, lying on his back, was beginning to see dimly. But suddenly he was blinded by a handful of dirt deliberately flung into his eyes by his antagonist. In that moment of shock his grip on the revolver was broken. In the next moment he felt a smashing darkness descend upon his brain, and in the midst of the darkness even the darkness ceased.

But the pocket miner fired again and again, until the revolver was empty. Then he tossed it from him and, breathing heavily, sat down on the dead man's legs.

The miner was sobbing and struggling for breath. "Measly skunk!" he panted; "a-campin' on my trail an' lettin' me do the work, an' then shootin' me in the back!"

He was half crying from anger and exhaustion. He peered at the face of the dead man. It was sprinkled with loose dirt and gravel, and it was difficult to distinguish the features.

"Never laid eyes on him before," the miner concluded his scrutiny. "Just a common an' ordinary thief, damn him! An' he shot me in the back! He shot me in the back!"

He opened his shirt and felt himself, front and back, on his left side.

"Went clean through, and no harm done!" he cried jubilantly. "I'll bet he aimed all right, all right; but he drew the gun over when he pulled the trigger—the cuss! But I fixed 'm! Oh, I fixed 'm!"

His fingers were investigating the bullet hole in his side, and a shade of regret passed over his face. "It's goin' to be stiffer'n hell," he said. "An' it's up to me to get mended an' get out o' here."

He crawled out of the hole and went down the hill to his camp. Half an hour later he returned, leading his pack horse. His open shirt disclosed the rude bandages with which he had dressed his wound. He was slow and awkward with his left-hand movements, but that did not prevent his using the arm.

The bight of the pack rope under the dead man's shoulders enabled him to heave the body out of the hole. Then he set to work gathering up his gold. He worked steadily for several hours, pausing often to rest his stiffening shoulder and to exclaim:

"He shot me in the back, the measly skunk! He shot me in the back!"

When his treasure was quite cleaned up and wrapped securely

into a number of blanket-covered parcels, he made an estimate of its value.

"Four hundred pounds, or I'm a Hottentot," he concluded. "Say two hundred in quartz an' dirt—that leaves two hundred pounds of gold. Bill! Wake up! Two hundred pounds of gold! Forty thousand dollars! An' it's yourn—all yourn!"

He scratched his head delightedly and his fingers blundered into an unfamiliar groove. They quested along it for several inches. It was a crease through his scalp where the second bullet had plowed.

He walked angrily over to the dead man.

"You would, would you?" he bullied. "You would, eh? Well, I fixed you good an' plenty, an' I'll give you decent burial, too. That's more'n you'd have done for me."

He dragged the body to the edge of the hole and toppled it in. It struck the bottom with a dull crash, on its side, the face twisted up to the light. The miner peered down at it.

"An' you shot me in the back!" he said accusingly.

With pick and shovel he filled the hole. Then he loaded the gold on his horse. It was too great a load for the animal, and when he had gained his camp he transferred part of it to his saddle horse. Even so, he was compelled to abandon a portion of his outfit—pick and shovel and gold pan, extra food and cooking utensils, and divers odd and ends.

The sun was at the zenith when the man forced the horses at the screen of vines and creepers. To climb the huge boulders the animals were compelled to uprear and struggle blindly through the tangled mass of vegetation. Once the saddle horse fell heavily and the man removed the pack to get the animal on its feet. After it started on its way again the man thrust his head out from among the leaves and peered up at the hillside.

"The measly skunk!" he said, and disappeared.

There was a ripping and tearing of vines and boughs. The trees surged back and forth, marking the passage of the animals through the midst of them. There was a clashing of steel-shod hoofs on stone, and now and again an oath or a sharp cry of command. Then the voice of the man was raised in song:

> *"Tu'n around an' tu'n yo' face*
> *Untoe them sweet hills of grace.*
> *(D' pow'rs of sin yo' am scornin'!)*
> *Look about an' look aroun',*
> *Fling yo' sin pack on d' groun'.*
> *(Yo' will meet wid d' Lord in d' mornin'!)"*

The song grew faint and fainter, and through the silence crept back the spirit of the place. The stream once more drowsed and whispered; the hum of the mountain bees rose sleepily. Down through the perfume-weighted air fluttered the snowy fluffs of the cottonwoods. The butterflies drifted in and out among the trees, and over all blazed the quiet sunshine. Only remained the hoofmarks in the meadow and the torn hillside to mark the boisterous trail of the life that had broken the peace of the place and passed on.

All Gold Cañon, from "All Gold Cañon" by Jack London. *The Century Magazine,* November, 1905. Reprinted by permission of *Current History.*

Bret Harte

The Outcasts of Poker Flat

Bret Harte's stories of the sorry characters who inhabited the gold camps made him world-famous. Despite their sentimentality and their heavy moralizing, his tales of brawls, hold-ups, and lynchings, of love requited and destinies fulfilled struck a chord with legions of readers bewitched by the great American West.

Today some of Harte's characters may strike us as trite—the prostitute with the heart of gold, the hard-hearted prospector who sacrifices himself for his friend. But it should be remembered that Harte invented many of these now-familiar characters; indeed, he may be said to have invented the Western itself. Whatever their faults, his stories continue to entertain us because we have never tired of the genre.

Harte was one of the few writers of the time who understood the significance of nature in the gold rush story. While his principal theme was the nature of men and women in adverse circumstances, the nature of the Sierra—the author of those circumstances—always lay just beneath the surface. It's a rare Harte story where mood is not established through reference to the mountain environment—the wandering breezes and nodding redwoods of "The Luck of Roaring Camp," the "remote and passionless" Sierra of "Tennessee's Partner."

No story better illustrates this than "The Outcasts of Poker Flat," a tale where nature emerges from beneath the surface to become a major factor in the story. Read it with the Sierra in mind: Harte's precipitous granite cliffs, circling pines, and traceless snows are the cliffs and pines and snows of today's Sierra too; through the medium of the mountains, we have a link with the long-ago outcasts of a self-righteous two-bit mining town, and their grim march into the unforgiving wilds.

AS MR. JOHN OAKHURST, gambler, stepped into the main street of Poker Flat on the morning of the 23d of November, 1850, he was conscious of a change in its moral atmosphere since the preceding night. Two or three men, conversing earnestly together, ceased as he approached, and exchanged significant glances. There was a Sabbath lull in the air, which, in a settlement unused to Sabbath influences, looked ominous.

Mr. Oakhurst's calm, handsome face betrayed small concern in these indications. Whether he was conscious of any predisposing cause was another question. "I reckon they're after somebody," he reflected; "likely it's me." He returned to his pocket the handkerchief with which he had been whipping away the red dust of Poker Flat from his neat boots, and quietly discharged his mind of any further conjecture.

In point of fact, Poker Flat was "after somebody." It had lately suffered the loss of several thousand dollars, two valuable horses, and a prominent citizen. It was experiencing a spasm of virtuous reaction, quite as lawless and ungovernable as any of the acts that had provoked it. A secret committee had determined to rid the town of all improper persons. This was done permanently in regard of two men who were then hanging from the boughs of a sycamore in the gulch, and temporarily in the banishment of certain other objectionable characters. I regret to say that some of these were ladies. It is but due to the sex, however, to state that their impropriety was professional, and it was only in such easily established standards of evil that Poker Flat ventured to sit in judgment.

Mr. Oakhurst was right in supposing that he was included in this category. A few of the committee had urged hanging him as a possible example and a sure method of reimbursing themselves from his pockets of the sums he had won from them. "It's agin justice,' said Jim Wheeler, "to let this yer young man from Roaring Camp—an entire stranger—carry away our money." But a crude sentiment of equity residing in the breasts of those who had been fortunate enough to win from Mr. Oakhurst overruled this narrower local prejudice.

Mr. Oakhurst received his sentence with philosophic calmness, none the less coolly that he was aware of the hesitation of his judges. He was too much of a gambler not to accept fate. With him life was at best an uncertain game, and he recognized the usual percentage in favor of the dealer.

A body of armed men accompanied the deported wickedness of Poker Flat to the outskirts of the settlement. Besides Mr. Oakhurst, who was known to be a coolly desperate man, and for whose

A RUSH FOR NEW DIGGINGS.

intimidation the armed escort was intended, the expatriated party consisted of a young woman familiarly known as "The Duchess;" another who had won the title of "Mother Shipton;" and "Uncle Billy," a suspected sluice-robber and confirmed drunkard. The cavalcade provoked no comments from the spectators, nor was any word uttered by the escort. Only when the gulch which marked the uttermost limit of Poker Flat was reached, the leader spoke briefly and to the point. The exiles were forbidden to return at the peril of their lives.

As the escort disappeared, their pent-up feelings found vent in a few hysterical tears from the Duchess, some bad language from Mother Shipton, and a Parthian volley of expletives from Uncle Billy. The philosophic Oakhurst alone remained silent. He listened calmly to Mother Shipton's desire to cut somebody's heart out, to the repeated statements of the Duchess that she would die in the road, and to the alarming oaths that seemed to be bumped out of Uncle

Billy as he rode forward. With the easy good humor characteristic of his class, he insisted upon exchanging his own riding horse, "Five-Spot," for the sorry mule which the Duchess rode. But even this act did not draw the party into any closer sympathy. The young woman readjusted her somewhat draggled plumes with a feeble, faded coquetry; Mother Shipton eyed the possessor of "Five-Spot" with malevolence, and Uncle Billy included the whole party in one sweeping anathema.

The road to Sandy Bar—a camp that, not having as yet experienced the regenerating influences of Poker Flat, consequently seemed to offer some invitation to the emigrants—lay over a steep mountain range. It was distant a day's severe travel. In that advanced season the party soon passed out of the moist, temperate regions of the foothills into the dry, cold bracing air of the Sierras. The trail was narrow and difficult. At noon the Duchess, rolling out of her saddle upon the ground, declared her intentions of going no farther, and the party halted.

The spot was singularly wild and impressive. A wooded amphitheatre, surrounded on three sides by precipitous cliffs of naked granite, sloped gently toward the crest of another precipice that overlooked the valley. It was, undoubtedly, the most suitable spot for a camp, had camping been advisable. But Mr. Oakhurst knew that scarcely half the journey to Sandy Bar was accomplished, and the party were not equipped or provisioned for delay. This fact he pointed out to his companions curtly, with a philosophic commentary on the folly of "throwing up their hand before the game was played out." But they were furnished with liquor, which in this emergency stood them in place of food, fuel, rest, and prescience. In spite of his remonstrances, it was not long before they were more or less under its influence. Uncle Billy passed rapidly from a bellicose state into one of stupor. Mr. Oakhurst alone remained erect, leaning against a rock, calmly surveying them.

Mr. Oakhurst did not drink. It interfered with a profession which required coolness, impassiveness, and presence of mind, and, in his own language, he "couldn't afford it." As he gazed at his recumbent fellow exiles, the loneliness begotten of his pariah trade, his habits of life, his very vices, for the first time seriously oppressed him. He bestirred himself in dusting his black clothes, washing his hands and face, and other acts characteristic of his studiously neat habits, and for a moment forgot his annoyance. The thought of deserting his weaker and more pitiable companions never perhaps occurred to him. Yet he could not help feeling the want of that excitement which, singularly enough, was most conducive to that calm equanimity for which he was notorious. He looked at the gloomy walls that rose a thousand feet sheer above the circling lines around him, at the sky ominously clouded, at the valley below, already deepening into shadow; and, doing so, suddenly he heard his own name called.

A horseman slowly ascended the trail. In the fresh, open face of the newcomer Mr. Oakhurst recognized Tom Simson, otherwise known as "The Innocent," of Sandy Bar. He had met him some months before over a "little game," and had, with perfect equanimity, won the entire fortune—amounting to some forty dollars—of that guileless youth. After the game was finished, Mr. Oakhurst drew the youthful speculator behind the door and thus addressed him: "Tommy, you're a good little man, but you can't gamble worth a cent. Don't ever try it over again." He then handed him his money back, pushed him gently from the room, and so made a devoted slave of Tom Simson.

There was a remembrance of this in his boyish and enthusiastic greeting of Mr. Oakhurst. He had started, he said, to go to Poker Flat to seek his fortune. "Alone?" No, not exactly alone; in fact (a giggle), he had run away with Piney Woods. Didn't Mr. Oakhurst remember Piney? She that used to wait on the table at the Temperance House? They had been engaged a long time, but old Jake Woods had objected, and so they had run away, and were going to Poker Flat to be married, and here they were. And they were tired out, and how lucky it was they had found a place to camp, and company. All this the Innocent delivered rapidly, while Piney, a stout, comely damsel of fifteen, emerged from behind the pine-tree, where she had been blushing unseen, and rode to the side of her lover.

Mr. Oakhurst seldom troubled himself with sentiment, still less with propriety; but he had a vague idea that the situation was not fortunate. He retained, however, his presence of mind sufficiently to kick Uncle Billy, who was about to say something, and Uncle Billy was sober enough to recognize in Mr. Oakhurst's kick a superior power that would not bear trifling. He then endeavored to dissuade Tom Simson from delaying further, but in vain. He even pointed out the fact that there was no provision, nor means of making a camp. But, unluckily, the Innocent met this objection by assuring the party that he was provided with an extra mule loaded with provisions, and by the discovery of a rude attempt at a log house near the trail. "Piney can stay with Mrs. Oakhurst," said the Innocent, pointing to the Duchess, "and I can shift for myself."

Nothing but Mr. Oakhurst's admonishing foot saved Uncle Billy from bursting into a roar of laughter. As it was, he felt compelled to return up the cañon until he could recover his gravity. There he confided the joke to the tall pine-trees, with many slaps of his leg, contortions of his face, and the usual profanity. But when he returned to the party, he found them seated by a fire—for the air had grown strangely chill and the sky overcast—in apparently amicable conversation. Piney was actually talking with an interest and animation she had not shown for many days. The Innocent was holding forth, apparently with equal effect, to Mr. Oakhurst and Mother Shipton, who was actually relaxing into amiability. "Is this yer a d—d picnic?" said Uncle Billy, with inward scorn, as he surveyed the sylvan group, the glancing firelight, and the tethered animals in the foreground. Suddenly an idea mingled with the alcoholic fumes that disturbed his brain. It was apparently of a jocular nature, for he felt impelled to slap his leg again and cram his fist into his mouth.

As the shadows crept slowly up the mountain, a slight breeze rocked the tops of the pine-trees and moaned through their long and gloomy aisles. The ruined cabin, patched and covered with pine boughs, was set apart for the ladies. As the lovers parted, they unaffectedly exchanged a kiss, so honest and sincere that it might have been heard above the swaying pines. The frail Duchess and the malevolent Mother Shipton were probably too stunned to remark upon this last evidence of simplicity, and so turned without a word to the hut. The fire was replenished, the men lay down before the door, and in few minutes were asleep.

Mr. Oakhurst was a light sleeper. Toward morning he awoke benumbed and cold. As he stirred the dying fire, the wind, which was now blowing strongly, brought to his cheek that which caused the blood to leave it,—snow!

He started to his feet with the intention of awakening the sleepers, for there was no time to lose. But turning to where Uncle Billy had been lying, he found him gone. A suspicion leaped to his brain, and a curse to his lips. He ran to the spot where the mules had been tethered—they were no longer there. The tracks were already rapidly disappearing in the snow.

The momentary excitement brought Mr. Oakhurst back to the fire with his usual calm. He did not waken the sleepers. The Innocent slumbered peacefully, with a smile on his good-humored, freckled face; the virgin Piney slept beside her frailer sisters as sweetly as though attended by celestial guardians; and Mr. Oakhurst, drawing his blanket over his shoulders, stroked his mustache and waited for the dawn. It came slowly in a whirling mist of snowflakes that dazzled and confused the eye. What could be seen of the landscape appeared magically changed. He looked over the valley, and summed up the present and future in two words, "Snowed in!"

A careful inventory of the provisions, which, fortunately for the party, had been stored within the hut, and so escaped the felonious fingers of Uncle Billy, disclosed the fact that with care and prudence they might last ten days longer. "That is," said Mr. Oakhurst *sotto voce* to the Innocent, "if you're willing to board us. If you ain't—and perhaps you'd better not—you can wait till Uncle Billy gets back with provisions." For some occult reason, Mr. Oakhurst could not bring himself to disclose Uncle Billy's rascality, and so offered the hypothesis that he had wandered from the camp and had accidentally stampeded the animals. He dropped a warning to the Duchess and Mother Shipton, who of course knew the facts of their associate's defection. "They'll find out the truth about us *all* when they find out anything," he added significantly, "and there's no good frightening them now."

Tom Simson not only put all his worldly store at the disposal of Mr. Oakhurst, but seemed to enjoy the prospect of their forced seclusion. "We'll have a good camp for a week, and then the snow'll melt, and we'll all go back together." The cheerful gayety of the young man and Mr. Oakhurst's calm infected the others. The Innocent, with the aid of pine boughs, extemporized a thatch for the roofless cabin, and the Duchess directed Piney in the rearrangement of the interior with a taste and tact that opened the blue eyes of that provincial maiden to their fullest extent. "I reckon now you're used to fine things at Poker Flat," said Piney. The Duchess turned away sharply to conceal something that reddened her cheeks through their professional tint, and Mother Shipton requested Piney not to "chatter." But when Mr. Oakhurst returned from a weary search for the trail, he heard the sound of happy laughter echoed from the rocks. He stopped in some alarm, and his thoughts first naturally reverted to the whiskey, which he had prudently cachéd. "And yet it don't somehow sound like whiskey," said the gambler. It was not until he caught sight of the blazing fire through the still blinding storm, and the group around it, that he settled to the conviction that it was "square fun."

Whether Mr. Oakhurst had cachéd his cards with the whiskey as something debarred the free access of the community, I cannot say. It was certain that, in Mother Shipton's words, he "didn't say 'cards' once" during that evening. Haply the time was beguiled by an accordion, produced somewhat ostentatiously by Tom Simson from his pack. Notwithstanding some difficulties attending the manipulation of this instrument, Piney Woods managed to pluck several reluctant melodies from its keys, to an accompaniment by the Innocent on a pair of bone castanets. But the crowning festivity of the evening was reached in a rude camp-meeting hymn which the lovers, joining hands, sang with great earnestness and vociferation. I fear that a certain defiant tone and Covenanter's swing to its chorus, rather than any devotional quality, caused it speedily to infect the others, who at least joined in the refrain:—

> "I'm proud to live in the service of the Lord,
> And I'm bound to die in His army."

The pines rocked, the storm eddied and whirled above the miserable group, and the flames of their altar leaped heavenward, as if in token of the vow.

At midnight the storm abated, the rolling clouds parted and the stars glittered keenly above the sleeping camp. Mr. Oakhurst, whose professional habits had enabled him to live on the smallest possible amount of sleep, in dividing the watch with Tom Simson somehow managed to take upon himself the greater part of that duty. He excused himself to the Innocent by saying that he had "often been a week without sleep." "Doing what?" asked Tom. "Poker!" replied Oakhurst sententiously. "When a man gets a streak of luck,—nigger-luck,—he don't get tired. The luck gives in first. Luck," continued the gambler reflectively, "is a mighty queer thing. All you know about it for certain is that it's bound to change. And it's finding out when it's going to change that makes you. We've had a streak of bad luck since we left Poker Flat,—you came along, and slap you get into it, too. If you can hold your cards right along you're all right. For," added the gambler, with cheerful irrelevance—

> " 'I'm proud to live in the service of the Lord,
> And I'm bound to die in His army.' "

The third day came, and the sun, looking through the white-curtained valley, saw the outcasts divide their slowly decreasing store of provisions for the morning meal. It was one of the peculiarities of that mountain climate that its rays diffused a kindly warmth over the wintry landscape, as if in regretful commiseration of the past. But it revealed drift on drift of snow piled high around the hut,—a hopeless, uncharted, trackless sea of white lying below the rocky shores to which the castaways still clung. Through the marvelously clear air the smoke of the pastoral village of Poker Flat rose miles away. Mother Shipton saw it, and from a remote pinnacle of her rocky fastness hurled in that direction a final malediction. It was her last vituperative attempt, and perhaps for that reason was invested with a certain degree of sublimity. It did her good, she privately informed the Duchess. "Just you go out there and cuss, and see." She then set herself to the task of amusing "the child," as she and the Duchess were pleased to call Piney. Piney was no chicken, but it was a soothing and original theory of the pair thus to account for the fact that she didn't swear and wasn't improper.

When night crept up again through the gorges, the reedy notes of the accordion rose and fell in fitful spasms and long-drawn gasps by the flickering campfire. But music failed to fill entirely the aching void left by insufficient food, and a new diversion was proposed by Piney,—story-telling. Neither Mr. Oakhurst nor his female companions caring to relate their personal experiences, this plan would have failed too, but for the Innocent. Some months before he had chanced upon a stray copy of Mr. Pope's ingenious translation of the Iliad. He now proposed to narrate the principal incidents of that poem—having thoroughly mastered the argument and fairly forgotten the words—in the current vernacular of Sandy Bar. And so for the rest of that night the Homeric demigods walked the earth. Trojan bully and wily Greek wrestled in the winds, and the great pines in the cañon seemed to bow to the wrath of the son of Peleus. Mr. Oakhurst listened with quiet satisfaction. Most especially was he interested in the fate of "Ashheels," as the Innocent persisted in denominating the "swift-footed Achilles."

So, with small food and much of Homer and the accordion, a week passed over the heads of the outcasts. The sun again forsook them, and again from leaden skies the snowflakes were sifted over the land. Day by day closer around them drew the snowy circle, until at last they looked from their prison over drifted walls of dazzling white, that towered twenty feet above their heads. It became more and more difficult to replenish their fires, even from the fallen trees beside them, now half hidden in the drifts. And yet no one complained. The lovers turned from the dreary prospect and looked into each other's eyes, and were happy. Mr. Oakhurst settled himself coolly to the losing game before him. The Duchess, more cheerful than she had been, assumed the care of Piney. Only Mother Shipton—once the strongest of the party—seemed to sicken and fade. At midnight on the tenth day she called Oakhurst to her side. "I'm going,' she said, in a voice of querulous weakness, "but don't say anything about it. Don't waken the kids. Take the bundle from under my head, and open it." Mr. Oakhurst did so. It contained Mother Shipton's rations for the last week, untouched. "Give 'em to the child," she said, pointing to the sleeping Piney. "You've starved yourself," said the gambler. "That's what they call it," said the woman querulously, as she lay down again, and turning her face to the wall, passed quietly away.

The accordion and the bones were put aside that day, and Homer was forgotten. When the body of Mother Shipton had been committed to the snow, Mr. Oakhurst took the Innocent aside, and showed him a pair of snowshoes, which he had fashioned from the old pack-saddle. "There's one chance in a hundred to save her yet," he said, pointing to Piney; "but it's there," he added, pointing toward Poker Flat. "If you can reach there in two days she's safe." "And you?" asked Tom Simson. "I'll stay here," was the curt reply.

The lovers parted with a long embrace. "You are not going, too?" said the Duchess, as she saw Mr. Oakhurst apparently waiting to accompany him. "As far as the cañon," he replied. He turned suddenly and kissed the Duchess, leaving her pallid face aflame, and her trembling limbs rigid with amazement.

Night came, but not Mr. Oakhurst. It brought the storm again and the whirling snow. Then the Duchess, feeding the fire, found that some one had quietly piled beside the hut enough fuel to last a few days longer. The tears rose to her eyes, but she hid them from Piney.

The women slept but little. In the morning, looking into each other's faces, they read their fate. Neither spoke, but Piney, accepting the position of the stronger, drew near and placed her arm around the Duchess's waist. They kept this attitude for the rest of the day. That night the storm reached its greatest fury, and, rending asunder the protecting vines, invaded the very hut.

Toward morning they found themselves unable to feed the fire, which gradually died away. As the embers slowly blackened, the Duchess crept closer to Piney, and broke the silence of many hours: "Piney, can you pray?" "No, dear," said Piney simply. The Duchess, without knowing exactly why, felt relieved, and, putting her head upon Piney's shoulder, spoke no more. And so reclining, the younger and purer pillowing the head of her soiled sister upon her virgin breast, they fell asleep.

The wind lulled as if it feared to waken them. Feathery drifts of snow, shaken from the long pine boughs, flew like white winged birds, and settled about them as they slept. The moon through the rifted clouds looked down upon what had been the camp. But all human stain, all trace of earthly travail, was hidden beneath the spotless mantle mercifully flung from above.

They slept all that day and the next, nor did they waken when voices and footsteps broke the silence of the camp. And when pitying fingers brushed the snow from their wan faces, you could scarcely have told from the equal peace that dwelt upon them which was she that had sinned. Even the law of Poker Flat recognized this, and turned away, leaving them still locked in each other's arms.

But at the head of the gulch, on one of the largest pine-trees, they found the deuce of clubs pinned to the bark with a bowie-knife. It bore the following, written in pencil in a firm hand:—

†

BENEATH THIS TREE

LIES THE BODY

OF

JOHN OAKHURST,

WHO STRUCK A STREAK OF BAD LUCK

ON THE 23D OF NOVEMBER 1850,

AND

HANDED IN HIS CHECKS

ON THE 7TH DECEMBER, 1850.

†

And pulseless and cold, with a derringer by his side and a bullet in his heart, though still calm as in life, beneath the snow lay he who was at once the strongest and yet the weakest of the outcasts of Poker Flat.

The Outcasts of Poker Flat, from *The Luck of Roaring Camp and Other Stories* by Bret Harte. Houghton Mifflin Company, 1903.

Mark Twain

The Fairest Picture

In 1861, young Samuel Clemens resigned after a two-week stint in the Confederate Army and lit out for the West, determined to strike it rich in the Nevada silver fields. A year later he had found a new occupation and, quite literally, had made a name for himself: Mark Twain, reporter for the Virginia City Territorial Enterprise. *During several years of roaming and writing in Nevada and California, Twain perfected the ironic, exaggerated style that made him famous, and built a reputation as "the wild humorist of the Pacific slope."*

Unlike most humorists of the last century, Twain remains as funny today as he was then. His account of an idyllic vacation spent at Lake Tahoe is at times hilarious. But for the modern mountain lover who may find nothing funny about the latter-day development of Lake Tahoe, there is a strong undercurrent of melancholy running through the story. Twain's report of the crystal clarity of the water, of air "the angels breathe"—of not a soul to be seen in two weeks!—staggers one's belief. To anyone who has sweltered in a weekend traffic jam at South Lake Tahoe or wandered the wilderness of Stateline, there is more irony in Twain's account than the great humorist could have mustered in the wildest flight of his imagination.

We had heard a world of talk about the marvelous beauty of Lake Tahoe, and finally curiosity drove us thither to see it. Three or four members of the Brigade had been there and located some timber-lands on its shores and stored up a quantity of provisions in their camp. We strapped a couple of blankets on our shoulders and took an ax apiece and started—for we intended to take up a wood ranch or so ourselves and become wealthy. We were on foot. The reader will find it advantageous to go horseback. We were told that the distance was eleven miles. We tramped a long time on level ground, and then toiled laboriously up a mountain about a thousand miles high and looked over. No lake there. We descended on the other side, crossed the valley and toiled up another mountain three or four thousand miles high, apparently, and looked over again. No lake yet. We sat down tired and perspiring, and hired a couple of Chinamen to curse those people who had beguiled us. Thus refreshed, we presently resumed the march with renewed vigor and determination. We plodded on, two or three hours longer, and at last the lake burst upon us—a noble sheet of blue water lifted six thousand three hundred feet above the level of the sea, and walled in by a rim of snow-clad mountain peaks that towered aloft full three thousand feet higher still! It was a vast oval, and one would have to use up eighty or a hundred good miles in traveling around it. As it lay there with the shadows of the mountains brilliantly photographed upon its still surface I thought it must surely be the fairest picture the whole earth affords.

We found the small skiff belonging to the Brigade boys, and without loss of time set out across a deep bend of the lake toward the landmarks that signified the locality of the camp. I got Johnny to row—not because I mind exertion myself, but because it makes me sick to ride backward when I am at work. But I steered. A three-mile pull brought us to the camp just as the night fell, and we stepped ashore very tired and wolfishly hungry. In a "cache" among the rocks we found the provisions and the cooking-utensils, and then, all fatigued as I was, I sat down on a boulder and superintended while Johnny gathered wood and cooked supper. Many a man who had gone through what I had, would have wanted to rest.

It was a delicious supper—hot bread, fried bacon, and black coffee. It was a delicious solitude we were in, too. Three miles away was a sawmill and some workmen, but there were not fifteen other human beings throughout the wide circumference of the lake. As the darkness closed down and the stars came out and spangled the great mirror with jewels, we smoked meditatively in the solemn hush and forgot our troubles and our pains. In due time we spread our blankets in the warm sand between two large boulders and soon fell asleep, careless of the procession of ants that passed in through rents in our clothing and explored our persons. Nothing could disturb the sleep that fettered us for it had been fairly earned, and if our consciences had any sins on them they had to adjourn court for that night, anyway. The wind rose just as we were losing consciousness, and we were lulled to sleep by the beating of the surf upon the shore.

It is always very cold on that lake-shore in the night, but we had plenty of blankets and were warm enough. We never moved a muscle all night, but waked at early dawn in the original positions, and got up at once, thoroughly refreshed, free from soreness, and brim full of friskiness. There is no end of wholesome medicine in such an experience. That morning we could have whipped ten such people as we were the day before—sick ones at any rate. But the world is slow, and people will go to "water cures" and "movement cures" and to foreign lands for health. Three months of camp life on Lake Tahoe would restore an Egyptian mummy to his pristine vigor, and give him an appetite like an alligator. I do not mean the oldest and driest mummies, of course, but the fresher ones. The air up there in the clouds is very pure and fine, bracing and delicious. And why shouldn't it be?—it is the same the angels breathe. I think that hardly any amount of fatigue can be gathered together that a man cannot sleep off in one night on the sand by its side. Not under a roof, but under the sky; it seldom or never rains there in the summer-time. I know a man who went there to die. But he made a failure of it. He was a skeleton when he came, and could barely stand. He had no appetite, and did nothing but read tracts and reflect on the future. Three months later he was sleeping out-of-doors regularly, eating all he could hold, three times a day, and chasing game over mountains three thousand feet high for recreation. And he was a skeleton no longer, but weighed part of a ton. This is no fancy sketch, but the truth. His disease was consumption. I confidently commend his experience to other skeletons.

I superintended again, and as soon as we had eaten breakfast we got in the boat and skirted along the lake-shore about three miles and disembarked. We liked the appearance of the place, and so we claimed some three hundred acres of it and stuck our "notices" on a tree. It was yellow-pine timber-land—a dense forest of trees a hundred feet high and from one to five feet through at the butt. It was necessary to fence our property or we could not hold it. That is to say, it was necessary to cut down trees here and there and make them fall in

such a way as to form a sort of inclosure (with pretty wide gaps in it).
We cut down three trees apiece, and found it such heartbreaking work
that we decided to "rest our case" on those; if they held the property,
well and good; if they didn't, let the property spill out through the
gaps and go; it was no use to work ourselves to death merely to save a
few acres of land. Next day we came back to build a house—for a
house was also necessary, in order to hold the property. We decided to
build a substantial log house and excite the envy of the Brigade boys;
but by the time we had cut and trimmed the first log it seemed
unnecesary to be so elaborate, and so we concluded to build it of
saplings. However, two saplings, duly cut and trimmed, compelled
recognition of the fact that a still modester architecture would satisfy
the law, and so we concluded to build a "brush" house. We devoted
the next day to this work, but we did so much "sitting around" and
discussing, that by the middle of the afternoon we had achieved only
a half-way sort of affair which one of us had to watch while the other
cut brush, lest if both turned our backs we might not be able to find it
again, it had such a strong family resemblance to the surrounding
vegetation. But we were satisfied with it.

We were landowners now, duly seized and possessed, and within
the protection of the law. Therefore we decided to take up our
residence on our own domain and enjoy that large sense of independence which only such an experience can bring. Late the next
afternoon, after a good long rest, we sailed away from the Brigade
camp with all the provisions and cooking-utensils we could carry
off—borrow is the more accurate word—and just as the night was
falling we beached the boat at our own landing.

If there is any life that is happier than the life we led on our timber
ranch for the next two or three weeks, it must be a sort of life which I
have not read of in books or experienced in person. We did not see a
human being but ourselves during the time, or hear any sounds but
those that were made by the wind and the waves, the sighing of the
pines, and now and then the far-off thunder of an avalanche. The
forest about us was dense and cool, the sky above us was cloudless
and brilliant with sunshine, the broad lake before us was glassy and
clear, or rippled and breezy, or black and storm-tossed, according to

Nature's mood; and its circling border of mountain domes, clothed with forests, scarred with landslides, cloven by cañons and valleys, and helmeted with glittering snow, fitly framed and finished the noble picture. The view was always fascinating, bewitching, entrancing. The eye was never tired of gazing, night or day, in calm or storm; it suffered but one grief, and that was that it could not look always, but must close sometimes in sleep.

We slept in the sand close to the water's edge, between two protecting boulders, which took care of the stormy night winds for us. We never took any paregoric to make us sleep. At the first break of dawn we were always up and running foot-races to tone down excess of physical vigor and exuberance of spirits. That is, Johnny was—but I held his hat. While smoking the pipe of peace after breakfast we watched the sentinel peaks put on the glory of the sun, and followed the conquering light as it swept down among the shadows, and set the captive crags and forests free. We watched the tinted pictures grow and brighten upon the water till every little detail of forest, precipice, and pinnacle was wrought in and finished, and the miracle of the enchanter complete. Then to "business."

That is, drifting around in the boat. We were on the north shore. There, the rocks on the bottom are sometimes gray, sometimes white. This gives the marvelous transparency of the water a fuller advantage than it has elsewhere on the lake. We usually pushed out a hundred yards or so from the shore, and then lay down on the thwarts in the sun, and let the boat drift by the hour whither it would. We seldom talked. It interrupted the Sabbath stillness, and marred the dreams the luxurious rest and indolence brought. The shore all along was indented with deep, curved bays and coves, bordered by narrow sand-beaches; and where the sand ended, the steep mountainsides rose right up aloft into space—rose up like a vast wall a little out of the perpendicular, and thickly wooded with tall pines.

So singularly clear was the water, that where it was only twenty or thirty feet deep the bottom was so perfectly distinct that the boat seemed floating in the air! Yes, where it was even *eighty* feet deep. Every little pebble was distinct, every speckled trout, every hand's-breadth of sand. Often, as we lay on our faces, a granite boulder, as large as a village church, would start out of the bottom apparently, and seem climbing up rapidly to the surface, till presently it threatened to touch our faces, and we could not resist the impulse to seize an oar and avert the danger. But the boat would float on, and the boulder descend again, and then we could see that when we had been exactly above it, it must still have been twenty or thirty feet below the surface. Down through the transparency of these great depths, the water was not *merely* transparent, but dazzlingly, brilliantly so. All objects seen through it had a bright, strong vividness, not only of outline, but of every minute detail, which they would not have had when seen simply through the same depth of atmosphere. So empty and airy did all spaces seem below us, and so strong was the sense of floating high aloft in mid-nothingness, that we called these boat excursions "balloon voyages."

We fished a good deal, but we did not average one fish a week. We could see trout by the thousand winging about in the emptiness under us, or sleeping in shoals on the bottom, but they would not bite—they could see the line too plainly, perhaps. We frequently selected the trout we wanted, and rested the bait patiently and persistently on the end of his nose at a depth of eighty feet, but he would only shake it off with an annoyed manner, and shift his position.

We bathed occasionally, but the water was rather chilly, for all it looked so sunny. Sometimes we rowed out to the "blue water," a mile or two from shore. It was as dead blue as indigo there, because of the immense depth. By official measurement, the lake in its center is one thousand five hundred and twenty-five feet deep!

Sometimes, on lazy afternoons, we lolled on the sand in camp, and smoked pipes and read some old well-worn novels. At night, by the camp-fire, we played euchre and seven-up to strengthen the mind—and played them with cards so greasy and defaced that only a whole summer's acquaintance with them could enable the student to tell the ace of clubs from the jack of diamonds.

We never slept in our "house." It never occurred to us, for one thing; and besides, it was built to hold ground, and that was enough. We did not wish to strain it.

By and by our provisions began to run short, and we went back to the old camp and laid in a new supply. We were gone all day, and reached home again about nightfall, pretty tired and hungry. While Johnny was carrrying the main bulk of the provisions up to our "house" for future use, I took the loaf of bread, some slices of bacon, and the coffee-pot, ashore, set them down by a tree, lit a fire, and went back to the boat to get the frying-pan. While I was at this, I heard a shout from Johnny, and looking up I saw that my fire was galloping all over the premises!

Johnny was on the other side of it. He had to run through the flames to get to the lake-shore, and then we stood helpless and watched the devastation.

The ground was deeply carpeted with dry pine-needles, and the fire touched them off as if they were gunpowder. It was wonderful to see with what fierce speed the tall sheet of flame traveled! My coffee-pot was gone, and everything with it. In a minute and a half the fire seized upon a dense growth of dry manzanita chapparal six or eight feet high, and then the roaring and popping and crackling was something terrific. We were driven to the boat by the intense heat, and there we remained, spell-bound.

Within half an hour all before us was a tossing, blinding tempest of flame! It went surging up adjacent ridges—surmounted them and disappeared in the cañon beyond—burst into view upon higher and farther ridges, presently—shed a grander illumination abroad, and dove again—flamed out again, directly, higher and still higher up the mountainside—threw out skirmishing parties of fire here and there, and sent them trailing their crimson spirals away among remote ramparts and ribs and gorges, till as far as the eye could reach the lofty mountain-fronts were webbed as it were with a tangled network of red lava streams. Away across the water the crags and domes were lit with a ruddy glare, and the firmament above was a reflected hell!

Every feature of the spectacle was repeated in the glowing mirror of the lake! Both pictures were sublime, both were beautiful; but that in the lake had a bewildering richness about it that enchanted the eye and held it with the stronger fascination.

We sat absorbed and motionless through four long hours. We never thought of supper, and never felt fatigue. But at eleven o'clock the conflagration had traveled beyond our range of vision, and then darkness stole down upon the landscape again.

Hunger asserted itself now, but there was nothing to eat. The provisions were all cooked, no doubt, but we did not go to see. We were homeless wanderers again, without any property. Our fence was gone, our house burned down; no insurance. Our pine forest was well scorched, the dead trees all burned up, and our broad acres of manzanita swept away. Our blankets were on our usual sand-bed, however, and so we lay down and went to sleep. The next morning we started back to the old camp, but while out a long way from shore, so great a storm came up that we dared not try to land. So I bailed out the seas we shipped, and Johnny pulled heavily through the billows till we had reached a point three or four miles beyond the camp. The storm was increasing, and it became evident that it was better to take the hazard of beaching the boat than go down in a hundred fathoms of water; so we ran in, with tall white caps following, and I sat down in the stern-sheets and pointed her head-on to the shore. The instant the bow struck, a wave came over the stern that washed crew and cargo ashore, and saved a deal of trouble. We shivered in the lee of a boulder all the rest of the day, and froze all the night through. In the morning the tempest had gone down, and we paddled down to the camp without any unnecessary delay. We were so starved that we ate up the rest of the Brigade's provisions, and then set out to Carson to tell them about it and ask their forgiveness. It was accorded, upon payment of damages.

We made many trips to the lake after that, and had many a hair-breadth escape and blood-curdling adventure which will never be recorded of any history.

The Fairest Picture, from *Roughing It* by Mark Twain. Harper & Bros., 1906.

Walt Whitman

Passage to India

The completion of the transcontinental railroad in 1869 brought California within reach of everyone. No longer did one need to be an adventurer to embark for the golden shore. Now for two dollars a night anyone could reserve a comfortable Pullman and speed coast to coast in a matter of days.

Completion of the railroad had not only practical value for the nation but symbolic value as well. After the trauma of the Civil War, a sense of promise sprang from the mere fact of spreading rails, linking citizen, city, and state, one with the other. The inexorable joining of East and West fulfilled a cherished American dream: the Union was not simply preserved, it was assured.

No one understood the importance of a unified America more clearly than Walt Whitman. Whitman, whose subject was always the dream of America, had experienced first-hand the wrenching nightmare of the Civil War. In "Passage to India," a plea for the unity of all nations, he portrayed the unity of his own through the symbol of a relentless west-bound train speeding across the Great Plains toward the Pacific. Here is the third stanza of that poem.

Passage to India!
Lo soul for thee of tableaus twain,
I see in one the Suez canal initiated, open'd,
I see the procession of steamships, the Empress Eugenie's leading
    the van,
I mark from on deck the strange landscape, the pure sky, the
    level sand in the distance,
I pass swiftly the picturesque groups, the workmen gather'd,
The gigantic dredging machines.

In one again, different, (yet thine, all thine, O soul, the same,)
I see over my own continent the Pacific railroad surmounting
every barrier,
I see continual trains of cars winding along the Platte carrying
freight and passengers,
I hear the locomotives rushing and roaring, and the shrill steam-
whistle,
I hear the echoes reverberate through the grandest scenery in the
world,
I cross the Laramie plains, I note the rocks in grotesque shapes,
the buttes,
I see the plentiful larkspur and wild onions, the barren, colorless,
sage-deserts,
I see in glimpses afar or towering immediately above me the
great mountains, I see the Wind river and the Wahsatch
mountains,
I see the Monument mountain and the Eagle's Nest, I pass the
Promontory, I ascend the Nevadas,
I scan the noble Elk mountain and wind around its base,
I see the Humboldt range, I thread the valley and cross the river,
I see the clear waters of lake Tahoe, I see forests of majestic
pines,
Or crossing the great desert, the alkaline plains, I behold enchant-
ing mirages of waters and meadows,
Marking through these and after all, in duplicate slender lines,
Bridging the three or four thousand miles of land travel,
Tying the Eastern to the Western sea,
The road between Europe and Asia.

(Ah Genoese thy dream! thy dream!
Centuries after thou art laid in thy grave,
The shore thou foundest verifies thy dream.)

Passage to India, from *Leaves of Grass* by Walt Whitman. David McKay, 1888.

Robert Louis Stevenson

A Grateful Mountain Feeling

For the California-bound train passenger despairing of the seemingly endless journey across the Nevada moonscape, the ride up into the cool wooded heights of the Sierra can seem like a rebirth. That at least was the reaction of the great Scottish writer Robert Louis Stevenson, who took the Union and Central Pacific railroads from New York to San Francisco in 1879. Stevenson, the author of Treasure Island, Kidnapped, *and* Dr. Jekyll and Mr. Hyde, *was embarked upon a most unusual mission. Several years earlier as a young bachelor, he had met a San Francisco woman named Fanny Osbourne when she vacationed in France. Fanny was already married, the mother of three children, and ten years Stevenson's senior. A most unorthodox woman, she packed a revolver and rolled her own cigarettes. Worse, she smoked them. By the standards of the times, she did not qualify as good marriage material.*

Nevertheless, Stevenson fell madly in love with her. When Mrs. Osbourne returned to California, he tried living without her. Failing in this, he took off on a desperate 6,000-mile journey from Scotland to San Francisco to wrest her from her husband. His heart soaring as he neared his destination, Stevenson wrote a rapturous account of the Sierra crossing at Donner Pass. His words are sure to ring true for anyone whose spirits lift at the thought of a trip to the high country.

Of all the next day I will tell you nothing, for the best of all reasons, that I remember no more than that we continued through desolate and desert scenes, fiery hot and deadly weary. But some time after I had fallen asleep that night, I was awakened by one of my companions. It was in vain that I resisted. A fire of enthusiasm and whisky burned in his eyes; and he declared we were in a new country, and I must come forth upon the platform and see with my own eyes. The train was then, in its patient way, standing halted in a by-track. It was a clear, moonlit night; but the valley was too narrow to admit the moonshine direct, and only a diffused glimmer whitened the tall rocks and relieved the blackness of the pines. A hoarse clamour filled the air; it was the continuous plunge of a cascade somewhere near at hand among the mountains. The air struck chill, but tasted good and vigorous in the nostrils—a fine, dry, old mountain atmosphere. I was dead sleepy, but I returned to roost with a grateful mountain feeling at my heart.

When I awoke next morning, I was puzzled for a while to know if it were day or night, for the illumination was unusual. I sat up at last, and found we were grading slowly downward through a long snowshed; and suddenly we shot into an open; and before we were swallowed into the next length of wooden tunnel, I had one glimpse of a huge pine-forested ravine upon my left, a foaming river, and a sky already coloured with the fires of dawn. I am usually very calm over the displays of nature; but you will scarce believe how my heart leaped at this. It was like meeting one's wife. I had come home again—home from unsightly deserts to the green and habitable corners of the earth. Every spire of pine along the hill-top, every trouty pool along that mountain river, was more dear to me than a blood relation. Few people have praised God more happily than I did. And thenceforward, down by Blue Cañon, Alta, Dutch Flat, and all the old mining camps, through a sea of mountain forests, dropping thousands of feet toward the far sea-level as we went, not I only, but all the passengers on board, threw off their sense of dirt and heat and weariness, and bawled like school-boys and thronged with shining eyes upon the platform and became new creatures within and without. The sun no longer oppressed us with heat, it only shone laughingly along the mountain-side, until we were fain to laugh ourselves for glee. At every turn we could see farther into the land and our own happy futures. At every town the cocks were tossing their clear notes into the golden air, and crowing for the new day and the new country. For this was indeed our destination; this was "the good country" we had been going to so long.

A Grateful Mountain Feeling, from *Across the Plains* by Robert Louis Stevenson. Charles Scribner's Sons, 1892.

SECTION III:
THE VACATIONERS

Even were it not for the drawing power of Yosemite Valley, the Sierra would assuredly attract its share of summer visitors. Deep forests of magnificent firs and pines, sparkling lakes teeming with trout, hiking trails leading into remote alpine wilderness—these would draw vacationers to the Sierra just as they attract visitors to the Tetons, the Cascades, and other great mountain ranges around the world.

But the Sierra has something that no other range has, and because of it the normally slow process of turning a wild mountain range into a vacationland was compressed into a few years. Upon its discovery, Yosemite Valley was immediately recognized not merely as an interesting place to visit, but as a very wonder of the world. It drew visitors to the Sierra as though the range were the site not of lakes and hiking trails, but of the pyramids or the Holy Grail.

This is no exaggeration. Here is Samuel Bowles writing about Yosemite Valley in the 1860s:

> The overpowering sense of the sublime, of awful desolation, of transcendent marvelousness and unexpectedness, that swept over us, as we reined our horses sharply out of green forests, and stood upon a high jutting rock that over-looked this rolling, upheaving sea of granite mountains, holding, far down in its rough lap, the vale of meadow and grove and river—such a tide of feeling, such stoppage of ordinary emotions, comes at rare intervals in any life. It was the confrontal of God face to face, as

in great danger, or sudden death. It was Niagara magnified. All that was mortal shrank back; all that was immortal swept to the front, and bowed down in awe.

More succinctly, another visitor of the day remarked: "I was never so near Heaven in my life."

The first tourists arrived in Yosemite Valley in 1855. Within a few decades the number of tourists had risen to 10,000 a year. No one who has visited Yosemite recently needs to be told that the number today is somewhat larger.[1]

Vacationers shortly discovered that there was more to the 30,000-square-mile Sierra than 7-square-mile Yosemite Valley. In the north, Lake Tahoe offered its own special charms—magnificent scenery, pure mountain air, water clear as glass—and soon developed its own special brand of overcrowding: traffic-choked highways, fast-food sprawl and, in a bizarre twist, casinos full of gamblers.

In the southern Sierra, Sequoia and Kings Canyon national parks, less accessible than Lake Tahoe and less spectacular than Yosemite, nevertheless drew the more enterprising vacationers, few of whom regretted the trip. Throughout the range a network of hiking trails sprang up, centered around the 211-mile-long John Muir Trail. Running along the crest of the range from Mount Whitney to Yosemite Valley, the Muir Trail has introduced countless thousands of hikers to the pleasures of high-country backpacking. Partly as a result of the trail's popularity, the once lonely High Sierra has become swamped with summer hikers. Permits are now required by the U.S. Forest Service and the National Park Service to enter the Sierra backcountry. Rutted trails and litter-strewn lakesides have led to the growth of a new environmental consciousness, an awareness of the need to tread lightly and respectfully on fragile nature. And they have led the seeker of solitude away from the maintained trails into the still-existing wild country to be found far from the beaten track in the off-trail High Sierra.

---

[1] 2.5 million in 1980

James H. Lawrence

The First Tourists

Following the entrance of the Mariposa Battalion into Yosemite Valley in 1851,[1] only one small matter remained to be cleared up before Yosemite would be ready to receive visitors. On its first foray into the valley, the battalion failed to locate any of the rebellious Indians it had been sent to eradicate. Two months later a division of the battalion under Captain John Bowling reentered the valley. Bowling's men captured a few Indians and killed one, the son of chief Teneiya. Then they hiked to Tenaya Lake, where they captured Teneiya and several dozen of his followers. The Indians were marched to Bowling's headquarters on the Fresno River and settled on a reservation.

Shortly thereafter, however, Teneiya and his band were released and allowed to return to their mountain home. Then in May 1852, an Indian boy was murdered near the camp of eight prospectors in Yosemite Valley. Teneiya's people retaliated, killing two of the miners.

With open warfare flaring, a company of soldiers under Lieutenant Tredwell Moore was sent on a punitive mission from Fort Miller to Yosemite, where they captured five Indians. Relying heavily on circumstantial evidence, Moore found the five guilty of the miners' murders and had them shot. Farther up the valley he captured several more of Teneiya's followers; these were hanged near Washington Column. Teneiya and the demoralized remnants of his band escaped over the Sierra, and the battle for Yosemite Valley was over.

With hostilities ended, rumors of the benign and beautiful valley spread quickly. An Englishman named James M. Hutchings thought that the time might be ripe for an illustrated magazine publicizing California, and Yosemite sounded like an ideal subject for the magazine. Hutchings and two friends engaged an artist and two Indian guides, and in June 1855 set off for a week in the valley. The first issue of Hutchings' Illustrated California Magazine *rolled off the press a year later.*

---

[1] See "Lafayette Bunnell: Discovery of the Yosemite," Section I.

147

Since Hutchings's visit might be characterized as a "business trip," the honor
of being the first tourists in Yosemite Valley fell to two groups which arrived two
months after Hutchings, in August 1855. Both parties had as grand a time
exploring and rollicking in the valley as any tourist might today. Years later, James
H. Lawrence, a member of one of the parties, recalled his "discovery" of Nevada
Fall, actually seen for the first time four years earlier by members of the Mariposa
Battalion.

Next morning, soon as it was fairly light, the cheerful crack of the
rifle awoke the slumbering echoes. Four of the best shots had been
detailed to replenish the commissary supplies, and in about half an
hour they came in loaded with mountain grouse.

"Looks like you had good luck."

"Struck a perfect streak."

"Did any of 'em get away?"

These were among the congratulatory greetings, to which the
response was that the woods were full of them; there were plenty left;
that they were fat as butter balls. The prospect of fresh meat in
unlimited quantities was encouraging. "Broil the youngest for breakfast and save the others for a grand stew," was the order of the *chef de
cuisine*—while we all volunteered in dressing the birds.

After breakfast we moved camp, and drove our stakes three or
four miles further up the valley, on the north side of the river nearly
opposite the Yosemite Fall. This became our permanent headquarters,
and was made the point of departure for all our exploration in and
about the valley.

Our first excursion was up the Cañon of Pyweah to Mirror Lake.
Pohono, or the Bridal Veil, came in for a share of our attention. As
surmised by Haughton, it was only a wreath of spray, which hung
pendant and gracefully swinging with the breeze. The great Yosemite
Fall was a thing of the past. It had left its impress on the naked rocks in
a broad stain, but a meager, trickling, straggling stream, lazily crawling
down the face of the seamed cliff, and wiggling among the jagged
rocks below, was all that was left of the grand fall, which, with its
roaring and thundering, strikes terror to the soul of the tourist who
ventures near it during the spring or earlier summer months.

Perilous attempts to penetrate the forbidding looking cañons were made. Usually one man was left to "keep camp"—sometimes two. This meant to go a fishing, and have dinner well under way before the rest of the party returned.

One evening, after a series of dare-devil escapades for no particular purpose, except to demonstrate how near a man can come to breaking his neck and miss it, some one suggested an expedition up the main river, above the valley. Haughton was appealed to for information. He favored the proposition, and said he would cheerfully make one of the party. As for information he had none to give; neither he nor any of the Boling Expedition ever dreamed of attempting it. They came on business—not to see sights or explore for new fields of wonder. Their mission was hunting Indians. They tracked their game up the Pyweah Cañon to their *rancheria,* where they captured them. As to the main river above the valley, he had taken a peep at it. There was no sign of a trail. It was a deep, rough cañon, filled with immense bowlders, through which the river seethed and roared with a deafening sound, and there had never been seen a foot-print of white man or Indian in that direction. The cañon was considered *impassable.*

There was a chorus of voices in response.

"That's the word."

"Say it again."

"Just what we are hunting."

"We want something rough."

"We'll tackle that cañon in the morning."

"An early start, now."

It was so ordered. "With the first streak of daylight you'll hear me crow," was Connor's little speech as he rolled himself in his blankets. Next morning we were up and alive, pursuant to programme. Everybody seemed anxious to get ahead.

Three of us—Milton J. Mann, G. C. Pearson, and the writer of this sketch—lingered to arrange the camp fixtures, for everybody was going up the cañon. When we came to the South Cañon, or Talool-weack, our friends were far in advance of us. We could hear them up the cañon shouting, their voices mingling with the roar of the waters. A brief consultation, and we came to the resolve to diverge from the main river and try to effect an ascent between that stream and the cañon. It looked like a perilous undertaking, and there were some doubts as to the result; nevertheless, the conclusion was to see how far we could go. Away up, up, far above us, skirting the base of what seemed to be a perpendicular cliff, there was a narrow belt of timber. That meant a plateau or strip of land comparatively level. If we could only reach that, it was reasonable to suppose that we could get around the face of the cliff. "Then we will see sights," was the expression of one of the trio. What we expected to discover somewhere up the main stream was a lake or perhaps a succession of lakes—such having been the result of the explorations up the Pyweah Cañon, and mountain lakes being not unfrequently noted as a feature of the sources of mountain streams.

But to reach the plateau—that was the problem. It was a fearful climb. Over and under and around masses of immense rocks, jumping across chasms at imminent risk of life and limb, keeping a bright lookout for soft places to fall, as well as for the best way to circumvent the next obstacle, after about three hours wrestling, "catch as catch can," with that grim old mountain side, we reached the timber. Here, as we had surmised, was enough of level ground for a foothold, and here we took a rest, little dreaming of the magnificent scene in store for us when we rounded the base of the cliff. . . .

The oft-quoted phrase, "A thing of beauty is a joy forever," was never more fully realized. The picture is photographed on the tablets of my memory in indelible colors, and is as fresh and bright to-day as was the first impression twenty-nine years ago. To the tourist who beholds it for the first time, the Nevada Fall, with its weird surroundings, is a view of rare and picturesque beauty and grandeur. The rugged cliffs, the summits fringed with stunted pine and juniper, bounding the cañon on the southern side, the "Cap of Liberty" standing like a huge sentinel overlooking the scene at the north, the foaming caldron at the foot of the fall, the rapids below, the flume where the stream glides noiselessly but with lightning speed over its polished granite bed, making the preparatory run for its plunge over the Vernal Fall, form a combination of rare effects, leaving upon the mind an impression that years cannot efface. But the tourist is in a measure prepared. He has seen the engravings and photographic views, and read descriptions written by visitors who have preceded him. To us it was the opening of a sealed volume. Long we lingered and admiringly gazed upon the grand panorama, till the descending sun admonished us that we had no time to lose in making our way campward.

Later, Lawrence and his friends discussed the future of Yosemite as a tourist attraction.

Our evenings were pleasant and sociable. Around the cheerful camp-fire we discussed the grandeur of our surroundings and the possibilities of the future. It was unanimously agreed that for beauty and sublimity of scenery the valley was without a peer: as people from all parts of the world visited Niagara Falls, and our own countrymen made the European tour for the special purpose of viewing the wonders of the Alps, why should not this wonder-land attract thousands from the Atlantic States and Europe, when its fame should become world-wide? An improved trail was suggested, and various places along the route, where steep and abrupt pitches could be avoided and an easy grade substituted, were mapped out and theoretically surveyed.

These subjects were argued at length, and particularly during the evening of our last day in the valley, when the discussion ran on till after midnight. Even the feasibility of a wagon road was suggested, and the contruction of a railroad was vaguely hinted at as one of the possibilities of the far-away future—sometime in the next century. "We will none of us live to see that," despairingly remarked one fellow; "nor is it likely that this place will become much of a resort during our life-time."

The First Tourists, from "Discovery of the Nevada Falls" by James H. Lawrence. *The Overland Monthly,* October, 1884.

James M. Hutchings

A Guide For Tourists

James Hutchings's visit to Yosemite Valley in 1855 changed his life. Thereafter, his mission in life became to spread the gospel of Yosemite to the rest of the world. He served alternately as innkeeper, guide, explorer, and publicist for the miraculous valley until his death in 1902.

One of Hutchings's major achievements was his publication of a series of magazines and books describing the wonders of Yosemite. Hutchings' Illustrated California Magazine *appeared in July 1856 and ran monthly for the next four years.* Scenes of Wonder and Curiosity in California, *essentially a tourist's guide to Yosemite Valley, was published in 1860 and went through numerous editions. Finally in 1886, Hutchings produced* In the Heart of the Sierras, *the classic volume on the lore and the lure of Yosemite.*

In Scenes of Wonder and Curiosity in California, *Hutchings provided the tourist of the 1860s with the following alluring description of the first night in the valley, and an excursion to Yosemite Falls.*

Then, weary as we are, it seems such a luxury to lie awake and listen to the splashing, washing, roaring, surging, hissing, seething sound of the great Yo-Semite Falls, just opposite; or to pass quietly out of a sheltering-place, and look up between the lofty pines and spreading oaks, to the granite cliffs, that tower up, with such majesty of form and boldness of outline, against the vast etherial vault of heaven; or watch, in the moonlight, the everchanging shapes and shadows of the water, as it leaps the cloud-draped summit of the mountain, and falls in gusty torrents on the unyielding granite, to be dashed to an infinity of atoms. Then to return to our fern-leaf couch, and dream of some tutelary genius, of immense proportions, extending over us his protecting arms—of his admonishing the water-fall to modulate the music of its voice into some gently soothing lullaby, that we may sleep and be refreshed.

Some time before the sun can get a good, honest look at us, deep down as we are in this awful chasm, we see him painting his rosy smiles upon the ridges, and etching light and shadows in the furrows of the mountain's brow, as though he took a pride in showing up, to the best advantage, the wrinkles time had made upon it; but all of us feel too fatigued fully to enjoy the thrilling grandeur and beauty that surrounds us.

Here it will not be out of place to remark that ladies or gentlemen—especially the former—who visit this valley to look upon and appreciate its wonders, and make it a trip of pleasurable enjoyment, should not attempt its accomplishment in less than three days from Mariposa, Coulterville, or Big-Oak Flat. If this is remembered, the enjoyment of the visit will be more than doubled.

RIDE TO THE CHO-LOOKE OR YO-SEMITE FALL.

After a substantial breakfast, made palatable by that most excellent of sauces, a good appetite, our guide announces that the horses are ready, and the saddle-bags well stored with such good things as will commend themselves acceptably to our attention about noon; and that the first place to visit is the Yo-Semite Fall.

Crossing a rude bridge over the main stream, which is here about sixty feet in width, and nine in depth, we keep down the northern bank of the river for a short distance, to avoid a large portion of the valley in front of the hotel, that is probably overflowed with water. On either side of our trail, in several places, such is the luxuriant growth of the ferns, that they are above our shoulders as we ride through them.

Presently we reach one of the most beautifully picturesque scenes that eye ever saw. It is the ford. The oak, dogwood, maple, cottonwood, and other trees, form an arcade of great beauty over the sparkling, rippling, pebbly stream, and, in the back-ground, the lower fall of the Yo-Semite is dropping its sheet of snowy sheen behind a dark middle distance of pines and hemlocks.

As the snow rapidly melts beneath the fiery strength of a hot summer sun, a large body of water, most probably, is rushing past, forming several small streams—which, being comparatively shallow,

Drawn by T. Hill.

THE CHIL-NOO-AL-NA FALLS.

NEAR WAWONA.

are easily forded. When within about a hundred and fifty yards of the fall, as numerous large boulders begin to intercept our progress, we may as well dismount, and, after fastening our animals to some young trees, make our way up to it on foot.

Now a change of temperature soon becomes perceptible, as we advance; and the almost oppressive heat of the centre of the valley is gradually changing to that of chilliness. But up, up, we climb, over this rock, and past that tree, until we reach the foot, or as near as we can advance to it, of the great Yo-Semite Fall, when a cold draught of air rushes down upon us from above, about equal in strength to an eight knot breeze; bringing with it a heavy shower of finely comminuted spray, that falls with sufficient force to saturate our clothing in a few moments. From this a beautiful phenomenon is observable—inasmuch as, after striking our hats, the diamond-like mist shoots off at an angle of about thirty-five or forty degrees, and as the sun shines upon it, a number of miniature rainbows are formed all round us.

Those who have never visited this spot, must not suppose that the cloud-like spray that descends upon us is the main fall itself, broken into infinitesimal particles, and becomes nothing but a sheet of cloud. By no means; for, although this stream shoots over the margin of the mountain, nearly seven hundred feet above, it falls almost in a solid body—not in a continuous stream exactly, but having a close resemblance to an avalanche of snowy rockets that appear to be perpetually trying to overtake each other in their descent, and mingle the one into the other, the whole composing a torrent of indescribable power and beauty.

Huge boulders, and large masses of sharp, angular rocks, are scattered here and there, forming the uneven sides of an immense, and apparently ever-boiling cauldron; around and in the interstices of which numerous dwarf ferns, weeds, grasses, and flowers, are ever growing, where not actually washed by the falling stream.

It is beyond the power of language to describe the awe-inspiring majesty of the darkly-frowning and overhanging mountain walls of solid granite that here hem us in on every side, as though they would threaten us with instantaneous destruction, if not total annihilation, did we attempt for a moment to deny their power. If man ever feels his utter insignificance at any time, it is when looking upon such a scene of appalling grandeur as this here presented. . . .

After lingering here for several hours, with inexpressible feelings of suppressed astonishment and delight, qualified and intensified by veneration, we may take a long and reluctant last upward gaze, convinced that we shall "never look upon its like again," until we pay it another visit at some future time; and, making the best of our way to where our horses are tied, proceed to endorse the truthfulness of the prognostications of our guide in the morning before starting, concerning appetites and lunch.

A Guide for Tourists, from *Scenes of Wonder and Curiosity in California* by J.M. Hutchings. Hutchings & Rosenfield, 1860.

Charles Loring Brace

A Visit with the Hutchingses

*In 1863 James Hutchings purchased the Upper Hotel near Yosemite Falls.
He renamed it the Hutchings House and the following summer took over as
proprietor of the hotel. For the next decade he and his wife Elvira played host to
as many as 57 guests a night. (The Hutchings House had really adequate
accommodations for only 28; the valley's hotels were crowded in those days too.)*

*Cultured and engaging, the Hutchingses were very popular with their guests.
Whatever social virtues they may have had, however, they were decidedly not cut
out for innkeeping. Author and philanthropist Charles Loring Brace, who boarded
at the Hutchings House in 1867 or 1868, provided this genial sketch of the trials
and the pleasures to be found there.*

ONE of the jokes current in the Valley is to carefully warn the
traveler, before coming to this hotel, "not to leave his bed-room door
unlocked, as there are thieves about!" On retiring to his room for the
night, he discovers to his amazement, that his door is a sheet, and his
partition from the adjoining sleeping-chamber also a cotton cloth.
The curtain-lectures and bed-room conversations conducted under
these circumstances, it may be judged, are discreet. The house,
however, is clean, and the table excellent; and Hutchings himself,
enough of a character alone to make up for innumerable deficiencies.
He is one of the original pioneers of the Valley, and at the same time
is a man of considerable literary abilities, and a poet. He was written a
very creditable guide-book on the Cañon. No one could have a finer
appreciation of the points of beauty, and the most characteristic
scenes of the Valley. He is a "Guide" in the highest sense, and loves the
wonderful region which he shows yearly to strangers from every quarter of the world. But, unfortunately, he is also hotel-keeper, waiter, and
cook—employments requiring a good deal of close, practical attention,

as earthly life is arranged. Thus we come down, very hungry, to a delicious breakfast of fresh trout, venison, and great pans of garden strawberries; but unfortunately, there are no knives and forks. A romantic young lady asks, in an unlucky moment, about the best point of view for the Nevada Fall. "Madam, there is but one; you must get close to the Upper Fall, just above the mist of the lower, and there you will see a horizontal rainbow beneath your feet, and the most exquisite—"

Here a strong-minded lady, whose politeness is at an end, "But here Hutchings, we have no knives and forks!" "Oh, beg a thousand pardons, madam!" and he rushes off; but meeting his wife on the way, she gives him coffee for the English party, and he forgets us entirely, and we get up good-naturedly and search out the implements ourselves. Again, from an amiable lady, "*Please,* Mr. Hutchings, another cup of coffee!" "Certainly, madam!" When the English lady from Calcutta asks him about some wild flowers, he goes off in a botanical and poetical disquisition, and in his abstraction brings the other lady, with great eagerness, a glass of water. Sometimes sugar is handed you instead of salt for the trout, or cold water is poured into your coffee; but none of the ladies mind, for our landlord is as handsome as he is obliging, and really full of information.

"Mr. Hutchings, how do you like it here in the winter?"

"Madam, I always retire then to my country seat, on the sunny side of the Valley" (pointing to a little cabin on the other side, out of the eternal shadow of rocks.) "I have it full of books, and I get a paper once in three months. At first, I used to think it quite romantic to watch the avalanches, but when a fresh one fell every half mile as I waded through the snow, I began to get enough of them. We have snow here ten feet deep, and I've slept in it like any bear sometimes, as I was backing my things in."

"Well, you are not much troubled with neighbors."

"No; I have only Leidig (his next neighbor), and the Diggers; that's what I like about it."

It was a very agreeable thing to us travelers that Mr. Hutchings had been able to lay out an excellent garden in the Valley. He brought in strawberries of several varieties, and most delicious flavor, by the pail full, and says that he has them all summer. The trout are a far inferior fish to our Eastern trout, and much less prettily marked. We saw the Indians catch them in the icy-cold stream which flowed by the door. The venison, too, seems not equal to ours, but it cannot be in full season yet. Mr. Hutchings is always ready for a philosophical remark. My wife had gone out and gathered some splended wild flowers, and arranged them about the room. "There, gentlemen," said he, "I have always said that the highest art was in producing beauty from the poorest materials."

There were several parties in the hotel. A San Francisco business party, who were doing the Valley, with the rapidity they sold ready-made clothes: then the English party from India—very pleasant people, and among them, an exceedingly pretty young lady, who was watched by us gentlemen with great admiration, as she was not only very pretty, but wore an exquisite long riding-dress, while our ladies were all in what must always be a hideous dress—bloomers or very short skirts. "But what will she do at the waterfalls, and in the swamps?" was the envious female whisper; but we, her admirers, were sure that an English woman would be practical; "She will come out with just the thing at the right moment!"

Alas! our ladies were right; she had to drop her beautiful plumes, and go in her petticoats, and finally borrow from her critics.

This party were just from the Himalayas, and said that these contained no pass so grand as this.

From this hotel there are excursions enough to occupy one for weeks, among the beautiful scenes of the Valley. Each morning the guide saddles the horses—which had been turned loose in the mountain pasture—and fastens them in front of the house; and after lunch has been packed, we set off in different directions, to see the famous points and objects. One of the most enjoyable features of the excursion is simply cantering up and down the valley, getting the new aspects which open freshly every half-mile, and are different each hour of the day. The wonderful thing about the Cañon, which will hereafter draw many an invalid here from distant lands, is its divine atmosphere. To me, just recovering from a tedious fever, it seemed the very elixir of life—cool, clear, stimulating, and filled with light and glory from the sun of the South, which here never seems in summer to have a cloud. . . . nothing can surpass its mild, invigorating climate, and harmonious and resplendent atmosphere. Life seems to have a new spring and hope under it. The charm of the Wonderful Valley is its cheerfulness and joy. Even the awe-inspiring grandeur and majesty of its features do not overwhelm the sense of its exquisite beauty, its wonderful delicacy, and color, and life, and joy.

As I recall those rides in the fresh morning or the dreamy noon, that scene of unequaled grandeur and beauty is forever stamped on my memory, to remain when all other scenes of earth have passed from remembrance—the pearly gray and purple precipices, awful in mass, far above one, with deep shadows on their rugged surfaces, dark lines of gigantic archways or fantastic images drawn clearly upon them, the bright white water dashing over the distant gray tops seen against the dark blue of the unfathomable sky, the heavy shadows over the valley from the mighty peaks, the winding stream, and peaceful greensward with gay wild-flowers below, the snowy summits of the Sierras far away, the atmosphere of glory illuminating all, and the eternal voice of many waters wherever you walk or rest! This is the Yosemite in memory!

A Visit with the Hutchingses, from *The New West* by Charles Loring Brace. G.P. Putnam & Son, 1869.

Mary Cone

On Horseback to the Yosemite

For the post-Civil War traveler in the West, a "trip to the Yosemite" was obligatory. Before the stagecoach road was put through in 1874, a tourist had to endure a rough and sometimes frightening horseback ride down the canyon into Yosemite Valley. In the early 1870s, writer Mary Cone made the trip on the back of a nag named Alek. Her account of the journey from Clark's resort in the Mariposa Grove to the valley furnishes an amusing sketch of the harrowing ride.

At eight o'clock the next morning we again mounted our horses. A ride of twenty-five miles would bring us to the Yosemite. Mentally, I was in a better condition than at starting in the previous day; because of the facility with which the mind becomes accustomed to danger, I could trust myself in my perilous position on the back of the horse with diminished trepidation and alarm. But physcially! Ah, well! what boots it to tell of the wounds and bruises? Alek seemed by this time to have clear and settled convictions in regard to his rider. That I had not much will of my own was self-evident to him, and that I did not dare assert what little I had in the face of opposition was equally apparent. These first impressions were not effaced throughout all the ten days that we afterward journeyed together. Another conviction was equally well fastened upon Alek's mind. He was conscious of having the advantage on the score of that practical knowledge which was necessary for the emergencies to come. I went over to his opinion before we had been fellow-travelers very long.

We—that is, Alek and I—always guarded the rear of the party, to see that no evil came upon them from behind. It is only another proof that good deeds are not always recognized and rewarded, that our services in this respect were not appreciated, or, if they were, it was with the silent thankfulness with which the earth receives rain from the clouds. There was nothing said about it! . . .

We went on still ascending till we were seven thousand four hundred feet above the ocean, more than three thousand above Clark's. In many places the trail led up the mountain as nearly perpendicularly as earth would stay; then it was rocky and rough, which seemed to add to the danger as well as the toilsomeness of the ascent. Something was gained by making the trail zig-zag, like a Virginia fence. I was interested in watching Alek, and seeing how thorough was his knowledge of the laws of gravitation and equipoise.

He would go to the very farthest verge of the angle, so that his head and almost his entire body sometimes would project beyond the path; then, making a fulcrum of his hind legs, he would turn himself with gravity and deliberation, go on to the next angle, and so repeat the process. At first, not having learned to confide entirely in his wisdom and judgment, I pulled the rein to prevent his going out of the track as I thought he intended. He never paid the slightest attention to my efforts, and I soon concluded it was better to content myself with being a shadow behind the throne and give up all power and authority to him, devoting myself with a single eye to the one business of keeping myself on his back. To this determination I adhered ever after. The appearance of the party was often very picturesque, viewed from the rear, which was always my standpoint of observation. The whole party wound their way up the hill one after another, some on one level and others on a higher, the different hues of the costumes distinguishing each from the other as they were now lost to sight and then appearing again, like the pieces in a kaleidoscope. The zig-zag of the trail increased the effect and strengthened the appeal to the imagination, making it easy to set one's self back in the stream of time to an era which antedates the birth of railroads and coaches, when brave knights went to the rescue of fair ladies, on gallant steeds, with spear and breastplate. Sometimes a song would be started, and one after another would join in until the chorus was swelled by the voices of all the company. The tones lingered in the valleys and were echoed by the hills, until Nature herself took up the refrain and seemed to complete the harmony. . . . So we went on, rather flagging as the day advanced, till we came to Inspiration Point, where we were to have our first view of the remarkable place we had come so far to see. As we neared the spot, silence fell upon the party—all were busy with their own thoughts. Faith was soon to be turned into sight. With our own eyes we should soon verify what had been told us of this wonderful valley, like which there was said to be no other. That supreme moment, desired so long, hoped for through years, was near at hand. Then there was, after all, a vague uncertainty as to what the sight would be to us individually. Would our hopes or our fears be realized? The veil would soon be lifted, and we should know for ourselves—no longer see through the eyes of others. We dismounted at a little distance, and were soon on the edge of the precipice. There it was—this trough hewn out of the mountains. Awe-struck I stood, mute, and almost immovable. I should have been glad to be all alone in this first interview with God manifest in so wonderful a way. The whole valley lay spread out like a map beneath us. El Capitan stood out most prominently, for it was exactly before us. The Half Dome also arrested attention whenever we looked toward the upper end of the valley. We did not know until afterwards all the different points. It was the grand whole that bewildered and overwhelmed us. Whatever of majesty that is made up of imaginable strength and massiveness was there. Whatever of sublimity, inconceivable height and unsounded depth can give was there.

On Horseback to the Yosemite, from *Two Years in California* by Mary Cone. S.C. Griggs and Co., 1876.

Various Poets

Paeans to Yosemite

In the wonders of the West, Americans found the source of pride they had been searching for. Unlike Europe, for which Americans still held a grudging envy, the United States was short on home-grown culture, unrefined in politics and society, and too young to have venerable traditions. But in the grand and unique West, in such splendid natural wonders as Yellowstone and Yosemite, the nations's citizens found something as worthy of their pride as a crown prince, a Beethoven, or a Gothic cathedral.

The surest way to express these newfound sentiments was in poetry, and in Yosemite the typical tourist was only too happy to oblige. Visitors penned their creations in letters to relatives, in diaries, in the margins of hotel guest books. High-flown poetry gushed forth like Nevada Fall in spring; the noble Cathedal Rocks, the brooding Half Dome, and lo! the sublime El Capitan! each inspired its share of rapturous verse. To be sure, the loftiness of this poetry was attributable in part to the style of the times; equally, however, it was a reflection of a new and deeply felt regard for the beauties of the natural world of America.

Untitled

My soul bowed down in wondering, humble awe,
When first thy peaks and water-falls I saw;
And every hour but shows how vain 'twould be
For my frail mind to hope to picture thee.
Thy spell shall live when those who view thee now,
Have passed with ages 'neath thy mighty brow,
And like thy mists, in gorgeous gleamings curled,
Our names have melted from this changing world.

—Mrs. Jean Bruce Washburn

The Falls of the Yo-Semite

(Stanza 1)

The voice of waters! ringing on the ear,
Awe-struck, amid the fearful solitude—
Alone with Nature! Torrents fitful gleam,
Rushing, and hurrying on, with maddening leap,
Into the depths below! The deafening shock
Of rapid whirlpools, leaping on the rocks—
Dancing and foaming, with their deep hoarse roar,
Like some huge monster—then, with maddening plunge,
Dashing to depths below, while o'er them towers
A mighty pyramid of misty cloud,
Rising on high to heaven;—such, such art thou,
Yo-Semite! . . .

—G.T. Sproat

The Half Dome

MONARCH mountain! whose clear image lies
      Reflected on the waters at thy base,
If thou wert animate, I could surmise
      Why steeply climb thy shoulders into space,
And why no woods, nor beetling ridges break
      The open view below thy marble face.
For then, unmoving, freely thou couldst take
Proud glimpse of self within the Mirror Lake.
      Thus while the coming sun unbinds the lace
Of cloud worn nightly on thy sovran brow,
And ruffling winds are pent, I fancy thou
      Art watching rapt beside the lake with me,
To see thy naked form appear. Lo, now
      It shows in its serene sublimity!

—Wilbur G. Zeigler

Yosemite

If thou in dreams hast stood upon some lofty crag,
Whose ragged peaks have torn to shreds the drifting clouds,
And down in wavy depths of amethystine blue
Beheld, like gossamer, a dim enchanted vale,
Where ghostly trees were lost in silver shrouding mist,
With river like a thread of coiling light and fire,
And beauty that was strange and weird as moonlight shade,
Then thou in fantasy hast seen the magic land.
If thou in dreams hast strayed, 'twixt giant walls of rock,
Domed with an arc of sky, and sad and shudd'ring felt
That space was lost, as high above thy bended head
The pendent stars were hung, for thee to count them all;
Then has thou in thy dreams beheld Yosemite!
Its monumental pines swing their long arms and sing
In low and solemn tones their melody of praise;
The roving river steals among the shrubs of green,
To rest and brood upon the bosom of a lake,
Where trees and clouds and cliffs are kissed by rising suns.
Here midst this shady calm the lofty giants loom
Like carven gods of old, defying still the sharp
Attack of waters mad, which down their rugged sides
In daring anger leap.
                          Thou lonely mountain vale!
Mysteriously hid in fastnesses of deep
Ravines, and towering trees, and melancholy hills,
Through ages thou hast been a hermitage of gods.
Thy rocks reëchoing the eagle's piercing scream,
Thy butments sounding back the thunder of the winds,
Thy pinnacles unmoved amid the shifting clouds,
Thy spires and minarets daring the lightning flash,
Thine awful, ponderous dome veiled in translucent mist,
Speak thy divinity. Thou matchless minster grand!
On ambient air, through thy strained light, the soul doth mount
Those heights celestial where thy gray and fading aisles,
Thine onyx-tinted walls, thy mighty parapets,

And thy stupendous nave, fade like a blissful dream,
And God Himself, thine Architect, stands forth revealed.

So standest thou, alone, unmoved, eternal Truth!
Revealed, unveiled to him who scales the heights of mind—
Feeling the fiercest onslaught of our narrow creeds
As but the touch of vultures' wings upon thy crags.

—Annie Elizabeth Cheney

"Untitled," from *In the Heart of the Sierras* by J.M. Hutchings. J.M. Hutchings, 1886.
"The Falls of the Yo-Semite," (Stanza 1), from *Hutchings' California Magazine,* August, 1860.
"The Half Dome," from *The Overland Monthly,* June, 1896.
"Yosemite," from *Arena,* October, 1894.

John Muir

The Range of Light

It is hard to think of John Muir as a visitor to the Sierra. So completely did Muir give himself to the range that today he seems a part of it, no less a feature of the Sierra than the streams, the glaciers and the high mountain passes.

But like everyone else, Muir first went to the Sierra as a visitor. What distinguished him from others was his single-mindedness of purpose. No mere stopover on a Cook's tour of the West, the Sierra was for Muir the beginning and the end, his sole reason for traveling to California, He later wrote that on his arrival by steamer in San Francisco in 1868, he stepped off the boat and asked the first person he saw how to get out of town.

"But where do you want to go?" asked the startled passerby.

"To any place that is wild," answered Muir.

He immediately set out for the Sierra, not by stagecoach or on horseback but on foot. When first he beheld the range looming before him, he was inspired to give it a name which has since become synonymous with the name Sierra Nevada.

So on the first of April, 1868, I set out afoot for Yosemite. It was the bloom-time of the year over the lowlands and coast ranges; the landscapes of the Santa Clara Valley were fairly drenched with sunshine, all the air was quivering with the songs of the meadowlarks, and the hills were so covered with flowers that they seemed to be painted. Slow indeed was my progress through these glorious gardens, the first of the California flora I had seen. Cattle and cultivation were making few scars as yet, and I wandered enchanted in long wavering curves, knowing by my pocket map that Yosemite Valley lay to the east and that I should surely find it. . . .

Looking eastward from the summit of the Pacheco Pass one shining morning, a landscape was displayed that after all my wanderings still appears as the most beautiful I have ever beheld. At my feet lay the Great Central Valley of California, level and flowery, like a lake of pure sunshine, forty or fifty miles wide, five hundred miles long, one rich furred garden of yellow *Compositae*. And from the eastern boundary of this vast golden flower-bed rose the mighty Sierra, miles in height, and so gloriously colored and so radiant, it seemed not clothed with light, but wholly composed of it, like the wall of some celestial city. Along the top and extending a good way down, was a rich pearl-gray belt of snow; below it a belt of blue and dark purple, marking the extension of the forests; and stretching along the base of the range a broad belt of rose-purple; all these colors, from the blue sky to the yellow valley smoothly blending as they do in a rainbow, making a wall of light ineffably fine. Then it seemed to me that the Sierra should be called, not the Nevada or Snowy Range, but the Range of Light. And after ten years of wandering and wondering in the heart of it, rejoicing in its glorious floods of light, the white beams of the morning streaming through the passes, the noonday radiance on the crystal rocks, the flush of the alpenglow, and the irised spray of countless waterfalls, it still seems above all others the Range of Light.

John Muir

A Sierra Wind Storm

Upon his arrival in the Sierra, John Muir quickly established himself not merely as an observer and appreciator of the Range of Light, but as one eager to participate in its most intimate—and often dangerous—processes. Thoreau was no coward and William Brewer no faint-hearted academic; but no naturalist before Muir and few if any after him have ever matched him in the extremes he was willing to go to in order to experience nature. As his adventure crawling about in a glacial crevasse illustrated,[1] Muir's goal was no less than to become one with the snow, the water, and the wind. He once rode an avalanche down into Yosemite Valley as though it were a bucking bronco; on his first visit to the rim of the valley, he stood on the lip of Yosemite Falls imagining he was a water droplet plunging off merrily into the void.

In his most famous such adventure, Muir took in the grand fury of a Sierra wind storm while clinging happily to the topmost branch of a 100-foot-tall Douglas fir.

One of the most beautiful and exhilarating storms I ever enjoyed occurred in December, 1874, when I happened to be exploring one of the tributary valleys of the Yuba. The sky and the ground and the trees had been thoroughly rain-washed and were dry again. The day was intensely pure, one of those incomparable bits of California winter, warm and balmy and full of white sparkling sunshine, redolent of all the purest influences of the spring, and at the same time enlivened with one of the most cordial wind-storms conceivable. Instead of camping-out as I usually do, I then chanced to be stopping at the house of a friend. But when the storm began to sound, I lost no time in pushing out into the woods to enjoy it. For on such occasions

---

[1]See "John Muir: The Discovery of Glaciers," Section I.

nature has always something rare to show us, and the danger to life and limb is hardly greater than one would experience crouching deprecatingly beneath a roof.

It was still early morning when I found myself fairly adrift. Delicious sunshine came pouring over the hills, lighting the tops of the pines, and setting free a stream of summery fragrance that contrasted strangely with the wild tones of the storm. The air was mottled with pine-tassels and bright green plumes, that went flashing past in the sunlight like pursued birds. But there was not the slightest dustiness,—nothing less pure than leaves, and ripe pollen, and flecks of withered bracken and moss. Trees were heard falling for hours at the rate of one every two or three minutes; some uprooted, partly on account of the loose, water-soaked condition of the ground; others broken straight across, where some weakness caused by fire had determined the spot. The gestures of the various trees made a delightful study. Young sugar-pines, light and feathery as squirrel-tails, were bowing almost to the ground; while the grand old patriarchs, whose massive boles had been tried in a hundred storms, waved solemnly above them, their long, arching branches streaming fluently on the gale, and every needle thrilling and ringing and shedding off keen lances of light like a diamond. The Douglass spruces, with long sprays drawn out in level tresses, and needles massed in a gray, shimmering glow, presented a most striking appearance as they stood in bold relief along the hill-tops, and so did the madronas in the dells with their red bark and bowed glossy leaves tilted every way, reflecting the sunshine in throbbing spangles like those one so often sees on the rippled surface of a glacier lake. But the silver-pines were now the most impressively beautiful of all. Colossal spires two hundred feet in height waved like supple golden-rods chanting and bowing low as if in worship, while the whole mass of their long, tremulous foliage was kindled into one continuous blaze of white sun-fire.

The force of the gale was such that the most steadfast monarch of them all rocked down to its roots with a motion plainly perceptible when one leaned against it. Nature was holding high festival, and every fiber of the most rigid giants thrilled with glad excitement.

I drifted on through the midst of this passionate music and motion, across many a glen, from ridge to ridge; often halting in the lee of a rock for shelter, or to gaze and listen. Even when the grand anthem had swelled to its highest pitch, I could distinctly hear the varying tones of individual trees—spruce, and fir, and pine, and leafless oak—and even the infinitely gentle rustle of the withered grasses at my feet. Each was expressing itself in its own way,—singing its own song, and making its own peculiar gestures,—manifesting a richness of variety to be found in no other forest I have yet seen. The coniferous woods of Canada, and the Carolinas, and Florida, are made up of trees that resemble one another about as nearly as blades of grass, and grow close together in much the same way. Coniferous trees, in general, seldom possess individual character, such as is manifest among oaks and elms. But the California forests are made up of a greater number of distinct species than any other in the world. And in them we find, not only a marked differentiation into special groups, but also a marked personality in almost every individual tree, giving rise to storm effects indescribably glorious.

Toward midday, after a long, tingling scramble through copses of hazel and ceanothus, I gained the summit of the highest ridge in the neighborhood; and then it occurred to me that it would be a fine thing to climb one of the trees to obtain a wider outlook and get my ear close to the AEolian music of its topmost needles. But under the circumstances the choice of a tree was a serious matter. One whose instep was not very strong seemed in danger of being blown down, or of being struck by others in case they should fall; another was branchless to a considerable height above the ground, and at the same time too large to be grasped with arms and legs in climbing; while others were not favorably situated for clear views. After thus cautiously casting about, I made choice of the tallest of a group of Douglass spruces that were growing close together like a tuft of grass, no one of which seemed likely to fall unless all the rest fell with it. Though comparatively young, they were about a hundred feet high, and their lithe, brushy tops were rocking and swirling in wild ecstasy. Being accustomed to climb trees in making botanical studies, I experienced no difficulty in reaching the top of this one, and never before did I enjoy so noble an exhilaration of motion. The slender tops fairly flapped and swished in the passionate torrent, bending and swirling backward and forward, round and round, tracing indescribable combinations of vertical and horizontal curves, while I clung with muscles firm braced, like a bobolink on a reed.

In its widest sweeps my tree-top described an arc of from twenty to thirty degrees, but I felt sure of its elastic temper, having seen others of the same species still more severely tried,—bent almost to the ground indeed, in heavy snows without breaking a fiber. I was therefore safe and free to take the wind into my pulses and enjoy the excited forest from my grand outlook. The view from here must be extremely beautiful in any weather. Now my eye roved over the piney hills and dales as over fields of waving grain, and felt the light running in ripples and broad swelling undulations across the valleys from ridge to ridge, as the shining foliage was stirred by corresponding waves of air. Oftentimes these waves of reflected light would break up suddenly into a kind of beaten foam, and again, after chasing one another in regular order, they would seem to bend forward in concentric curves, and disappear on some hill-side, like sea-waves on a shelving shore. The quantity of light reflected from the bent needles was so great as to make whole groves appear as if covered with snow, while the black shadows beneath the trees greatly enhanced the effect of the silvery splendor.

Excepting only the shadows there was nothing somber in all this wild sea of pines. On the contrary, notwithstanding this was the winter season, the colors were remarkably beautiful. The shafts of the pine and libocedrus were brown and purple, and most of the foliage was well tinged with yellow, and the laurel groves, with the pale undersides of their leaves turned upward, made masses of gray; and then there was many a dash of chocolate color from clumps of manzanita, and jet of vivid crimson from the bark of the madronas, while the ground on the hill-sides, appearing here and there through openings between the groves, displayed masses of pale purple and brown.

The sounds of the storm corresponded gloriously with this wild exuberance of light and motion. The profound bass of the naked branches and boles booming like water-falls; the quick, tense vibrations of the pine needles, now rising to a shrill, whistling hiss, now falling to a silky murmur; the rustling of laurel groves in the dells, and the keen metallic click of leaf on leaf—all heard in easy analysis when the attention was calmly bent.

The varied gestures of the multitude were seen to fine advantage, so that one could recognize the different species at a distance of several miles by this means alone, as well as by their forms and colors, and the way they reflected the light. All seemed strong and comfortable, as if really enjoying the storm, while responding to its most enthusiastic greetings. We hear much nowadays concerning the universal struggle for existence, but no struggle in the common meaning of the word was manifest here; no recognition of danger by any tree, no deprecation; but rather an invincible gladness as remote from exultation as from fear.

I kept my lofty perch for hours, frequently closing my eyes to enjoy the music by itself, or to feast quietly on the delicious fragrance that was streaming past. It was less marked than that produced during warm rain, when so many balsamic buds and leaves are steeped like tea; but, from the chafing of rosiny branches against one another, and the incessant attrition of myriads of needles, the gale was spiced to a very tonic degree. And besides the fragrance from these local sources there were traces of scents brought from afar. For this wind came first from the sea, rubbing against its fresh, briny waves; then distilled through the redwoods, threading rich ferny gulches, and spreading itself in broad undulating currents over many a flower-enameled ridge of the coast; then across the golden plains, up the purple foothills, and into these piney woods with the varied incense gathered by the way.

Winds are advertisements of all they touch, however much or little we may be able to read them; telling their wanderings even by their scents alone. Mariners detect the flowery perfume of land-winds far at sea, and sea-winds carry the fragrance of dulse and tangle far inland, where it is quickly recognized, though mingled with the scents of a thousand land-flowers. As an illustration of this, I might tell here that I breathed sea-air on the Firth of Forth, in Scotland, while a boy; then was taken inland to Wisconsin, where I remained nineteen years; then without in all this time having breathed one breath of the sea, I walked quietly, alone, from the middle of the Mississippi Valley to the Gulf of Mexico, on a botanical excursion, and while in Florida, far from the coast, my attention wholly bent on the splendid tropical vegetation, I suddenly recognized a sea-breeze, as it came sifting through the palmettoes and blooming vine tangles, which at once awakened and set free a thousand dormant associations, and made me a boy in Scotland again, as if all the intervening years were annihilated.

Most people like to look at mountain rivers, and bear them in mind; but few care to look at the winds, though far more beautiful and sublime, and though they become at times about as visible as flowing water. When the north winds in winter are making upward sweeps over the curving summits of the Alps, the fact is sometimes published with flying banners half a mile long. Those portions of the winds thus embodied can scarce be wholly invisible, even to the darkest imagination. And when we look around over an agitated forest, we may see something of the wind that stirs it, by its effects upon the trees. Yonder it descends in a rush of water-like ripples, and sweeps over the bending trees from hill to hill. Nearer, we see detached plumes and leaves, now speeding by on level currents, now whirled in eddies, or, escaping over the edges of the whirls, carried rapidly aloft on grand, upswelling domes of air, or tossed on flame-like crests, smooth, deep currents, cascades, falls, and swirling eddies, singing around every tree and leaf, and over all the varied topography of the region with telling changes of form, like mountain rivers conforming to the features of their channels.

After tracing the Sierra streams from their fountains to the plains, marking where they bloom white in falls, glide in crystal plumes, surge gray and foam-filled in bowlder-choked gorges, and slip through the woods in long, tranquil reaches—after thus learning their language and forms in detail, we may at length hear them chanting all together in one grand anthem, and comprehend them all in clear inner vision, covering the range like lace. But even this glorious spectacle is far less sublime and not a whit more substantial than what we may behold of these storm-streams of air in the woods.

We all travel the milky way together, trees and men; but it never occurred to me until this storm-day, while swinging in the wind, that trees are travelers, in the ordinary sense. They make many journeys, not very extensive ones, it is true; but our own little comes and goes are only little more than tree-wavings—many of them not so much.

When the storm began to abate, I dismounted and sauntered down through the calming woods. The storm-tones died away, and, turning toward the east, I beheld the countless hosts of the forests hushed and tranquil, towering above one another on the slopes of the hills like a devout audience. The setting sun filled them with amber light, and seemed to say, while they listened, "My peace I give unto you."

As I gazed on the impressive scene, all the so-called ruin of the storm was forgotten, and never before did these noble woods appear so fresh, so joyous, so immortal.

A Sierra Wind Storm, from "A Wind Storm in the Forests of the Yuba" by John Muir. *Scribner's Monthly,* November, 1878.

Joseph LeConte

Rambling Through
the High Sierra

No word caught the spirit of 19th Century vacationing better than "ramble."
The tourists of the day didn't spend their time shopping for souvenirs or
queuing up to buy gasoline; they rambled. To Glacier Point, to Mirror Lake, to
Bridalveil Fall. Rambling was lighthearted, self-motivated, inquisitive, mean-
dering; it's an element of vacationing that has all but disappeared from today's
somber, obligatory, packaged tours of the national parks.

Joseph LeConte, professor of geology and natural history at the University of
California in 1870, was a rambler. In the lazy summer of that year, LeConte
and several of his students decided to have some fun, so they took off for a vacation
in the Sierra. LeConte hadn't been on a horse or an adventure like this for years.
But so what?

After much bustle, confusion, and noisy preparation, saddling,
cinching, strapping blanket rolls, packing camp utensils and provisions, we are fairly ready at 10A.M. Saluted by cheers from manly
throats, and handkerchief-waving by the white hands of women, we
leave Oakland at a sweeping trot, Hawkins leading the pack; while the
long handle of our frying-pan, sticking straight up through a hole in
the bag, and the merry jingling of *tin* pans, *tin* cups and coffee pot—
"tintinnabulation"—proclaimed the nature of our mission.

In LeConte's memoir of the vacation, A Journal of Ramblings Through
the High Sierra of California, *he gave an engaging acccount of his party's*
visit to Tenaya Lake and Tuolumne Meadows, in the company of a fellow rambler
they ran into, John Muir.

Ramblers Phelps, Bolton, Perkins, Prof. Le Conte, Soulé, Linderman, Cobb
Stone, Hawkins, Pomeroy

This afternoon we went on to Lake Tenaya. The trail is very blind, in most places detectable only by the blazing of trees, and very rough. We traveled most of the way on a high ridge. When [within] about two miles of our destination, from the brow of the mountain ridge upon which we had been traveling, Lake Tenaya burst upon our delighted vision, its placid surface set like a gem amongst magnificent mountains, the most conspicuous of which are [the] Mt. Hoffmann group on the left, and Cathedral Peak beyond the lake. From this point we descended to the margin of the lake, and encamped at 5 P.M. on the lower end of the lake, in a fine grove of tamaracks, near an extensive and beautiful meadow. We built an immense fire, and had a fine supper of excellent bread and delicious mutton. Our appetites were excellent; we ate up entirely one hind-quarter of mutton and wanted more.

After supper, I went with Mr. Muir and sat on a high rock jutting into the lake. It was full moon. I never saw a more delightful scene. This little lake, one mile long and a half-mile wide, is actually embosomed in the mountains, being surrounded by rocky eminences two thousand feet high, of the most picturesque forms, which come down to the very water's edge. The deep stillness of the night; the silvery light and deep shadows of the mountains; the reflection on the water, broken into thousands of glittering points by the ruffled surface; the gentle lapping of the wavelets upon the rocky shore—all these seemed exquisitely harmonized with one another and the grand harmony made answering music in our hearts. Gradually the lake surface became quiet and mirror-like, and the exquisite surrounding scenery was seen double. For an hour we remained sitting in silent enjoyment of this delicious scene, which we reluctantly left to go to bed. Tenaya Lake is about eight thousand feet above sea-level. The night air therefore is very cool.

I noticed in many places today, especially as we approached Lake Tenaya, the polishings and scorings of ancient glaciers. In many places we found broad, flat masses so polished that our horses could hardly maintain their footing in passing over them. It is wonderful that in granite so decomposable these old glacial surfaces should remain as fresh as the day they were left by the glaciers. But if ever the polished surface scales off, then the disintegration proceeds as usual.

The destruction of these surfaces by scaling is in fact continually going on. Whitney thinks the polished surface is hardened by pressure of the glacier. I cannot think so. The smoothing, I think, prevents the retention of water, and thus prevents the rotting. Like the rusting of iron, which is hastened by roughness, and still more by rust, and retarded, or even prevented, by cleaning and polishing, so rotting of rock is hastened by roughness, and still more by commencing to rot, and retarded or prevented by grinding down to the *sound* rock and then polishing.

Today, while cooking midday meal, the wind was high and the fire furious. I singed my whiskers and mustache and badly burned my hand with boiling-hot bacon fat.

AUGUST 10.—Early start this morning for Soda Springs and Mt. Dana. Phelps and his mare entertained us while getting off this morning with an amusing bucking scene. The interesting performance ended with the grand climactic feat of flying head foremost over the head of the horse, turning a somersault in the air, and alighting safely on his back. After this exhilarating diversion, we proceeded on our way, following the trail on the right hand of the lake. Onward we go in single file, I leading the pack, over the roughest and most precipitous trail (if trail it can be called) I ever saw. At one moment we lean forward, holding to the horse's mane, until our noses are between the horse's ears; at the next, we stand in the stirrups, with our backs leaning hard against the roll of blankets behind the saddle.

Thus we pass, dividing our attention between the difficulties of the way and the magnificence of the scenery, until 12 M., when we reached Soda Springs, in the splendid meadows of the upper Tuolumne River.

Our trail this morning has been up the Tenaya Cañon, over the divide, and into the Tuolumne Valley. There is abundant evidence of an immense former glacier, coming from Mt. Dana and Mt. Lyell group, filling the Tuolumne Valley, overrunning the divide, and sending a branch down the Tenaya Cañon. The rocks in and about Tenaya Cañon are everywhere scored and polished. We had to dismount and lead over some of these polished surfaces. The horses' feet slipped and sprawled in every direction, but none fell. A conspicuous feature of the scenery on Lake Tenaya is a granite knob, eight hundred feet high, at the upper end of the lake and in the middle of the cañon. This knob is bare, destitute of vegetation, round and polished to the very top. It has evidently been enveloped in the icy mass, and its shape has been determined by it. We observed similar scorings and polishings on the sides of the cañon, to an equal and much greater height. Splendid view of the double peaks of the Cathedral, from the Lake Tenaya and from the trail. Looking back from the trail soon after leaving the lake, we saw a conspicuous and very picturesque peak, with a vast amphitheater, with precipitous sides, to the north, filled with a grand mass of snow, evidently the fountain of an ancient tributary of the Tenaya Glacier. We called this *Coliseum Peak*. So let it be called hereafter, to the end of time.[1]

The Tuolumne Meadow is a beautiful grassy plain of great extent, thickly enameled with flowers, and surrounded with the most magnificent scenery. Conspicuous amongst the hundreds of peaks visible are Mt. Dana, with its grand symmetrical outline and purplish red color; Mt. Gibbs, of gray granite; Mt. Lyell and its group of peaks, upon which great masses of snow still lie; and the wonderfully picturesque group of sharp, inaccessible peaks (viz., Unicorn Peak, Cathedral Peaks, etc.), forming the Cathedral group.

Soda Springs is situated on the northern margin of the Tuolumne Meadow. It consists of several springs of ice-cold water, bubbling up from the top of a low reddish mound. Each spring itself issues from the top of a small subordinate mound. The mound consists of carbonate of lime, colored with iron deposited from the water. The water contains principally carbonates of lime and iron, dissolved in excess of carbonic acid, which escapes in large quantities, in bubbles. It possibly, also, contains carbonate of soda. It is very pungent, and delightful to the taste. Before dinner we took a swim in the ice-cold water of the Tuolumne River.

About 3 P.M. commenced saddling up, intending to go on to Mt. Dana. Heavy clouds have been gathering for some time past. Low mutterings of thunder have also been heard. But we had already been so accustomed to the same, without rain, in the Yosemite, that we

---

[1]Today this mountain is called Tenaya Peak.

Looking west from Muir Pass

thought nothing of it. We had already saddled, and some had mounted, when the storm burst upon us. "Our provisions—sugar, tea, salt, flour—must be kept dry!" shouted Hawkins. We hastily dismounted, constructed a sort of shed of blankets and india-rubber cloths, and threw our provisions under it. Now commenced peal after peal of thunder in an almost continuous roar, and floods of rain. We all crept under the temporary shed, but not before we had gotten pretty well soaked. So much delayed that we were now debating— after the rain—whether we had not better remain here overnight. Some were urgent for pushing on, others equally so for staying. Just at this juncture, when the debate ran high, a shout, "Hurrah!" turned all eyes in the same direction. Hawkins and Mr. Muir had scraped up the dry leaves underneath a huge prostrate tree, set fire and piled on fuel, and already, see!—a glorious blaze! This incident decided the question at once. With a shout, we all ran for fuel, and piled on log after log, until the blaze rose twenty feet high. Before, shivering, crouching, and miserable; now, joyous and gloriously happy.

The storm did not last more than an hour. After it, the sun came out and flooded all the landscape with liquid gold. I sat alone at some distance from the camp and watched the successive changes of the scene—first, the blazing sunlight flooding meadow and mountain; then the golden light on mountain peaks, and then the lengthening shadows on the valley; then a roseate bloom diffused over sky and air, over mountain and meadow. Oh, how exquisite! I never saw the like before. Last, the creeping shadow of night, descending and enveloping all.

Rambling Through the High Sierra, from *A Journal of Ramblings Through the High Sierra of California* by Joseph LeConte. The Sierra Club, 1960. Reprinted by permission of The Sierra Club.

James Bradley Thayer

With M. and Mr. Emerson

The philosophy that guided John Muir was Transcendentalism, the New England-based system of thought whose principal proponents were Ralph Waldo Emerson and Henry David Thoreau. For the Transcendentalist, nature was where truth was revealed; in the wilderness one found not evil and debasement, but the possibility for improving oneself through the discovery of God's laws. Wrote Emerson: "In the woods we return to reason and faith."

John Muir embraced this viewpoint utterly; it's hard to find a page of his writings that doesn't reflect the Transcendentalist philosophy. Everyone knows that Muir always carried a spartan supply of tea and bread with him on his journeys through the High Sierra. Few realize that he toted along a copy of The Prose Works of Ralph Waldo Emerson *as well.*

Small wonder that when Muir learned that Emerson planned to visit Yosemite Valley in May 1871, he was beside himself with excitement. He sent a note to Emerson suggesting that the two take off together for "a month's worship with Nature in the high temples of the great Sierra Crown beyond our holy Yosemite."

Muir was disappointed to discover that at 68, Emerson was more the philosopher of nature than the participant. Not only was he not up to the proposed journey through the Sierra; his fussy party of hangers-on refused even to allow the great man to camp out in the Mariposa Grove with Muir.

Nevertheless the two men met and immediately forged a warm and mutually respectful friendship. They spent several days together, talking and taking in the sights of Yosemite. This extraordinary incident was later recalled by James Bradley Thayer, one of the twelve members of Emerson's party.

That evening (Monday) there came an admiring, enthusiastic letter for Mr. Emerson from M., a young man living in the valley, and tending a saw-mill there. He was a Scotchman by birth, who had come to this country at the age of eleven, and was a graduate at Madison University, in Wisconsin. Some friends near San Francisco had written him that Mr. Emerson was coming, and they had also told Mr. Emerson about him. He had read Mr. Emerson's books, but had never seen him, and wrote now with enthusiasm, wishing for an opportunity to come to him. The next morning Mr. Emerson asked my company on horseback for a visit to M. So he mounted his pied mustang, and we rode over, and found M. at the saw-mill alone. He was an interesting young fellow, of real intelligence and character, a botanist mainly, who, after studying a year or two at Madison, had "zigzagged his way," he said, "to the Gulf of Mexico, and at last had found this valley, and had got entangled here,—in love with the mountains and flowers; and he did n't know when he should get away." He had built the sawmill for Hutchings, and was now working it. He had heretofore tended sheep at times,—even flocks of twenty-five hundred. Occasionally he rambled among the mountains, and camped out for months; and he urged Mr. Emerson, with an amusing zeal, to stay and go off with him on such a trip. He lodged in the saw-mill, and we climbed a ladder to his room. Here he brought out a great many dried specimens of plants which he had collected, and hundreds of his own graceful pencil-sketches of the mountain peaks and forest trees, and gave us the botanical names, and talked of them with enthusiastic interest. All these treasures he poured out before Mr. Emerson, and begged him to accept them. But Mr. Emerson declined; wishing leave, however, to bring his friends to see them. Other calls were interchanged that day and the next; and when we left, two days later, to see the great trees of the Mariposa grove, M. joined our horseback party. . . .

In the morning we were off at eight o'clock for the Mariposa grove. Galen Clarke, our landlord, a solid, sensible man from New Hampshire, was the State guardian of the great trees, and now accompanied us, *honoris causa*. It was a sunny and pleasant ride. M. talked of the trees; and we grew learned, and were able to tell a sugar pine from a yellow pine, and to name the silver fir, and the "libocedrus," which is almost our arbor-vitae and second cousin to the great sequoia. By and by M. called out that he saw the sequoias. The general level was now about fifty-five hundred feet above the sea;

the trees stood a little lower, in a hollow of the mountain. They were "big trees," to be sure; and yet at first they seemed not so very big. We grew curious, and looked about among them for a while; and soon began to discover what company we were in. . . .

We passed along from one collection of the trees to another. Sometimes there were fifty of them near together; and then, again, they were scattered. There were some young ones; "That is good!" one said to himself; "they are not, then, a mere decaying thing of the past." These young ones were thrifty and perfectly proportioned: nothing could be more symmetrical,—so firmly planted, as they were, so straight, with so clean a stem and so shapely a foliage. The top in the perfect tree, as M. pointed out to us, is just a parabola, and not at all the peaked shape of a pine; it is akin to the cedar and the juniper. Now and then, in the old trees, the top slopes off ungracefully and sharp, as if it had got up too far out of the hollow, and did not like the air; this was the result of fire, M. thought, or something else that had destroyed the original top. Its Indian name, so we were told, is Wahwonah.

We sat down to lunch near a hut, and had a chance to rest and to look about us more quietly. M. protested against our going away so soon: "It is," said he, "as if a photographer should remove his plate before the impression was fully made;" he begged us to stay there and camp with him for the night. After lunch Mr. Emerson, at Clarke's request, chose and named a tree. This had been done by one distinguished person and another, and a sign put up to commemorate it. Mr. Emerson's tree was not far from the hut; it was a vigorous and handsome one; although not remarkably large, measurably fifty feet in circumference at two and a half feet from the ground. He named it Samoset, after our Plymouth sachem; having at first doubted a little over Logan. He had greatly enjoyed the day. "The greatest wonder," said he, "is that we can see these trees and not wonder more."

We were off at about three o'clock, and left M. standing in the forest alone; he was to pass the night there in solitude, and to find his way back to the valley on foot. We had all become greatly interested in him, and hated to leave him. His name has since grown to be well known at the East, through his valuable articles in the magazines.

With M. and Mr. Emerson, from *A Western Journey with Mr. Emerson* by James Bradley Thayer. Little, Brown and Company, 1884.

Ralph Waldo Emerson

The Right Man[1]

John Muir was disillusioned when he realized that Ralph Waldo Emerson, the great architect of Transcendentalism, was in fact too soft to camp out among the sequoias.

"But he was past his prime," Muir consoled himself, "and was now a child in the hands of his affectionate but sadly civilized friends, who seemed as full of old-fashioned conformity as of bold intellectual independence."

The Brahmin Emerson could not accept Muir's total embracing of the wilderness life. Nevertheless, he was so impressed by Muir that he added him to "My Men"—the list of esteemed men Emerson had met which included Carlyle, Coleridge and Wordsworth.

One of Muir's customs was to collect incense-cedar sprigs and send them to friends. In response to a gift of one of these, Emerson wrote the following letter to Muir.

CONCORD 5 *February,* 1872

MY DEAR MUIR:

Here lie your significant cedar flowers on my table, and in another letter; and I will procrastinate no longer. That singular disease of deferring, which kills all my designs, has left a pair of books brought home to send to you months and months ago, still covering their inches on my cabinet, and the letter and letters which should have accompanied, to utter my thanks and lively remembrance, are either unwritten or lost, so I will send this *peccavi*, as a sign of remorse.

I have been far from unthankful—I have everywhere testified to

---

[1] The Right Man, from *The Life and Letters of John Muir, Volume I,* edited by W.F. Badè. Copyright 1923 by Houghton Mifflin Company. Copyright renewed 1951 by John Muir Hanna. Reprinted by permission of Houghton Mifflin Company.

my friends, who should also be yours, my happiness in finding you—
the right man in the right place—in your mountain tabernacle, and
have expected when your guardian angel would pronounce that your
probation and sequestration in the solitudes and snows had reached
their term, and you were to bring your ripe fruits so rare and precious
into waiting society.

I trust you have also had, ere this, your own signals from the
upper powers. I know that society in the lump, admired at a distance,
shrinks and dissolves, when approached, into impracticable or
uninteresting individuals, but always with a reserve of a few unspoiled
good men, who really give it its halo in the distance.And there are
drawbacks also to solitude, who is a sublime mistress, but an intolerable wife. So I pray you to bring to an early close your absolute contracts with any yet unvisited glaciers or volcanoes, roll up your
drawings, herbariums and poems, and come to the Atlantic Coast.
Here in Cambridge Dr. Gray is at home, and Agassiz will doubtless
be, after a month or two, returned from Terra del Fuego—perhaps
through San Francisco—or you can come with him. At all events, on
your arrival, which I assume as certain, you must find your way to this
village, and my house. And when you are tired of our dwarf surroundings, I will show you better people.

 With kindest regards
Yours

R. W. Emerson

I send two volumes of collected essays by book-post.

*The two men never saw each other again. "There remained many a forest to
wander through," Muir wrote later, "many a mountain and glacier to cross,
before I was to see his Wachusett and Monadnock, Boston and Concord. It was
seventeen years after our parting on the Wawona ridge that I stood beside his grave
under a pine tree on the hill above Sleepy Hollow. He had gone to higher Sierras,
and, as I fancied, was again waving his hand in friendly recognition."*

Stewart Edward White

Life in Camp

In 1890, the U.S. Bureau of the Census declared that the U.S. frontier no longer existed. The United States was populated, more or less, coast to coast; henceforth its people were condemned to experience what little wilderness remained as play actors—hunters, anglers, mountain climbers—rather than as true frontiersmen.

Americans have never quite got used to the idea. And since the demise of the frontier, there has been a steady market for books and articles that portray the frontier experience—the rugged life on the trail, the camp and campfire under the stars. Stewart Edward White was one of the first writers to capitalize on the public's hunger for such works. Around the turn of the century he wrote a series of books, including The Claim Jumpers, The Forest, *and* Blazed Trail Stories, *that resurrected the fondly remembered life on the frontier. Several of his books were slightly fictionalized accounts of his summer trips in the Sierra. In* The Pass *(1906) he described for his civilized readers the joys of life in a rustic wilderness camp near Elizabeth Pass in the southern Sierra.*

AFTER far wandering a permanent camp is a great refreshment to the spirit.

You start in animated by the utmost vigor. There are so many things to be done, and they all occur to your mind at once. After breakfast you seize the axe and take to the brush. The search for straight saplings forking at required heights becomes absorbing. You cut them and drag them to camp and stick them in their appointed places. There is an amplitude to these preparations in delicious contrast to the direct utilitarianism of your camp-making while on trail. So must have felt the founder of Cologne Cathedral, his soul big and tranquil with the thought of the three hundred years of building that were to follow. You make a shelter and a bed. The former is beautiful and permanent; we put up the little balloon silk tent, which heretofore had been used only as a pack cloth. The bed you arrange carefully, smoothing the ground with the back of the axe swung adze-wise between your legs, laying parallel two generous lengths of logs well pegged to prevent rolling, filling between them first with dry pine needles, then with balsam fans thatched carefully springy side up. It is fun to cut balsam. The thicket is warm with the radiation of sun from fragrant piney things. You clip and clip away with the hatchet, bathed in tepid odors and buzzy sounds. It is a leisurely occupation that you cannot hurry, and so you lapse gladly into that half-dreamy state to be acquired only in the woods, wherein the golden afternoon seems to comprise several eternities. Then you return to camp, and begin feverishly the construction of a table.

It is a very ingenious table, supported by three saplings suspended between two trees. Across them you lay wands, and over the wands you spread your oilcloth. The bench you make of hewn logs (be sure

Camp at Hodgdon's near Yosemite's Big Oak Flat Entrance

they are dry, otherwise you may stick to your seat), supported on cross-pieces between forked branches driven into the ground. You place your eating utensils, and feel the creator's joy.

Then remain a dozen other affairs. The fireplace is elaborate; the saddles are conceded a rack. And you make a woodpile.

Ordinarily, while traveling, you cook with what you can pick up, or chop in two by a stroke or so of the axe. Now you cut the nearest pine logs into lengths, and lug these lengths into camp on your shoulders, staggering uncertainly. And then you hit with your axe a mighty whack lengthwise, and insert a wedge of hard wood in the crack thus made, and beat the wedge in until it is buried, and then insert another wedge lower down, until at last the log splits in two with a great tearing of wood fibers. Whereupon you attack the halves in like manner, and then the quarters, until in the final result you are possessed of a number of slender split posts. You lay one of these posts over your chopping log. A full swing of the axe bites deep and slanting. You reverse the blade and whack mightily on the end. The slender post breaks at the point of the axe cut, and at last you lay aside with pride the first stick of firewood.

There is a joy in the clean, accurate labor—a pleasure in stretching your muscles. And the gleaming yellow piles grow almost like magic.

By now you are fully in the vein. You are tired; but you do not know enough to feel so. A score of desirable little tasks crowd on your intention. You will put up shelves, and make a meat safe, and sweep the forest floor, and dig a garbage pit, and rope in the camp, and——

"Look here!" complains your companion, "don't you think we'd better call this a day? I'm hungry!"

You glance up with surprise. The pines are silhouetting against the west. Shadows are half-tree high already, and the coolness of evening is creeping very cautiously, very slowly down through the lowest thickets. The sparrows and vireos seem to have fallen silent. A pensive melody of thrushes steals in and out of the forest aisles.

You straighten your back, and suddenly feel very tired. The day is indeed done.

And next morning very early you awaken and look straight up at the sky. The pine tops touch it shyly—you could almost imagine that gently swaying in the wind they had brushed the stars away. A great singing of birds fills the air. So innumerable are the performers that it is difficult to distinguish the individuals. The result might be called a tremendous and composite chattering. Only here the tone of the chattering is supremely musical, so that the forest seems to be echoing to the voice of some single melodious creature.

Nearby a squirrel, like a fussy little old gentleman, jerks about nervously.

"Dear, dear!" says he. "*Look* at those people! *Look* at those people!"

After he has repeated this a few score of times he fusses away, probably to report to the proper officers that he must object, he really must object to such persons being admitted to his club. The sun strikes through the woods and glorifies a dogwood just to the left of its direct line of illumination. The light partly reflects from, partly shines through the delicate leaves, until the whole bush becomes ethereal, a gently glowing soul of itself. You stretch luxuriously, and extend your legs, and an unwonted feeling of satisfaction steals over you. You wonder why. The reason comes in due time. It is this: a whole glorious woodland day lies before you, and in it is no question of pack rope, horse or trail. You can do just exactly as much or as little as you please.

Probably you elect to putter around camp. There are innumerable things to do, and you can have fun at any one of them. To sit straddle a log, tinkering away at a new latigo for your saddle is joy, especially if you can look up every now and then to a very blue sky not much beyond very tall trees. Little items of repair have long been awaiting this leisure. Also there is laundry, with a glorious chance to wash everything washable, even down to the long-suffering dish rag. I should advise one of the cold-water soaps, as it is difficult to scare up anything big enough to boil clothes in.

And if you are fond of cooking, now is your chance to indulge in the most astounding culinary orgies. Simple puddings, cakes, and other bakings are quite within the reach of the ingenious camp cook: there is necessary only the widest possible interpretation of recipes, and the completest audacity in substitution. If you have no eggs, why, never mind. Perhaps dried prunes will do. Try it, anyway. I once made a very good pudding out of the remains of boiled macaroni, some cold cornmeal mush, sugar, cinnamon and raisins. This when baked through, and well browned atop proved to be marvelously popular. I admit it does not sound very good.

The cooking zeal is cumulative. There comes a day when you cook from morning until evening, and then triumphantly announce a feast. If you possess real enthusiasm, you get up menus and table decorations. Here is one we gave at Lake Charlotte, eleven thousand feet up,[1] in honor of the birthday of our old friend Spoopendyke. Your true celebrant in the woods always makes his feast an occasion, even if he has to invent one.

Clam Soup à la Dieu Sait Quoi

Fried Trout à la Lac Charlotte

Bacon à l' Axlegrease

Scrambled Eggs à la Tin Can

Bread	Corn Bread	Biscuits

Vegetables à l' Abercrombie

Boiled Potatoes		Baked Beans
Rice Pudding	Strawberries	Spice Cake
Nuts		Raisins

On the reverse came the

Wine List

Tea	.	.	.	In the Large Pot
Coffee	.	.	.	In the Small Pot
Cocoa	.	.	Make it Yourself, Darn You	
Water	.	.	.	Go to the Spring
Lemonade	.	.	In the Small Bottle	
Whiskey	.	.	Drink, $10; Smell, 25c.	
	Cigars	Pipes	Cigarettes	

After a brilliant climax of this sort, you generally settle back to a more leisurely gait. Other things engage your attention. You hunt, you fish, you explore the immediately surrouding country.

And then little by little you run down, like a clock that has not been wound. There is plenty of venison in camp; fishing palls. You

---

[1]Today Charlotte Lake's elevation is given as 10,370'.

lie around during endless golden hours, shifting with the sun, watching the rainbow colors in your eyelashes, soaking in comfort and rest as thirsty ground takes up water. In the evening you swap yarns and hold academic discussions around the campfire. If it were not for the fact that you have to chop wood for that campfire you could take root and your brains would turn out budding little green branches. The academic discussions are lazily delivered, and irresponsible, oh, utterly irresponsible! The ordinary rules of coherency and probability are quite relaxed. You hear the most extraordinary stories, and still more extraordinary theories. . . .

A tentative chilly little night wind ventures across the dying fire. The incandescent coals, with their halls and galleries magnificent, sink together with a faint sound. In a moment they begin to film over. The features of your companions grow indistinct. Outside noises come more clearly to your attention, for strangely enough the mere fact of firelight seems to hold at a distance not only the darkness but the sounds that people it. The rush of waters, the sighing of winds, the distant mournful owl-notes, or sleepy single chirp of some momentarily awakened day-bird—these come closer with the reassured shadows creeping down to pounce on the dying fire.

In the group some one raps a pipe sharply twice. Some one else stretchs and sighs. The stir of leaves tells of reluctant risings.

"Time to turn in, boys; good-night," says one.

In a moment you and the faint glow in the ashes are left alone together.

Life in Camp, from *The Pass* by Stewart Edward White. The Outing Publishing Company, 1906.

William Frederic Badè

A Dash Up Mount Whitney

Anyone familiar with the vast assortment of outings now offered by the Sierra Club may be surprised to learn that in the club's infancy, some of its board members resisted the idea of an outings program. But William Colby, one of the greatest of the early club leaders, believed that members should be given the opportunity to enjoy the wilds of the Sierra in relative comfort during summer vacations. With the strong encouragement of John Muir, he pressed the issue and ultimately won over the club leadership.

In the beginning, Sierra Club outings, soon known as High Trips, took place only once a year. Colby himself organized and led the outings for 29 years. High Trips differed markedly from the small, low-impact trips the Sierra Club now considers mandatory. As many as 200 participants spent a month trekking in the Sierra, aided by 50 packers and commissary staff members. Ten tons of provisions and five tons of miscellaneous equipment were packed in to support this army.

Theology professor William Frederic Badè joined the 1903 High Trip from Mineral King to the Kern River Canyon. Badè later served as president of the club for three years and as editor of the Sierra Club Bulletin *for twelve. In his account of the 1903 trip, he described a four-day "dash" to the top of Mount Whitney by more than a hundred climbers.*

One of the motives of the Club's officers in selecting the Kern Cañon for last summer's outing was the desire to give mountain-climbers a chance to make the ascent of Mt. Whitney. The second party had arrived at the camp soon after the first, swelling its population to over two hundred. Many had come expressly to join in the dash to "the top of the United States." The distance from the camp to the mountain was about eighteen miles as the crow flies when he has not too much distracting business on the way. But a trail over the extremely corrugated surface of the Sierra Nevada easily doubles an air-line measurement, for it must follow the line of least resistance along the path of rivers, circumvent mountains, follow the backs of ridges, hit meadows enough to keep life in the pack-animals, and not miss the fords and the gaps. Thus it was not surprising that the real distance to Mt. Whitney was placed somewhere between thirty and forty miles. A pioneer party, composed of about forty persons under the leadership of Professor Le Conte, started on the 5th of July, making the ascent succesfully, and by dint of forced marches returning to Camp Olney in six days. The main party, composed of one hundred and eight persons, started on the 9th of July, and planned to make the trip in seven days. Most of the members of both parties were seasoned climbers, including a number of Mazamas from Portland. The approach to Mt. Whitney was made by the Volcano Creek trail and the return by the Kern River Cañon. The size of the party and the limited number of pack-animals available produced some unexpected complications, with the result that some of us, without our sleeping-bags in a freezing temperature, cheerfully slept away part of the first night between a log and a fire. Onward and upward we went the next day, still following Volcano Creek, whose teeming population of famous golden trout was laid under tribute to our rods and appetites. Volumes might be written on what we saw this and the following day, as our path led over lava-beds, past an extinct crater where but recently Nature blew her volcanic forges, over closely matted rosettes of a rare and beautiful evening primrose (*Enothera xylocarpa*), over golden acres of *Mimuli,* through zone after zone of vegetation, over the sandy waste of the Siberian outpost, into the deeply carved cañon of Rock Creek, hard by the spire of Mt. Guyot, to the third night's camping-ground on Crabtree Meadows. To-morrow Mt. Whitney!

A quintet of adventurous spirits started soon after 1 o'clock in the morning, hoping to reach the top by sunrise. Unfortunately the distance of the camp from the base involved loss of time in picking the trail where it led over streams and meadows. Silently we filed on through the night, the leaders changing places occasionally to take turns in picking the trail. Even at that early hour the titanic character of our surroundings was manifest; the deep glaciated gorge, mountainous boulders, the dark depths of Guitar Lake, near where Professor

Langley made his famous investigation of the color of the sun, and on our left rose the majestic granite hulk of Mt. Whitney. On its shoulder sparkled the diadem of the Pleiades, displaying a dozen or more brilliants where ordinarily but six are dimly visible. Over all brooded a silence so profound that it seemed as if a bit of eternity had been slipped into the place of one of our noisy days. An easy climb brought us to the "chimney,"—a rift in a five-hundred-foot precipice. This part of the climb called for caution and skill. To start a loose rock was to jeopardize the lives of climbers beneath. The "chimney" surmounted, there was a steady, but comparatively easy, climb of fifteen hundred feet to the summit. When we were halfway up the mountainside the rising sun threw the shadow of Whitney westward over the cul-de-sac of a valley we had just left and bathed in rosy light the wilderness of snow-ribbed summits to the north and west. To convey an impression of the phenomenon is beyond the power of language. Far down at the approach to the "chimney" the main party, under the direction of Secretary Colby and Mr. Parsons, was dimly discernible as a wavering line. A few minutes after 7 the quintet was at the top, and members of the main party kept arriving steadily until, about the middle of the forenoon, all had safely conquered the mountain—one hundred and three persons. Considering the size of the party and the height of the mountain (14,522 ft.),[1] July 12th deserves to be remembered in connection with one of the most remarkable achievements in the history of mountaineering.

A Dash Up Mount Whitney, from "On the Trail with the Sierra Club" by William Frederic Badè. *Sierra Club Bulletin,* January, 1904. Reprinted by permission of The Sierra Club.

---

[1]Mount Whitney's height is today calculated at 14,495 feet.

SECTION IV:
THE NATURALISTS

From the beginning, the history of the Sierra's explorers, immigrants and mountain climbers has been characterized by the sure mark of progress. We read of the discovery of remote lakes and canyons, the opening of passes, and the ascents of more and more difficult climbing routes, and get the sense of a well-ordered plan, a campaign moving confidently from one clear advance to the next.

But that is not true for the study of the range's natural history. Progress is only incidental to the work of the naturalist, whose business it is to describe what is there—to open our eyes to the obvious. The task calls not so much for building on the work of others as for patience and clarity of thought. One can read the notes on Sierra flora that John Frémont composed during his winter crossing of the Sierra in 1844 and be satisfied that, under the circumstances, he did about as well as anyone could do today. To be sure, Frémont's notes pale in comparison with the engrossing tale that Mary Austin told decades later in *The Land of Little Rain*; but the differences are ones of extent and literary quality, not a century of progress. Austin's most urgent need as she made her observations was to remain attentive to her work. Frémont's rather more pressing task was to save his skin.

This is not to say that naturalists have made no progress whatever toward understanding the Sierra's natural history. Much has been learned about the range's botany, geology and meteorology. A controversy over the proper classification of sequoia trees raged for many years following their discovery, and only in the past few decades have botanists agreed on the classification *Sequoiadendron giganteum*.

199

Even more notable was the long debate among geologists over the causes of the formation of Yosemite Valley. When John Muir postulated that glaciers had been responsible for the valley's unique architecture, he was ridiculed by nearly every responsible geologist. It was not until 1930 that the studies of Francois Matthes confirmed to everyone's satisfaction that Muir had been right.

One might argue that the recent emergence of the science of ecology and of our recognition that complex relationships exist among all objects in nature is the clearest evidence of progress in the natural sciences. Here again, however, the example of the far-sighted John Muir proves otherwise.

"When we try to pick out anything by itself," Muir wrote nearly a century ago, "we find it hitched to everything else in the universe."

James M. Hutchings

A Curiously Delusive Dream

No feature of the Sierra has attracted more attention than the sequoia trees.
Upon their discovery the sequoias, the most massive trees in the world, were greeted
by the general public with a degree of awe today reserved for rock stars and Super
Bowl champions. Some of the trees were cut down simply because they were so
huge, a tribute to their novelty if not to their rarity. The bark shells of entire
sequoia trunks were shipped to New York and London and put on display. Dance
pavilions, a bowling alley, even a small hotel were erected on the enormous
stumps. Few people seemed to realize that sequoias were in fact trees and not
freaks.

Probably the first white men to see sequoias were members of the Walker party
in 1833.[1] *But the trees didn't become widely known until 1852, when a hunter*
named Augustus T. Dowd stumbled onto a grove of them in Calaveras County.
In In the Heart of the Sierras, *James M. Hutchings related the story of*
Dowd's at-first-unbelievable discovery.

In the spring of 1852, Mr. A. T. Dowd, a hunter, was employed by
the Union Water Company, of Murphy's, Calaveras County, to
supply the workmen engaged in the construction of their canal, with
fresh meat, from the large quantities of game running wild on the
upper portion of their works. While engaged in this calling, having
wounded a grizzly bear, and while industriously pursuing him, he
suddenly came upon one of those immense trees that have since
become so justly celebrated throughout the civilized world. All
thoughts of hunting were absorbed and lost in the wonder and
surprise inspired by the scene. "Surely," he mused, "this must be
some curiously delusive dream!" But the great realities indubitably

---

[1]See "Zenas Leonard: Across the Giddy Heights," Section I.

confronting him were convincing proof, beyond question, that they were no mere fanciful creations of his imagination.

Returning to camp, he there related the wonders he had seen, when his companions laughed at him; and even questioned his veracity, which, previously, they had considered to be in every way reliable. He affirmed his statement to be true; but they still thought it "too big a story" to believe, supposing that he was trying to perpetrate upon them some first-of-April joke.

For a day or two he allowed the matter to rest; submitting, with chuckling satisfaction, to their occasional jocular allusions to "his big tree yarn," but continued hunting as formerly. On the Sunday morning ensuing, he went out early as usual, but soon returned in haste, apparently excited by some great event, when he exclaimed, "Boys, I have killed the largest grizzly bear that I ever saw in my life. While I am getting a little something to eat, you make every preparation for bringing him in; all had better go that can possibly be spared, as their assistance will certainly be needed."

As the big tree story was now almost forgotten, or by common consent laid aside as a subject of conversation; and, moreover, as Sunday was a leisure day, and one that generally hangs the heaviest of the seven on those who are shut out from social or religious intercourse with friends, as many Californians unfortunately were and still are, the tidings were gladly welcomed, especially as the proposition was suggestive of a day's intense excitement.

Nothing loath, they were soon ready for the start. The camp was almost deserted. On, on they hurried, with Dowd as their guide, through thickets and pine groves; crossing ridges and cañons, flats, and ravines, each relating in turn the adventures experienced, or heard of from companions, with grizzly bears, and other formidable tenants of the mountains, until their leader came to a halt at the foot of the immense tree he had seen, and to them had represented the approximate size. Pointing to its extraordinary diameter and lofty height, he exultingly exclaimed, "Now, boys, do you believe my big tree story? That is the large grizzly I wanted you to see. Do you now think it a yarn?" By this ruse of their leader all doubt was changed into certainty, and unbelief into amazement; as, speechless with profound awe, their admiring gaze was riveted upon those forest giants.

But a short season was allowed to elapse before the trumpet-tongued press proclaimed abroad the wonder; and the intelligent and devout worshipers, in nature and science, flocked to the Big Tree Groves of Calaveras, for the purpose of seeing for themselves the astounding marvels about which they had heard so much.

A Curiously Delusive Dream, from *In the Heart of the Sierras,* by J.M. Hutchings. J.M. Hutchings, 1886.

Anonymous

A Carpeted Saloon

So excited was the public's response to the discovery of sequoias one would have thought a live saber-toothed tiger had been captured in the California forests. In 1854 the trunk of a downed seqouia was shipped to New York City and placed on public exhibition in the Racket Court of the Union Club at Number 596 Broadway. An anonymous pamphleteer turned out the following breathless description of the tree.

The acquisition, by the United States, of the vast territories upon the Pacific, every day unfolds some new wonder, giving importance and interest to that wild and beautiful region, while it adds to our national greatness and wealth. It is to the indomitable enterprise of the citizens of the United States, that the world is mostly indebted, not only for the development of those exhaustless sources of natural wealth, the golden streams from which overrun and enrich every part of our country, but also for a variety of vegetable discoveries of equal value and importance to mankind.

The natural treasures of this vast continent, even now, three hundred and sixty-two years from the time of its discovery, are just beginning to be known, and every day develops some new feature in the vegetable or mineral kingdom, unnoticed by the people of any previous age. Nothing, however, has yet been discovered in the new world, that will convey to the mind a conception of the immensity of its forests, or the grandeur of its timber, so much as to look upon the great tree—the majestic monarch of the wood recently felled upon the slopes of the Sierra Nevada, in California, and now for the first time offered for public exhibition in the Atlantic States.

This mountain of wood, while standing in its native forest, measured three hundred and twenty feet in height, and ninety-five

204

feet in circumference. Its age would appear fabulous but for the self-evident testimony it bears in its wood. Professor Lobb, . . . in speaking of its great age, says, that judging from the number of its concentric rings, its age has been estimated at THREE THOUSAND YEARS.

Of this vegetable monster, fifty feet of the bark from the lower part of the trunk, is put in natural form for exhibition. It was first exhibited in San Francisco, and has never been shown at any other place, except

Pavilion built on the stump of a sequoia big tree

the Racket Court, adjoining the Metropolitan Hotel, Broadway, New York. The tree at the Crystal Palace is two thirds smaller in diameter than this, and is not even half as large as the old sycamore, exhibited in this city some twenty years ago. In fact it is so insignificant, after all the pompous parade made about its height and age, that visitors to the Palace show are obliged to enquire for its whereabouts.

GIGANTEA AMERICUS is the name which the proprietor of the great California Tree has bestowed upon it, as its kind is not mentioned in any of the works upon Botany or Natural History. The interior of the tree presents a spacious carpeted saloon, with seats around its circumference for forty persons, and room for a piano. On one occasion one hundred and forty children belonging to a Sunday School, accompanied by their teachers, entered within it at one time without inconvenience. Thirty-two couples have waltzed inside of it at once in perfect harmony, and a banquet has been spread within its colossal bark walls, at which nearly one hundred persons partook together. . . .

A vast deal of labor was required to level this monster to the earth, and after almost incredible toiling with pump augers, axes and saws, it finally fell prostrate—the crash can neither be imagined nor described—the jar of the hill was perceived for miles, as though an earthquake had passed that way. . . .

A piece of wood will be shown which was cut from the tree across the whole diameter. In this piece will be seen the concentric rings denoting its great age, and also several charred places near its center, showing where fires had been kindled against its trunk many centuries ago by the aboriginals.

This is the identical tree described in the February number of the London Illustrated News, Gleason's Pictorial for October last, and noticed by the leading scientific journals. . . .

It was . . . seen standing in its natural state by Senator Gwinn, Mr. Adams, of the Express Company, and several other gentlemen whose veracity may be relied on.

A Carpeted Saloon, from "Description of the Great Tree, Recently Felled upon the Sierra Nevada, California, now placed for Public Exhibition in the spacious Racket Court of the Union Club, No. 596, Broadway, adjoining the Metropolitan Hotel, New York." 1854.

Edwin Way Teale

Autumn in the Sequoias

Since their discovery, the magnificent sequoias have inspired legions of writers to record their impressions of the big trees. Predictably, the results have been mixed. One poet, unable to contain his soaring imagination, called the General Sherman Tree "my barked behemoth, my noble architect of woodsy destiny."

Another lost control of his metaphors altogether: "This battleship, this blunderbuss, this sombre Trojan horse . . ."

Fortunately, a few writers have paused long enough to collect their thoughts before committing them to paper. Thirty years ago, Edwin Way Teale, one of our most celebrated naturalists, took an autumn-long trip from Cape Cod to California. As the journey wound to a close, he and his wife Nellie spent two memorable days in the Wawona (Mariposa) Grove.

Wawona Grove, the first and most famous of the sequoia sanctuaries, was waist-deep in snow when we reached it. But the road had been plowed out as far as the Grizzly Giant. This 3,700-ton patriarch, with a trunk that has a circumference of forty-six feet 90 feet above ground, is believed to be at least 3,800 years old. All the arts that make this printed page possible, even to the invention of paper, occurred within its lifetime. With 100 or 150 feet of its top gone, the Grizzly Giant still towers to a height of 209 feet. Six times in a single storm this tree was struck by lightning. Yet it has endured, in spite of fire and thunderbolt, for nearly forty centuries.

While the coastal redwoods were seen by the Spaniards as early as 1769, these mountain redwoods, *Sequoia gigantea*, were not discovered until 1833 when the exploring party led by Joseph Walker crossed the Sierra Nevada in the region of Yosemite. As compared to the 2,000,000 acres originally covered by the coastal trees, the total for all the high-country groves of *Sequoia gigantea* is only about 30,000 acres. Unlike the taller redwoods, the more massive and older sequoias do not grow in pure stands. They are mixed with other trees such as the great sugar pines we saw dangling their eighteen-inch cones from the tips of their upper branches. A sequoia is several hundred years old before it begins to reproduce. This it does with cones hardly two inches long. So numerous are they that two small branches were once found to hold 480. Each cone is packed with from 150 to 300 seeds so small they range from an eighth to a quarter of an inch in length. The little western chickaree with its finely tufted ears never seems to get enough sequoia seeds. In a single day one of these squirrels may cut down as much as a bushel of cones.

When we first came to the grove it was enveloped in the age-old calm of these greater redwoods, a hush that was almost complete. Blue-tinted shadows ran across the snow of open spaces, the oldest tree shadows we had ever seen, cast by the same trunks on this same position of the earth for ten or twenty centuries before the *Golden Hinde* carried Sir Francis Drake to the Pacific. Under the snow the spreading roots of some of the titan trees extended through an acre of soil. In one place where the sun's rays descended between two shadow paths we saw a shining mote, the form of an amazingly hardy gnat, dancing in the light surrounded by the blur of its wings. Here side by side in nature's vast machine were the largest and one of the smallest of its cogs—the long, slowly revolving life cycle of the sequoia and the swiftly completed existence of the gnat.

Looking up along the grooved cinnamon-red trunks of the many-autumned trees we saw the brilliant green of western lichen running in lines up the ridgetops of the bark. This same growth mantled the upper branches of the Grizzly Giant and here and there green blotches stood out on the snow where tufts of the lichen had fallen. At times we heard the far-away surf-sound of wind coming toward us through the treetops. In the changeable mountain weather it approached in single, isolated waves with a recognizable front. Each time we would hear the sound grow in volume, pass high overhead with "a rushing like the rushing of mighty waters," then sweep on and become faint in the distance, leaving the great trees once more wrapped in stillness.

Only three times during our two afternoons in this snow-covered sequoia grove did other visitors appear. Once it was a couple from British Columbia, another time a farm family from Nebraska and the third time an elderly man bundled in robes and sitting alone in the back of a limousine driven by a liveried chauffeur. Occasionally the profound hush of the forest was broken by the calling of a white-headed woodpecker, the voice of a Steller's jay or the small clinking sounds of feeding nuthatches. Whenever we remained motionless for any length of time we became aware of a slow, almost imperceptible drift of tiny bark fragments raining down from the trees. Where these particles collect in depressions on the trunks, mountain chickadees and thin-billed nuthatches sometimes take dust baths high above the ground. Woodpeckers, on occasion, excavate their nest holes entirely within the bark of the sequoias. For no other tree has so heavy an outer layer; on large trunks it may be as much as two feet thick.

One of the secrets of the sequoia's longevity is the protection against fire and injury provided by this bark. The wood of the big tree is particularly brittle. It fractures across the grain. In consequence the trunk of a felled sequoia breaks into such small sections that nearly 80 per cent of the wood is unsuitable for lumber. This characteristic, together with the remote and mountainous location of its grove, has played a major role in saving it from the axe and saw. And the abundant supply of tannin it contains brings it immunity from the attacks of insects and fungus. Wherever the trunk of a sequoia is cut the wood turns jet black as the tannin oxidizes on contact with the air. John Muir, in this very grove, use to make the ink he used by dissolving in water flakes of reddish gum obtained from the cones of the big trees. Letters he wrote with this tannin-rich sequoia ink are still legible more than seventy years later.

All through the Yosemite country, wherever you go, you cross the trail of this remarkable man and hear echoes of the days he spent there. With a sack of bread over his shoulder and a notebook tied to his belt, Muir roamed alone among the mountains making the pioneer studies on which his early books were based. It was in Wawona Grove, then known as Mariposa Grove, that Muir camped with Theodore Roosevelt in 1903. Thirty-two years earlier he had shown the same sequoias to Ralph Waldo Emerson.

"The wonder is," Emerson had remarked, "that we can see these trees and not wonder more."

When, after only a few hours' visit, the Emerson party prepared to leave the grove, Muir remonstrated:

"It is as though a photographer should remove his plate before the impression was fully made."

Always he was amazed by the rich and distinguised visitors who came to Yosemite and then rushed away again, so "time-poor" they could spare no more than a day or so to see the glories of the mountains.

"I have not yet in all my wanderings," he wrote to his sister, "found a single person so free as myself. When in the woods I sit at times for hours watching birds or squirrels or looking down into the faces of flowers without suffering any feeling of haste."

Since Muir's day the margin of time in the average man's life has widened as working hours have become shorter. Yet the demands on that time have been ever increasing. Hazlitt's wish for "a little breathing space to muse on indifferent matters" is a desire that seems each year harder to fulfill. When the famous Sierra Club was formed, one of the early members told me, a primary purpose was to induce people to come to Yosemite. Now in summer the cars move bumper to bumper and the problem is what to do with all the people who come. Time and space—time to be alone, space to move about—these may well become the great scarcities of tomorrow. Freedom as John Muir knew it, with its wealth of time, its unregimented days, its latitude of choice, such freedom seems more rare, more difficult to attain, more remote with each new generation.

We were thinking of John Muir and of space and time that day when we left the sequoias—those trees so full of years, so independent of the clock. The last of the autumn days were slipping away. In the life of the sequoia those days represented but an infinitesimal flicker of time. But to us they would round out the season. They would bring to a close our long westward pilgrimage through the fall. During this journey we had wandered as we wished. We had changed our plans to suit the day. We had, for the space of a whole glorious autumn, been time-rich.

Bret Harte

The Calaveras Skull

One of the most curious discoveries ever made in the Sierra was that of a human skull, brought up from the bottom of a mine shaft in Calaveras County in 1866. Two theories were advanced to explain the origin of the skull. One proposed that it was of ancient origin—"the oldest known human being" in the estimation of one excited local newspaper editor: "This fossil proves that he was here before the mastodon was known to exist."

The other said it was a hoax.

Professor J.D. Whitney, head of the California State Geological Survey, believed that the skull was an authentic fossil. After exhaustive study, he reported to the California Academy of Natural Sciences that the skull belonged to the Pliocene epoch, and was thus several million years old.

Writer Bret Harte knew better. Harte was no scientist; but as a man with first-hand experience in the gold fields, he understood the hazards of a mine shaft far better than did Professor Whitney. In "To the Pliocene Skull (A Geological Address)," a sarcastic Harte advanced his own rather prosaic theory of the origin of the Calaveras Skull.

"Speak, O man, less recent! Fragmentary fossil!
 Primal pioneer of pliocene formation,
 Hid in lowest drifts below the earliest stratum
     Of volcanic tufa!

"Older than the beasts, the oldest Palaeotherium;
 Older than the trees, the oldest Cryptogami;
 Older than the hills, those infantile eruptions
     Of earth's epidermis!

"Eo—Mio—Plio—whatsoe'er the 'cene' was
That those vacant sockets filled with awe and wonder,—
Whether shores Devonian or Silurian beaches,—
    Tell us thy strange story!

"Or has the professor slightly antedated
By some thousand years thy advent on this planet,
Giving thee an air that's somewhat better fitted
    For cold-blooded creatures?

"Wert thou true spectator of that mighty forest
When above thy head the stately Sigillaria
Reared its columned trunks in that remote and distant
    Carboniferous epoch?

"Tell us of that scene,—the dim and watery woodland,
Songless, silent, hushed, with never bird or insect,
Veiled with spreading fronds and screened with tall clubmosses,
    Lycopodiacea,—

"When beside thee walked the solemn Plesiosaurus,
And around thee crept the festive Ichthyosaurus,
While from time to time above thee flew and circled
    Cheerful Pterodactyls.

"Tell us of thy food,—those half-marine refections,
Crinoids on the shell and Brachipods *au naturel*,—
Cuttlefish to which the *pieuvre* of Victor Hugo
    Seems a periwinkle.

"Speak, thou awful vestige of the earth's creation,
Solitary fragment of remains organic!
Tell the wondrous secret of thy past existence,—
    Speak! thou oldest primate!"

Even as I gazed, a thrill of the maxilla,
And a lateral movement of the condyloid process,
With post-pliocene sounds of healthy mastication,
    Ground the teeth together.

And from that imperfect dental exhibition,
Stained with express juices of the weed nicotian,
Came these hollow accents, blent with softer murmurs
    Of expectoration:

"Which my name is Bowers, and my crust was busted
Falling down a shaft in Calaveras County;
But I'd take it kindly if you'd send the pieces
    Home to old Missouri!"

The Calaveras Skull, from *Complete Poetical Works* by Bret Harte. Houghton
Mifflin Company, 1902.

Theodore H. Hittell

Grizzly Adams

In the fall of 1852 animal trainer James Capen "Grizzly" Adams took up residence in a remote valley on a branch of the Merced River. It was hardly a move that might have been expected to lead to fame and fortune. Yet within four years Adams was the renowned proprietor of the Mountaineer Museum in San Francisco, which featured "the largest collection of wild animals ever exhibited on the Pacific Coast"; four years after that he and P.T. Barnum were partners in a hugely successful wild animal show on Broadway in New York City.

Adams was not a naturalist in the modern sense of the word. He captured wild animals not for scientific study but to supply menageries and to serve himself as pack animals. (His trained grizzly bear Lady Washington toted 200-pound loads for Adams on hunting expeditions.)

Nevertheless, he was a keen and interested observer of wildlife, and he enjoyed a fond and respectful relationship with many of his animals. The fact that he exploited these animals for personal gain and killed many others on hunting expeditions does not really distinguish him from wildlife biologists today who study and dispatch research animals in the respectable surroundings of their laboratories.

In the spring of 1854 Adams captured two grizzly cubs near Little Yosemite Valley in what is now Yosemite National Park. One of the cubs became Adams's most famous trained bear, Ben Franklin. He narrated the tale of the capture of the cubs to his biographer, Theodore H. Hittell.

My next adventure, and the most fortunate of all my career, was the capture of Ben Franklin, the flower of his race, my firmest friend, the boon companion of my after-years. . . .

We had moved to the head waters of the Merced River. On the first hunt there, I discovered a grizzly's den, and no sooner had my eyes fallen upon it, than I forgot all other hunting; I thought and dreamed of nothing else but how to take it;—this, at once, became all my ambition. . . .

In a short time after arriving, which was late in the afternoon, I climbed a tree, and reconnoitred the entire ravine. From that position, I observed and chose a spot for concealment in a bunch of junipers, on the opposite side of the cañon, and about a hundred yards distant from the den; and, upon cautiously crawling up, found, as I had anticipated, that it afforded a fair view of its mouth at the same time that it screened me entirely from observation. Though it was impossible to see far into the den, I soon ascertained its character to be similar to that usually dug by the California grizzly;—in form something like an oven, having an entrance three or four feet in diameter and six or ten feet long, with a larger space, or den proper, rounded out at the extremity, intended for the lying-in place of the dam and the bedding of the cubs. A number of such dens I had seen in the Sierra, varying only according to their position and the quality of the ground in which they were excavated. The ravine here was rugged and narrow; and the den penetrated its steep, bushy side, about fifty feet above the bed of the stream, at this time dry, which formed the bottom of the cañon.

After making these observations, and satisfying myself that my position was the most judicious possible, being convinced that there were cubs in the place, I went back to the mule, built up a little fire for her protection, and then, leaving her to herself, I took my blankets, returned to my post in the juniper bushes, and commenced my watch, which I kept up unremittingly till morning. . . .

As the light of dawn began to peep, the thought struck me to discharge my rifle for two reasons: first, to see what effect it would have; and, again, to put in a fresh charge. Upon doing so, the report echoed off among the hills, as if they were playing with the unaccustomed sound. It had barely died away, when there seemed to be a snuffing underground, very faint at first, but growing louder and louder, until there was no mistaking it for the growl of a bear. I climbed a small tree, and looked and listened attentively, in hopes of seeing her; but the sound died away in a few minutes, and again all was silent. . . . Shortly after mid-day I got a short nap, and in the evening went back and built a fire near the mule; but before dark I

ADAMS AND BEN FRANKLIN.

was at my post again, and there I remained, shivering, till morning.

About daybreak there was again a noise in the den, and I thought the old bear might be stirring, and prepared for her reception; but it was a vain expectation; for in a short time all was quiet, and it seemed as if she never would show herself. As the morning advanced, however, I discharged my rifle again, and was gratified, not only with a snuff in the den, but also with the sight of the occupant's head and paws, as she came to the mouth of her stronghold; but the most gratifying circumstance was the yelping of cubs, which could now be distinctly heard. . . .

Adams prepared for his encounter with the grizzly. But the bear quickly reentered her den. Another day and night passed with no further activity, and Adams understandably began to grow impatient.

Daylight came, but the bear still remained housed, and I began to think she would not make her appearance. My watching was now becoming very irksome, and, feeling much like bringing the adventure to an issue, I determined to rouse her. There was some danger in this; for my plan would probably attract her directly to me, and, as sure as she should see me, I knew she would give no time to draw an aim. Before putting my plan into execution, therefore, I stuck my cap full of green twigs, and stationed myself in such a manner in the bushes that it would take a nice eye to discern my form, even though looking directly towards me. Having thus disposed myself, cocking and drawing my rifle, I uttered one of those terrific yells with which I have so often started the grizzly to his feet. It echoed like the roar of a lion up the cañon; and in a moment afterwards there was a booming in the den like the puffing and snorting of an engine in a tunnel, and the enraged animal rushed out, growling and snuffing, as if she could belch forth the fire of a volcano. She rose upon her hind feet, and exhibited a monster form,—limbs of terrible strength. She looked around in every direction; but in a few moments, seeing nothing to attack, she sat down upon her haunches, with her back towards me and her face towards the opposite side of the cañon, as if her enemy were there.

During these few minutes I stood as motionless as a statue, hardly breathing, waiting and watching an opportunity to fire. Had I met such an animal unawares, in an unexpected place, her ferocity would have made me tremble; but after my long watch I was anxious to commence the attack, and felt as steady as a piece of ordnance upon a battery. As I watched, I saw her turn her head towards the den; and, fearing she would retire, I gave a low, sharp whistle, which brought her to her feet again, with her breast fronting directly towards me. It was then, having my rifle already drawn, that I fired; and in an instant, dropping the rifle, I drew my pistol in one hand and my knife in the other. The bear, as the ball slapped loudly in the fat of her breast, staggered and fell backwards, and began pawing and biting the ground,—a sure sign of a deadly hurt. Copious streams of crimson blood also gushed from her breast, and I knew that they came from the fountainhead. The work was, indeed, nearly done; but so anxious was I to complete it at once, that I commenced leaping over the bushes to plunge my knife in her dying heart; when, gathering her savage strength, she rose, and, with one last, desperate effort, sprang towards me. The distance between us was only thirty feet, but, fortunately, full of brush, and she soon weakened with the prodigious energy requisite to tear her way through it. I discharged the six shots of my revolver, the last of which struck under the left ear, and laid her still for a moment; when, leaping forwards, I plunged my knife to her vitals. Again she endeavored to rise, but was so choked with blood that she could not. I drew my knife across her throat, and after a few convulsive struggles she expired.

My feelings, as she thus lay dead at my feet, it would be difficult to describe. I looked at the hills around, to see if any eye had beheld my success; but all was silence. I looked to the heavens; but all was quiet, only a vulture was circling like a speck in the distant ether. I was alone in the gorge, and, as I looked upon the dead monster, felt like Alexander sated with victory and wishing another foe to engage, worthy of my prowess. . . .

No sooner was the dam dead, than I turned towards the den, and determined to enter it without delay. Approaching its mouth, accordingly, I knelt, and tried to peer in; but all was dark, silent, and ominous. What dangers might lurk in that mysterious gloom, it was impossible to tell; nor was it without a tremor that I prepared to explore its depths. I trembled for a moment at the thought of another old bear in the den; but on second thought I assured myself of the folly of such an idea; for an occurrence of this kind would have been against all experience. But in such a situation, a man imagines many things, and fears much at which he afterwards laughs; and therefore, though there was really no difficulty to anticipate, I carefully loaded my rifle and pistol, and carried my arms as if, the next instant, I was to be called upon to fight for life. Being thus prepared, I took from my pocket a small torch made of pine splinters, lighted it, and, placing my rifle in the mouth of the den, with the torch in my left and the pistol in my right hand, I dropped upon my knees and began to crawl in.

The entrance consisted of a rough hole, three feet wide and four feet high. It extended inwards nearly horizontally, and almost without a turn, for six feet, where there was a chamber, six or eight feet in diameter and five feet high, giving me room to rise upon my knees, but not to stand up;—and its entire floor was thickly carpeted with leaves and grass. On the first look, I could see no animals, and felt grievously disappointed; but, as I crawled around, there was a rustling in the leaves; and, bending down with my torch, I discovered two beautiful little cubs, which could not have been over a week old, as their eyes, which open in eight or ten days, were still closed. I took the little sprawlers, one after the other, by the nape of the neck, lifted them up to the light, and found them very lively. . . .

Upon his return to camp, Adams gave one of the cubs to his hunting companion Solon.

He thought that this was more than his share; but I insisted upon his receiving it, and he did so with a thankful heart. He asked me the story of the capture, and I told it, from the moment of my leaving camp to my return. He wondered much at my patient watching in the juniper bushes, and said he would not have done it, but still he wished he had been with me;—and thus we went on talking, till the dying embers admonished us of the lateness of the hour. Before retiring, Solon christened his cub General Jackson; I remarked that

General Jackson was a great man in his way, but I would call my bear
Ben Franklin,—a greater name. Such was the manner that, in one and
the same day, I captured and christened my noble Ben.

Grizzly Adams, from Theodore H. Hittell, *The Adventures of James Capen
Adams* (New York: Charles Scribner's Sons, 1911) Reprinted courtesy Charles
Scribner's Sons.

Mary Austin

The Streets of the Sierra

Mary Austin's realm was the desolate country that spreads south and east of the Sierra, the endless desert lands, the region she called the Country of Lost Borders. As a young woman she lived in several of the towns that lay in the eastern shadow of the Sierra—Lone Pine, Independence, Kearsarge and Bishop. Her interest in California's native peoples led her to venture out into the Mojave Desert to study the Indians of the region. What began as a hobby soon became a consuming interest; Austin's studies of American Indian culture occupied her for much of the rest of her life, and her writings on the subject became a distinguished addition to the literature.

If Austin's eyes gazed naturally east from her home, her legs carried her west up into the High Sierra often enough for her to come to know that wild country too. With the insight of a naturalist, she understood the need to absorb the mountains slowly.

"The real heart and core of the country are not to be come at in a month's vacation," she wrote. "One must summer and winter with the land and wait its occasions."

In her best-known book, The Land of Little Rain, *published in 1903, Austin recounted a few of the occasions of the Sierra's splendid river canyons, which she called "the streets of the Sierra."*

All streets of the mountains lead to the citadel; steep or slow they go up to the core of the hills. Any trail that goes otherwhere must dip and cross, sidle and take chances. Rifts of the hills open into each other, and the high meadows are often wide enough to be called valleys by courtesy; but one keeps this distinction in mind,—valleys are the sunken places of the earth, cañons are scored out by the glacier ploughs of God. They have a better name in the Rockies for these hill-fenced open glades of pleasantness; they call them parks. Here and there in the hill country one comes upon blind gullies fronted by high stony barriers. These head also for the heart of the mountains; their distinction is that they never get anywhere.

All mountain streets have streams to thread them, or deep grooves where a stream might run. You would do well to avoid that range uncomforted by singing floods. You will find it forsaken of most things but beauty and madness and death and God. Many such lie east and north away from the mid Sierras, and quicken the imagination with the sense of purposes not revealed, but the ordinary traveler brings nothing away from them but an intolerable thirst.

The river cañons of the Sierras of the Snows are better worth while than most Broadways, though the choice of them is like the choice of streets, not very well determined by their names. There is always an amount of local history to be read in the names of mountain highways where one touches the successive waves of occupation or discovery, as in the old villages where the neighborhoods are not built but grow. Here you have the Spanish Californian in *Cero Gordo* and piñon; Symmes and Shepherd, pioneers both; Tunawai, probably Shoshone; Oak Creek, Kearsarge,—easy to fix the date of that christening,— Tinpah, Paiute that; Mist Cañon and Paddy Jack's. The streets of the west Sierras sloping toward the San Joaquin are long and winding, but from the east, my country, a day's ride carries one to the lake regions. The next day reaches the passes of the high divide, but whether one gets passage depends a little on how many have gone that road before, and much on one's own powers. The passes are steep and windy ridges, though not the highest. By two and three thousand feet the snow-caps overtop them. It is even possible to win through the Sierras without having passed above timber-line, but one misses a great exhilaration.

The shape of a new mountain is roughly pyramidal, running out into long shark-finned ridges that interfere and merge into other thunder-splintered sierras. You get the saw-tooth effect from a distance, but the near-by granite bulk glitters with the terrible keen polish of old glacial ages. I say terrible; so it seems. When those glossy domes swim into the alpenglow, wet after rain, you conceive how long and imperturbable are the purposes of God.

Never believe what you are told, that midsummer is the best time to go up the streets of the mountain—well—perhaps for the merely idle or sportsmanly or scientific; but for seeing and understanding, the best time is when you have the longest leave to stay. And here is a hint if you would attempt the stateliest approaches; travel light, and as much as possible live off the land. Mulligatawny soup and tinned lobster will not bring you the favor of the woodlanders.

Every cañon commends itself for some particular pleasantness; this for pines, another for trout, one for pure bleak beauty of granite buttresses, one for its far-flung irised falls; and as I say, though some are easier going, leads each to the cloud shouldering citadel. First, near the cañon mouth you get the low-heading full-branched, one-leaf pines. That is the sort of tree to know at sight, for the globose, resin-dripping cones have palatable, nourishing kernels, the main harvest of the Paiutes. That perhaps accounts for their growing accommo-datingly below the limit of deep snows, grouped sombrely on the valleyward slopes. The real procession of the pines begins in the rifts with the long-leafed *Pinus Jeffreyi*, sighing its soul away upon the wind. And it ought not to sigh in such good company. Here begins the manzanita, adjusting its tortuous stiff stems to the sharp waste of boulders, its pale olive leaves twisting edgewise to the sleek, ruddy, chestnut stems; begins also the meadow-sweet, burnished laurel, and the million unregarded trumpets of the coral-red pentstemon. Wild life is likely to be busiest about the lower pine borders. One looks in hollow trees and hiving rocks for wild honey. The drone of bees, the chatter of jays, the hurry and stir of squirrels, is incessant; the air is odorous and hot. The roar of the stream fills up the morning and evening intervals, and at night the deer feed in the buckthorn thickets. It is worth watching the year round in the purlieus of the long-leafed pines. One month or another you get sight or trail of most roving mountain dwellers as they follow the limit of forbidding snows, and more bloom than you can properly appreciate.

Whatever goes up or comes down the streets of the mountains, water has the right of way; it takes the lowest ground and the shortest passage. Where the rifts are narrow, and some of the Sierra cañons are not a stone's throw from wall to wall, the best trail for foot or horse winds considerably above the watercourses; but in a country of cone-bearers there is usually a good strip of swardy sod along the cañon floor. Pine woods, the short-leafed Balfour and Murryana of the high Sierras, are sombre, rooted in the litter of a thousand years, hushed, and corrective to the spirit. The trail passes insensibly into them from the black pines and a thin belt of firs. You look back as you rise, and strain for glimpses of the tawny valley, blue glints of the Bitter Lake, and tender cloud films on the farther ranges. For such pictures the pine branches make a noble frame. Presently they close in wholly; they draw mysteriously near, covering your tracks, giving up the trail indifferently, or with a secret grudge. You get a kind of impatience with their locked ranks, until you come out lastly on some high, windy dome and see what they are about. They troop thickly up the open ways, river banks, and brook borders; up open swales of dribbling springs; swarm over old moraines, circle the peaty swamps and part and meet about clean still lakes; scale the stony gullies; tormented, bowed, persisting to the door of the storm chambers, tall priests to pray for rain. The spring winds lift clouds of pollen dust, finer than frankincense, and trail it out over high altars, staining the snow. No doubt they understand this work better than we; in fact they know no other. "Come," say the churches of the valleys, after a season of dry years, "let us pray for rain." They would do better to plant more trees.

It is a pity we have let the gift of lyric improvisation die out. Sitting islanded on some gray peak above the encompassing wood, the soul is lifted up to sing the Iliad of the pines. They have no voice but the wind, and no sound of them rises up to the high places. But the waters, the evidences of their power, that go down the steep and stony ways, the outlets of ice-bordered pools, the young rivers swaying with the force of their running, they sing and shout and trumpet at the falls, and the noise of it far outreaches the forest spires. You see from these conning towers how they call and find each other in the slender gorges; how they fumble in the meadows, needing the sheer nearing walls to give them countenance and show the way; and how the pine woods are made glad by them.

The Streets of the Sierra, from *The Land of Little Rain* by Mary Austin. Houghton Mifflin Company, 1903.

John Burroughs

Yosemite Is Home

Unlike his friend and fellow naturalist John Muir, John Burroughs is scarcely remembered today, and read even less. Yet at the turn of the century Burroughs's books and articles on natural history enjoyed immense popularity. His essays focused in sparkling detail on the hidden lives of insects, birds, flowers and fish. Neither as grand as Muir's mountains and sequoias, nor as threatened with destruction, Burroughs's subjects were small and safe, and the author himself more the quiet observer than the crusader. These facts may help to explain why Burroughs has fallen into obscurity while Muir has endured.

A confirmed Easterner, Burroughs visited Yosemite Valley just once, in 1909. It was not the towering granite walls that won his heart but a robin, the first he had seen since leaving his home on New York's Hudson River.

"He struck the right note, he brought the scene home to me, he supplied the link of association. There he was, running over the grass or perching on the fence, or singing from the tree-top in the old familiar way. Where the robin is at home, there at home am I."

Burroughs expanded on the idea of Yosemite as home in an article in which he compared Yosemite with the Grand Canyon.

GOING from the Grand Cañon to Yosemite is going from one sublimity to another of a different order. The cañon is the more strange, unearthly, apocryphal, appeals more to the imagination, and is the more overwhelming in its size, its wealth of color, and its multitude of suggestive forms. But for quiet majesty and beauty, with a touch of the sylvan and pastoral, too, Yosemite stands alone. One could live with Yosemite, camp in it, tramp in it, winter and summer in it, and find nature in her tender and human, almost domestic moods, as well as in her grand and austere. But I do not think one could ever feel at home in or near the Grand Cañon; it is too unlike anything we have ever known upon the earth; it is like a vision of some strange colossal city uncovered from the depth of geologic time. You may have come to it, as we did, from the Petrified Forests, where you saw the silicified trunks of thousands of gigantic trees or tree ferns, that grew millions of years ago, most of them uncovered, but many of them protruding from banks of clay and gravel, and in their interiors rich in all the colors of the rainbow, and you wonder if you may not now be gazing upon some petrified antediluvian city of temples and holy places exhumed by mysterious hands and opened up to the vulgar gaze of to-day. You look into it from above and from another world and you descend into it at your peril. Yosemite you enter as into a gigantic hall and make your own; the cañon you gaze down upon, and are an alien, whether you enter it or not. Yosemite is carved out of the most majestic and enduring of all rocks, granite; the

Mrs. Glynn's house in Yosemite Valley, 1894

Grand Cañon is carved out of one of the most beautiful but perishable, red carboniferous sandstone. There is a maze of beautiful and intricate lines in the latter, a wilderness of temple-like forms and monumental remains, alcoves and amphitheaters, salients and entering angles, escarpments and retaining walls and noble architectural profiles that delight while they bewilder the eye. Yosemite has much greater simplicity, and is much nearer the classic standard of beauty. Its grand and austere features predominate, of course, but underneath these and adorning them are many touches of the idyllic and the picturesque. Its many waterfalls fluttering like white lace against its vertical granite walls, its smooth level floor, its noble pines and oaks, its open glades, its sheltering groves, its bright clear winding river, its soft voice of many waters, its flowers, its birds, its grass, its verdure, even its orchards of blooming apple-trees, all inclosed in this tremendous granite frame—what an unforgetable picture it all makes, what a blending of the sublime and the homelike and familiar it all is! It is the waterfalls that make the granite alive, and burst into bloom as it were. What a touch they give, how they enliven the scene! What music they evoke from these harps of stone!

The first leap of Yosemite Falls is sixteen hundred feet—sixteen hundred feet of a compact mass of snowy rockets shooting downward and bursting into spray around which rainbows flit and hover. The next leap is four hundred feet, and the last six hundred. We tried to get near its foot and inspect the hidden recess in which this airy spirit again took on its more tangible form of still, running water, but the spray over a large area about its foot fell like a summer shower, drenching the trees and rocks, and holding the inquisitive tourist off at a good safe distance. We had to beat a retreat with dripping garments before we had got within fifty yards of the foot of the fall. At first I was surprised at the volume of water that came hurrying out of the hidden recess of dripping rocks and trees—a swiftly flowing stream, thirty or forty feet wide and four or five feet deep. How could that comparatively narrow curtain of white spray up there give birth to such a full robust stream? But I saw that in making the tremendous leap from the top of the precipice, the stream was suddenly drawn out, as we stretch a rubber band in our hands, and that the solid and massive current below was like the rubber again relaxed. The strain was over, and the united waters deepened and slowed up over their rocky bed.

Yosemite for a home or a camp, the Grand Cañon for a spectacle.

Yosemite Is Home, from "The Spell of the Yosemite" by John Burroughs. *The Century Magazine,* November, 1910. Reprinted by permission of *Current History.*

Clara Barrus

A Portrait of Muir

John Muir, the greatest of Sierra naturalists: what was he like?
In 1909, Clara Barrus accompanied Muir and his friend John Burroughs on
visits to the Petrified Forest, the Grand Canyon and Yosemite Valley. Muir was
now past 70, but no less spry, opinionated or Scottish for the wear. Clearly taken by
him, Barrus later drew the following appealing portrait of her famous companion.

Mr. Muir's forte is in monologue. He is one of the most engaging
talkers imaginable, discursive, grave, and gay, relating thrilling
adventures, side-splitting anecdotes, choice quotations, apt charac-
terizations, scientific data, enthusiastic descriptions, sarcastic comments, scornful denunciations, inimitable mimicry. All this and
much more one will get, if one but lets him talk on uninterruptedly
as he listeth. . . .

Mr. Muir takes great pleasure in taking down or cutting under
almost any remark you chance to make, though it is always from a fun-
loving motive, never in a spirit of unkindness. I once heard him say,
"There is nothing I hate as those three things—dirt,—physical and
moral dirt,—confusion, and cruelty, especially cruelty." And one
look into his kindly face would convince you that compassion and
benevolence are in the very warp and woof of his character.

Concerning his liking for talk, one evening I heard him say, as he
half apologized for having monopolized the conversation, "Johnny, I
like the feel of words in my mouth better than bread," and those of us
who knew his opinion of bread realized the force of the remark.

One is drawn to him, above all else, for some rare quality he has
acquired in the mountain solitudes that gives him a pathetic seriousness and a certain wistfulness and furtiveness, like the wild things in
nature. With all this, one has the feeling that his love of nature is a

consecration; that, much as he has loved home and friends and humankind, he has loved nature more, and has obeyed some imperative need of his own in yielding to the *wanderlust,* which, with him, has not occupied a few years of his youth, but has been the master passion of his life. . . .

Those days in the petrified forests we ate our luncheons on the trunks of trees uprooted millions of years ago, Mr. Muir talking while we ate. When others congregated to eat, the Scot seemed specially impelled to talk. With a fine disregard for food, he sat and crumbled dry bread in his fingers, occasionally putting a bit in his mouth, talking while the eating was going on.

On this and other occasions we saw how insensible to fatigue Mr. Muir was when he could command companionship, and how independent of sleep. "Sleep!" he would exclaim. "Why, you can sleep when you get back home, or, at least, in the grave. That's what I consoled myself with when I was too cold and hungry to sleep, when camping out, with the night and stars."

Mr. Burroughs, on the contrary, is specially dependent upon sleep and food in order to do his best work. On our arrival at the Grand Cañon in the morning, after a night of travel and fasting and little sleep, all the rest of us felt the need of refreshing ourselves, and taking breakfast before we would even take a peep at the great rose-purple abyss out there a few steps from the hotel. The teasing Scot jeered at us for thinking of eating when there was that sublime spectacle to be seen. Although he deigned to breakfast with us, he preceded us to the rim of the cañon, where he stood in silent contemplation as we approached. Turning, he waved toward the great abyss and said: "There! Empty your heads of all vanity, and look!" And we did look, overwhelmed by what must be the most truly sublime spectacle this earth has to offer—a veritable terrestial Book of Revelation, as Mr. Burroughs said.

The next day we descended over four thousand feet in the cañon, to within a thousand feet of the river, several hours later making the ascent to the rim, the only part of the excursion that met Mr. Muir's approval. "Climb, climb, if you would see the glories," was always the burden of his cry.

One day, feeling acutely aware of our incalculable privilege, I said,

"To think of having the Grand Cañon, and John Burroughs and John Muir thrown in!"

"I wish Muir *was* thrown in, sometimes," retorted Mr. Burroughs, with a twinkle in his eye, "when he gets between me and the cañon."

. . . Once when some one asked Mr. Muir if he did not feel lonely in those years when he spent much time in the high Sierra away from everybody, he replied: "There is no loneliness except in the city. A mountain range, or even a continent, cannot separate friends." It seems strange, yet is is true, that this wanderer, who can find his way on the trackless desert, in deep forests, and on the mountains, even when the trails are covered and the snow is waist-deep, is almost as helpless as a child when he finds himself alone in a city of only a few thousand inhabitants. Even in Pasadena he had to be piloted about, and in Los Angeles he was hopelessly at sea. One day, however, he came over from the latter city to our cottage in Pasadena, and, on being asked how he had got there, said triumphantly, "By Jove, I came all the way from Hooker's alone to-day, and only made one mistake!"

. . . As we came into the deep-walled inclosure of Yosemite Valley, and looked up in amazement at its stupendous, sheer granite walls, three thousand and more feet high, and saw also the tender, winsome beauty of it all, we were awed into reverent silence, mighty El Capitan guarding the entrance, granite domes and spires roundabout, foaming waterfalls, stately trees, and the river, which we had seen tumbling over boulders as we came hither, now lazily coursing along through pastoral meadows.

"How is that for a piece of masonry, Johnny?" asked Mr. Muir, as we came to El Capitan. The next day, when we were journeying toward Half Dome and Mr. Muir was telling how probably the glacier had worn off at least half a mile from its top, and then had sawed right down through the valley, he turned and asked, "John, how is that for a piece of work?" Mr. Burroughs answered him, "Oh, Lord, that's too much, Muir." He said that it stuck in his crop—this theory that ice alone accounts for this great valley cut out of the solid rocks. On our way up Nevada Fall, I heard Mr. Muir telling him of the glacial scourings that he had seen on the top of Half Dome, and of their traces all along as the glaciers had sawed down through this valley; and

Mr. Burroughs had protested: "But, Muir, the million years before the ice age—what was going on here then?"

"Oh, God knows," said Mr. Muir; but he added that he had found slate fragments on the top of Half Dome, which he adduced as further proof of his theory.

When we stood as near as we could get to the thundering Yosemite Fall, and looked up at that body of water, which in a series of three great leaps has a fall of twenty-six hundred feet, Mr. Burroughs exclaimed in reverent wonder, "Great God Almighty!" and seemed more deeply moved than I had noticed him to be at any of the wonders we had yet seen.

As we neared Register Rock, a granite boulder weighing, they estimated, between twenty and thirty thousand tons, Mr. Muir said, "Think of the roar when that came down, and the smell like sulphur, and the red glow!"

The second day in Yosemite, one of us was lamenting that we could not see the giant sequoias, climb to Glacier Point, go to the tops of various falls, and do many other things. Mr. Muir retorted, "I puttered around here for ten years, and you expect to see and do everything in four days!" And again: "You come in here, and then excuse yourselves to God, who has kept these glories waiting for you by saying, 'I've got to go back to Slabsides,'[1] or, 'We want to go to Honolulu.' "

I shall never forget the sight of him that May day as we rushed excitedly down the trail to the foot of Nevada Fall, and saw the hilarous, tumbling waters throwing up glistening fountains of spray. With great bounds he leaped down the trail, and, on reaching the foot, threw up his arms and shouted exultantly, "Ha!" There was something almost demoniacal in his glee: his spirit and the wild free spirit of the madly rushing waterfall seemed to be saluting each other. One had a glimpse of the wild, ecstatic moods he must have experienced when, alone, he came upon those glorious scenes in the years that are gone.

As we were resting on the rocks after our climb to Nevada Fall, he showed me a tiny fern (*pellaea densa*)—"one of the bonniest of our father's bairns"—and said "Will you keep it, if I pick it for you?"

---

[1]Burroughs's home on the Hudson River.

receiving assurance before he would remove it from its shelter in the rock. Just to hear him name certain flowers is a privilege; his face grows tender, and his voice is a caress as he speaks of his darlings— Calypso, Bryanthus, and Cassiope, and declares that "Heaven itself would not be heaven without them."

I see that I have kept Mr. Burroughs somewhat in the background. But so it was on our Western tour; when the Scot was there, he occupied the center of the stage, and we were content to have it so, for Mr. Muir was on his native heath.

The night of our return from Nevada Fall we found shelter in the hospitable Camp Ahwahnee, where, as happy dwellers in tents, we tasted the charm of the ideal way of living in Yosemite.

Sitting about the huge camp-fire, under the noble spruces and firs, we saw the moon rise over Sentinel Rock, lending the crowning touch to this ideal scene. After the other campers had gone to rest we lingered, loath to bring to its close a day so replete with sublimity and beauty. Mr. Burroughs summed it up as he said good night: "A day with the gods of eld—a holy day in the temple of the gods."

The next day as we reluctantly left the valley, turning back for one more glance, I surprised a wistful parting look on Mr. Muir's countenance, and, as he faced forward, he confessed: "I hate to think any time I'm leaving the valley that it is for the last time." Later, as one tried to voice the gratitude we felt at the inestimable privilege of seeing all this wondrous beauty under his guidance, he said: "You were pretty good people when you went into the valley, but you are a good deal better now. Life is richer."

A Portrait of Muir, from "With John O'Birds and John O'Mountains in the Southwest" by Clara Barrus. *The Century Magazine,* August, 1910. Reprinted by permission of *Current History.*

Francois Matthes

Cockscomb Crest

John Muir's theory that glaciers were the principal architects of the Yosemite landscape had not been confirmed by the time he died in 1914. The debate lingered on until 1930, when the celebrated geologist Francois Matthes published his "Geologic History of the Yosemite Valley." This comprehensive study at last confirmed Muir's glacial theory to the satisfaction of everyone.

Matthes was a fitting successor to Muir as an interpreter of Sierra geology. Like Muir, he fell in love with Yosemite at the age of 30 and never escaped from its spell. His geological research took him far afield, but he returned to the Sierra again and again to resume his study of his favorite range. In his technical papers he wrote with the thoughtful lay person in mind, never sacrificing scientific accuracy, but striving for something rare in professional journals: readability.

In Matthes's article on "Cockscomb Crest" he explained the origins of the strange and spectacular pinnacles—Unicorn, Echo, Cathedral, and the rest— that surround Cathedral Pass in Yosemite National Park.

The significance of this peculiar style of mountain architecture, which is not prevalent in the Sierra Nevada, has been hinted at by more than one writer. Muir and Chase both have suggested that the sharp pinnacles and crests may be summits that were never overridden by the ice of the Glacial Epoch; that stood out above even the highest ice-floods and escaped being planed down and rounded off as were the massive shoulders of the mountain pedestals under them. This explanation, though only conjectural, was eminently reasonable, and it is a genuine satisfaction, now that the region has been submitted to a systematic and detailed study, to be able to confirm its correctness and to corroborate with positive and abundant evidence the surmise of these two keen and perceptive observers. . . .

In the Sierra Nevada indications of at least two great ice-floods have been clearly recognized by several observers—two ice-floods that occurred manifestly at widely different times, the later culminating probably only twenty thousand years ago, the earlier, perhaps as much as several hundred thousand years ago. The evidence is the more readily established as the later ice-flood was the smaller and less extensive of the two and left undisturbed the moraines—that is, the ridges of ice-carried rock debris—that mark the limits of the earlier ice-flood. In no part of the Sierra Nevada have these facts been ascertained with more precision than in the Yosemite region and the High Sierra immediately above it. Thus it is now definitely known that the later ice-flood invaded the Yosemite Valley only as far as the Bridalveil Meadows, whereas the earlier ice-flood advanced eleven miles farther down the Merced Canyon, coming to a halt a short distance beyond El Portal.

It will be clear from this that there must be from the Bridalveil Meadows upward throughout the Yosemite region and adjoining the High Sierra not one but two "ice-lines," each marking the culmination of an ice-flood. The pursuit of these two ice-lines up towards the crest of the range was, indeed, for the better part of two seasons the writer's most engrossing occupation. He traced them in detail and mapped them along the length of the Yosemite, up through the Little Yosemite and the upper Merced Basin and all its tributary canyons, and also up through Tenaya Canyon and the great Tuolumne Basin and its tributary canyons. The result, it may be said, was to him, as glacialist, a genuine surprise. The two ice-lines, which in the lower Yosemite lie several thousand feet apart in altitude, were found to approach each other as they ascend the range and ultimately to coalesce at its crest. One might reasonably have expected the extensive and deep ice-fields and glaciers of the earlier epoch to have come from a Sierra crest completely domed over with smoothly sloping, unbroken snow-fields, and the relatively modest ice-stream of the later epoch to have flowed forth from cirques filled only to moderate depth, and partitioned from one another by bare rock crests and "arêtes" rising high above the ice; but, curiously, it appears that the snow conditions along the Sierra crest were substantially the same in both epochs. *The snows that fed the vast glaciers of the earlier epoch filled the summit cirques to no greater depth than did the snows that formed the smaller glaciers of the later epoch.* The significance of this remarkable coincidence need not be here discussed—it would lead too far afield; suffice it for our purpose that the fact has been established.

A few figures will help to give more definiteness to one's conception of the relation of the two ice-lines. The later Yosemite Glacier ended at the Bridalveil Meadows at an altitude of 3900 feet, but the lateral moraines left by the earlier ice-stream on either side of the Yosemite chasm lie 2700 feet above this spot. At the head of the valley the later glacier attained a depth of about 1500 feet, but the lateral moraines of the earlier glacier still lie 2400 feet higher. Within the next few miles the two ice-lines converge with remarkable rapidity. In the Little Yosemite, for instance, they are only 600 feet apart. There the later ice rose within 100 feet of the top of Moraine Dome, but the earlier ice passed over it with a depth of over 500 feet. Opposite Lake Merced the difference in altitude between the two ice-lines dwindles to 400 feet, and thence upward, to the ultimate source of the glacier under Mount Lyell, the difference steadily decreases until it becomes a vanishing quantity.

Following the ice-lines up through Tenaya Canyon, they are found to be 2100 feet apart in altitude opposite Half Dome. That rock monument was engulfed by the earlier ice up to within 700 feet of its summit, but even the foot of its great cliff rose 800 feet above the surface of the later glacier. At the head of Tenaya Canyon the earlier ice rose only 900 feet higher than the later ice, and still farther up, on the divide between the Tenaya and Tuolumne basins, the two ice-lines are only 400 feet apart. In the great upper Tuolumne Basin, which held an ice-field embracing 140 square miles, the earlier and later ice-floods differed only 200 feet in level, as is to be inferred from the two ice-lines on Ragged Peak. And on the Cathedral Range, which was in large measure the generator of this immense ice-field, being the great hedge behind which the wind-blown snows accumulated, the difference was least of all. From Cathedral Peak eastward to Mount Lyell it lessened by degrees until at length it became insignificant.

The figures are but very few out of many scores determined by the writer on both ice-lines. Indeed, the total number of determinations made was large enough to enable him to construct a contour map of each ice surface. These contour maps, he is happy to say, have furnished excellent proof of the mutual concordance and consistency of the data.

The group of pinnacled mountains, it will be clear from the foregoing, stands in a region where the two ice-floods reached substantially the same height. Most of the work of paring away the sides of the pinnacles and crests was done by the earlier ice-flood, which was the one of greater duration, but the later ice-flood undoubtedly did much to accentuate the effect produced by the first. It is a significant fact that farther down on the Sierra flank, where the ice-lines diverge widely in altitude, and where the fluctuations in level of each of the floods no doubt were of considerable amplitude, no attenuated pinnacles or crests rising abruptly from ice-rounded mountains are to be found.

In Greenland, which is one of the few parts of the earth even now under the dominion of the ice, an Eskimo word is commonly used to designate those barren rocky summits that protrude here and there above the rapidly descending glaciers forming the fringes of the vast and otherwise continual glacial mantle. That word is *nunatak*. Physiographers throughout the world have adopted it as a technical term for rocky summits rising above surrounding ice-sheets and glaciers. The pinnacles and crests of the Cathedral Range might, therefore, be referred to as *former nunataks*. But the appropriateness and desirability of so styling them are, in the writer's opinion, open to question.

For one thing, it must be borne in mind that the pinnacles and crest were not the only summits of the Cathedral Range, nor of the entire High Sierra, that remained uncovered by the ice. There were many larger and more massive summits of varying shapes and designs, and even occasional plateau-like tracts. Only half a mile to the southwest of Unicorn Peak, for instance, stands a massive peak of blunted, pyramidal form (still unnamed, although higher than Unicorn) that rose several hundred feet above the ice. Parsons Peak and the broad-topped mountain (still unnamed) northeast of Vogelsang Pass are examples of elevated plateaus that remained emergent. Surely no one would think of placing these in the same class with the attenuated crest of Unicorn Peak, the triangular teeth of Echo Peak, or the ethereal spires of the Cathedral. "Former nunatak" might do in a generic and vague sense for all of them, but there is clearly need of a distinctive term for the more fragile, evanescent forms. What is more, there is need, it seems to the writer, of a term from the Sierra Nevada itself, if possible from the locality where the type is found in its purest form.

Now, as a matter of fact, neither Unicorn, Echo, nor Cathedral represents a "pure type" of mountain sculpture. In each the paring effect of the ice is somewhat obscured or even outweighed by other influences, either by the headward gnawing of local cirque glaciers or by peculiarities of the structure of the rock. When closely analyzed each is found to present a rather complex case. But fortunately there are in the same neighborhood three other peaks or crests each of which might well be taken as a type example.

The first of these is that narrow, linear, bladelike crest southwest of the Cathedral Pass and overlooking Long Meadow, which has been aptly named Columbia's Finger. On the topographic map the name is misplaced, and as a consequence there has arisen some confusion as to the identity of the feature to which it is supposed to refer. The writer himself is willing to admit some uncertainty on his own part, but, if form be the main criterion—and it certainly should be in a case of this sort—then the name surely belongs to the crest just mentioned. For that crest terminates southward in a tall, columnar rock pinnacle that seems to point heavenward like a slender, tapering finger. It is especially impressive when viewed endwise, from the direction of Long Meadow, and doubtless it was named by someone who traveled through that flat on his way to Soda Springs. The case is parallel to that of Unicorn Peak, which was named unquestionably by someone in the Tuolumne Meadows, and whose crest does not resemble a pointing horn except when viewed endwise, from one particular direction.

The second crest in question rises a scant mile to the north of Columbia's Finger, and is of exactly the same narrow, linear type. It even duplicates the latter's terminal pinnacle, but only in what, by contrast, might be called a "stubby thumb." More perfectly modeled even than Columbia's Finger, this crest eloquently tells its story—one wonders that it should still be without a name.

The third crest is a much more imposing feature than either of the foregoing. Rising abruptly from a long-drawn ridge as even-topped as the roof of a house, about a mile south of the Unicorn, it attracts the eye at once by its wonderful symmetry and the supreme boldness of its design. Seen endwise it seems but a narrow blade, springing almost without transition from the broad mountain under it. From certain directions it is suggestive of the upper half of an ornamental "fleur-de-lis," but from most view points it resembles nothing so much as a splendidly sculptured, gigantic cockscomb. Indeed, it stands planted upon the ice-smoothed ridge as a cockscomb surmounts the proud head of a cock. . . .

The writer does not claim to be a connoisseur in poultry; nevertheless, he believes that the likeness to a lobate cockscomb is fairly close—as close as one might expect to find in a piece of mountain sculpture. . . .

There is a special advantage in the adoption of the name that is worth pointing out. Not only is the appellation Cockscomb apt because it is descriptive of the form of this crest, but it would also be an extremely convenient generic term for the designation of all similarly sculptured crests—of all crests such as those previously described, which owe their attentuated linear forms to the paring action of the ice that split upon them and passed on either side without overwhelming them. It would admirably serve the physiographer's needs as standing for the type of mountain sculpture of which the beautiful crest under discussion is the finest example known.

Cockscomb Crest, from "Cockscomb Crest" by Francois Matthes. *Sierra Club Bulletin,* January, 1920. Reprinted by permission of The Sierra Club.

Kenneth Rexroth

Sacco and Vanzetti[1]

If, as many students of natural history would agree, the business of the naturalist is to open our eyes to the obvious, then surely one does not need to be a scientist in order to be a naturalist. No less than a geologist or a botanist, a poet with the patience, the intelligence, and the clear eye of a Kenneth Rexroth can help us to see and make sense of the baffling world around us.

Rexroth is widely regarded as one of the major American poets of the 20th Century. Before his death in 1982, he won acclaim not only as a poet but as a writer, a painter, and a translator of poetry in five languages as well. Rexroth's poetry is notable for a directness and clarity that make even his most difficult poems, in the words of one critic, "seem as natural as campfire talk." The comparison is apt, for Rexroth hiked and climbed extensively in the Sierra, and spent many an evening beside a campfire pondering his wild surroundings. As a result, even a casual perusal of his poetry is sure to turn up a line or two that recalls the Sierra:

*Coming back over the col between
Isosceles Mountain and North Palisade,
I stop at the summit and look back
At the storm gathering over the white peaks
Of the Whitney group and the colored
Kaweahs . . .*

— "Strength Through Joy"

At noon a flock of humming birds passed south,
Whirling in the wind up over the saddle between
Ritter and Banner . . .

      — *"Toward an Organic Philosophy"*

In "Blues" and "Climbing Milestone Mountain, August 22, 1937," the
natural surroundings of the Sierra led Rexroth to remember Nicola Sacco and
Bartolomeo Vanzetti, the Boston workingmen executed in 1927 for what many,
including Rexroth, believe to have been their political beliefs.

BLUES

The tops of the higher peaks
Of the Sierra Nevada
Of California are
Drenched in the perfume of
A flower which grows only there—
The blue *Polemonium*
Confertum eximium,
Soft, profound blue, like the eyes
Of impregnable innocence;
The perfume is heavy and
Clings thickly to the granite
Peaks, even in violent wind;
The leaves are clustered,
Fine, dull green, sticky, and musky.
I imagine that the scent
Of the body of Artemis
That put Endymion to sleep
Was like this and her eyes had the
Same inscrutable color.
Lawrence was lit into death
By the blue gentians of Kore.
Vanzetti had in his cell
A bowl of tall blue flowers
From a New England garden.
I hope that when I need it
My mind can always call back
This flower to its hidden senses.

CLIMBING MILESTONE MOUNTAIN,
AUGUST 22, 1937

For a month now, wandering over the Sierras,
A poem had been gathering in my mind,
Details of significance and rhythm,
The way poems do, but still lacking a focus.
Last night I remembered the date and it all
Began to grow together and take on purpose.
    We sat up late while Deneb moved over the zenith
And I told Marie all about Boston, how it looked
That last terrible week, how hundreds stood weeping
Impotent in the streets that last midnight.
I told her how those hours changed the lives of thousands,
How America was forever a different place
Afterwards for many.
              In the morning
We swam in the cold transparent lake, the blue
Damsel flies on all the reeds like millions
Of narrow metallic flowers, and I thought
Of you behind the grille in Dedham, Vanzetti,
Saying, "Who would ever have thought we would make this
    history?"
Crossing the brilliant mile-square meadow
Illuminated with asters and cyclamen,
The pollen of the lodgepole pines drifting
With the shifting wind over it and the blue
And sulphur butterflies drifting with the wind,
I saw you in the sour prison light, saying,
"Goodbye comrade."
             In the basin under the crest
Where the pines end and the Sierra primrose begins,
A party of lawyers was shooting at a whiskey bottle.
The bottle stayed on its rock, nobody could hit it.
Looking back over the peaks and canyons from the last lake,
The pattern of human beings seemed simpler
Than the diagonals of water and stone.
Climbing the chute, up the melting snow and broken rock,
I remembered what you said about Sacco,

How it slipped your mind and you demanded it be read
    into the record.
Traversing below the ragged arête,
One cheek pressed against the rock
The wind slapping the other,
I saw you both marching in an army
You with the red and black flag, Sacco with the rattlesnake
    banner.
I kicked steps up the last snow bank and came
To the indescribably blue and fragrant
Polemonium and the dead sky and the sterile
Crystalline granite and final monolith of the summit.
These are the things that will last a long time, Vanzetti,
I am glad that once on your day I have stood among them.
Some day mountains will be named after you and Sacco.
They will be here and your name with them,
"When these days are but a dim remembering of the time
When man was wolf to man."
I think men will be remembering you a long time
Standing on the mountains
Many men, a long time, comrade.

Gary Snyder

The Back Country[1]

Pulitzer Prize winner Gary Snyder is that rare poet who has found acceptance among serious critics and unsophisticated readers alike. As in the poetry of Kenneth Rexroth, one of Snyder's major influences, nature plays an important role in many of Snyder's poems. In the primitive world of mountains and rivers, he has discovered an idiom for illustrating one of his principal themes, the integrity of all nature.

Some of Snyder's poetry is based on his experiences as a trail builder in the Sierra for the U.S. Forest Service. In "Bubbs Creek Haircut" he crosses Forester Pass to "the realm of fallen rock"—

> *a deva world of sorts—it's high*
> *   it is a view that few men see, a point*
> *   bare sunlight*
> *   on the spaces*
> *empty sky*
> *   moulding to fit the shape of what ice left*
> *of fire-thrust, or of tilted, twisted, faulted*
> *   cast-out from this lava belly globe.*

The following two poems are from Snyder's collection, **The Back Country.** *The setting is the northern reaches of Yosemite National Park along Piute Creek.*

---

[1]The Back Country, Gary Snyder, *The Back Country.* Copyright © 1968 by Gary Snyder. Reprinted by permission of New Directions Publishing Corporation.

A WALK

Sunday the only day we don't work:
Mules farting around the meadow,
                    Murphy fishing,
The tent flaps in the warm
Early sun: I've eaten breakfast and I'll
                    take a walk
To Benson Lake. Packed a lunch,
Goodby. Hopping on creekbed boulders
Up the rock throat three miles
                    Piute Creek—
In steep gorge glacier-slick rattlesnake country
Jump, land by a pool, trout skitter,
The clear sky. Deer tracks.
Bad place by a falls, boulders big as houses,
Lunch tied to belt,
I stemmed up a crack and almost fell
But rolled out safe on a ledge
                    and ambled on.
Quail chicks freeze underfoot, color of stone
Then run cheep! away, hen quail fussing.
Craggy west end of Benson Lake—after edging
Past dark creek pools on a long white slope—
Lookt down in the ice-black lake
                    lined with cliff
From far above: deep shimmering trout.
A lone duck in a gunsightpass
                    steep side hill
Through slide-aspen and talus, to the east end,
Down to grass, wading a wide smooth stream
Into camp. At last.
                    By the rusty three-year-
Ago left-behind cookstove
Of the old trail crew,
Stoppt and swam and ate my lunch.

TRAIL CREW CAMP AT BEAR VALLEY, 9000 FEET.
NORTHERN SIERRA—WHITE BONE AND THREADS
OF SNOWMELT WATER

Cut branches back for a day—
trail a thin line through willow
      up buckbrush meadows,
      creekbed for twenty yards
   winding in boulders
     zigzags the hill
into timber, white pine.

gooseberry bush on the turns.
hooves clang on the riprap
     dust, brush, branches.
   a stone
  cairn at the pass—
strippt mountains hundreds of miles.

sundown went back
     the clean switchbacks to camp.
bell on the gelding,
stew in the cook tent,
black coffee in a big tin can.

THE "INDIAN TRAIL" UP THE MOUNTAIN.

James M. Hutchings and two companions on the first attempt to climb Half Dome, 1869

SECTION V:
THE MOUNTAINEERS

Perhaps no other sport with the possible exception of sailing boasts a literature that is as rich and as extensive as the literature of mountaineering. The principal adversary of both sailors and mountaineers is nature, an opponent far more likely to inspire thoughtful writing than a team of players wearing helmets and numbers on their backs. The object of the game that sailors and mountaineers play involves neither a ball, a bat nor a net; indeed, the object is so intriguing and yet so baffling—and therefore so conducive to ruminating upon—that although many have tried, no one has yet been able to put into words precisely what it is. Both sports involve discovery, so, like explorers, many climbers and sailors can scarcely wait to get home so that they can sit down and write about their adventures. Nowhere is this more evident than among the mountaineers of the Sierra Nevada, as a glance at the six-foot shelf of Sierra Club *Bulletins* dating back to 1893 will attest. Open any volume and you'll discover a treasure trove of climbing tales, some remarkable and worth reading, most merely ordinary but still important as historical documents. It's doubtful that there is a mountain in the entire Sierra that has not served as the subject of a thorough report in the *Bulletin* or some other mountaineering journal.

Publishing is not for everyone, of course, and most mountaineers are content simply to record their adventures in a diary or notebook. In failing to publicize their climbs, they continue a tradition begun by the Indians of the Sierra, who left no records whatever of the mountains they ascended. We can be sure, however, from relics found near the summits of many Sierra peaks, that whites were not the first Californians to climb in the range.

Moreover, if we can believe the legend of the Lost Arrow recorded in Section I, even the techniques of the modern rock climber were not unknown to the Indians. Tee-hee-neh's descent to the base of the Lost Arrow covered a distance of more than 200 feet, an entirely respectable rappel by today's standards. (Few climbers today, however, would be willing to trade their perlon ropes for Tee-hee-neh's tamarack saplings.)

Documented climbing in the Sierra began when John C. Frémont and Charles Preuss ascended Red Lake Peak near Carson Pass. Frémont mentions the ascent in his journal for February 14, 1844.[1] Extensive investigations by Sierra historians Francis P. Farquhar and Vincent P. Gianella have determined that Frémont's was the first account of an identifiable mountain ascent in the Sierra.

The honor of making the first ascent of a major peak in the range (Red Lake Peak is only 10,061 feet in altitude) fell probably to a man named Tom Clark, who in 1860 climbed Mount Tom, the 13,652-foot mountain near Bishop now named after him. Within a decade, three of the finest writers ever to climb in the Sierra— Clarence King, William Brewer, and John Muir—had arrived in the range, and the era of mountaineering writing had begun.

Choosing a representative selection from the huge body of Sierra mountaineering literature is clearly no easy task. What follows is one such selection, chosen not merely to highlight the historically important Sierra climbs, but to reflect the richness, interest and diversity of the literature as well.

---

[1]See "John Charles Frémont: Crossing Carson Pass," Section I.

Dan DeQuille

Snow-shoe Thompson

If being able to survive in and even enjoy mountains under the worst possible conditions is the mark of the true mountaineer, then John A. "Snow-shoe" Thompson may have been the greatest mountaineer in Sierra history. His legend, which was huge at the time of his death in 1876, has not diminished appreciably in the years since. Every winter from 1856 until 1876, Thompson ferried the U.S mails alone across the Sierra from Placerville to Carson Valley. Through twenty winters he was the sole communication link between California and the East Coast. Traveling on skis (called "snow-shoes" in those days), Thompson braved blizzards and freezing cold, averaging 36 miles a day for the 180-mile round trip, despite the burden of a pack that sometimes weighed 100 pounds. The payoff sounds like one concocted by a Hollywood screen writer but apparently it was true: Snow-shoe always brought the mail in on time.

Much of what we know about Thompson derives from an article about him that appeared in Overland Monthly *in October 1886. Author Dan DeQuille, a reporter for the Virginia City* Territorial Enterprise, *interviewed Thompson a few months before he died and collected scores of newspaper articles about him. Why DeQuille waited ten years to publish the story of this legendary character we don't know; perhaps it took him ten years to come to believe the story himself.*

While traveling in the mountains, Snow-shoe Thompson never carried blankets, nor did he even wear an overcoat. The weight and bulk of such articles would have encumbered and discommoded him. Exercise kept him warm while traveling, and when encamped he always built a fire. He carried as little as possible besides the bags containing the mail. During the first year or two after he went into the business, he carried a revolver. Finding, however, that he had no use for such a weapon, and it being of the first importance to travel as light as possible, he presently concluded to leave his pistol at home.

All that he carried in the way of provisions was a small quantity of jerked beef, or dried sausage, and a few crackers or biscuits. He never carried provisions that required to be cooked. The food that he took into the mountains was all of a kind that could be eaten as he ran. For drink he caught up a handful of snow, or lay down for a moment and quaffed the water of some brook or spring. He never took with him brandy, whisky, or liquor of any kind. He was a man that seldom tasted liquor.

Snow-shoe never stopped for storms. He always set out on the day appointed, without regard to the weather, and he traveled by nights as well as in the daytime. He pursued no regular path—in a trackless waste of snow there was no path to follow—but kept to a general route or course. By day he was guided by the trees and rocks, and by night looked to the stars, as does a mariner to his compass . . . .

Snow-shoe's night camps—whenever the night was such as prevented him from pursuing his journey, or when it was necessary for him to obtain sleep—were generally made wherever he happened to be at the moment. He did not push forward to reach particular points, as springs or brooks. He was always able to substitute snow for water, without feeling any bad effect. He always tried, however, to find the stump of a dead pine, at which to make his camp. After setting fire to the dry stump, he collected a quantity of fir or spruce boughs, with which he constructed a sort of rude couch or platform on the snow. Stretched upon his bed of boughs, with his feet to his fire, and his head resting upon one of Uncle Sam's mail bags, he slept as soundly as if occupying the best bed ever made; though, perhaps, beneath his couch there was a depth of from ten to thirty feet of snow . . . .

During his twenty winters in the Sierra, Snow-shoe Thompson had plenty of occasion to save lost souls, who, unlike himself, were merely human. Once such was James Sisson, who in December 1856 lay twelve days in a cabin in Lake Valley, his feet frozen, his life slowly ebbing away.

There was some flour in the cabin, and on this Sisson had subsisted. He was in the cabin four days without a fire. During this time he ate the flour raw, just as it came from the sack. On the fifth day, while rummaging about the shanty, he had the good fortune to find some matches. These were where no one would have thought of looking for matches, as they were scattered about under some hay that lay on the floor.

After finding the matches, Sisson made a fire and thawed out his boots, when he was able to get them off. For four days he had lain in the cabin with his boots frozen to his feet. When found by Mr. Thompson eight days later, Sisson's legs were purple to the knees. Sisson was confident from the appearance of his legs that mortification had set in. He knew that unless his legs were amputated, he must soon die. As he could expect no assistance from the outside world, he had concluded to himself undertake to perform the required operation. There was an ax in the cabin, and with this he had determined to cut off his frozen legs. But for the opportune arrival of Thompson, Sisson would the next day have attempted to disjoint his legs at the knees; for that was the day he had fixed upon for undertaking the operation.

At the time he found Sisson, Thompson was on his way from Placerville to Carson Valley. It was in the night, and on coming to the log house—which was occupied in the summer as a trading post— Thompson halted for a moment, and was knocking the snow off his shoes by striking them against the cabin, when he heard some one cry out. Going inside, he found Sisson situated as related above. A considerable amount of provision had been left in the cabin in the fall, but all except the flour had been stolen by the Indians.

Thompson chopped a supply of wood for the unfortunate man, and making him as comfortable as was possible with the means at hand, left for Genoa to obtain assistance. While Thompson was cutting the wood, Sisson called out to him and begged him not to dull the ax—the place being full of rocks—as he might yet want it for the purpose of taking off his legs. Sisson was firmly of the opinion that when Thompson left him he would never see him again. He thought Thompson would never be able to get down out of the mountains, and was of the opinion that in case he did succeed in reaching the valley, he would not attempt to return to the cabin.

Mr. Thompson told Sisson he would surely return and take him away, and advised him not to think of attempting to amputate his legs, as on cutting the arteries he would bleed to death. But Sisson had thought of that. He intended to make a sort of compress or tourniquet of some pieces of balingrope, which he would twist round his legs with a stick, in such a way that a bit of rock would be pressed upon the arteries. Then with fire-brands he would sear the ends of the arteries, and the raw flesh of the stumps of his legs. Sisson's mind was so much occupied with his plans for the amputation of his legs, that Thompson was almost afraid to leave the ax where he could get hold of it: he did so only upon receiving from Sisson a solemn promise that he would wait three days before attempting to use it on his knees.

On leaving the cabin, Thompson traveled all night, and early next morning arrived at Genoa. He there raised a party of six men—W. B. Wade, Harris, Jacobs, and other old settlers—to return with him and bring Sisson down to the valley. By Thompson's advice the party carried with them a few tools for use in making a sled. Snow-shoes were also hastily constructed for the men composing the relief party. As none of these men had ever done much traveling on show-shoes, they furnished Thompson not a little amusement during the journey, by their mishaps and involuntary antics.

After much hard work, the party arrived at the lone cabin late in the evening, to the great joy of Sisson, who at sight of so many men felt that he was saved.

That night they constructed a hand-sled on which to carry the frozen man down to Carson Valley. In the morning they awoke to find that nearly two feet of snow had fallen; there was a depth of eight feet before. The new snow made it very hard to get along with the hand-sled. Under Sisson's weight it plowed deeply along, and at times was buried almost out of sight.

The first day the party got no farther than to Hope Valley, where they encamped. Sisson was made as comfortable as possible on a bed of boughs. As they had expected to reach Genoa in one day, they had taken along with them no blanket, and but few other comforts, for the frozen man.

The second day they reached Genoa, and at once procured the medical assistance which Sisson's case so urgently demanded. The doctors found that it would be necessary to amputate both of Sisson's feet. Before the operation could be performed, however, the physician said he must have some chloroform. As Show-shoe Thompson never did things by halves, he at once set out, crossed the Sierra and traveled all the way to Sacramento, in order to get the required drug.

Finally the long-delayed operation was performed. Sisson survived it, and at last accounts, was living somewhere in the Atlantic States.

According to DeQuille, when Thompson was overtaken by a storm before he could make camp, he simply stood on a rock dancing a "midnight jig" to keep himself warm. In the melodramatic conclusion to his article, DeQuille makes reference to this frenetic—and exceedingly wise—practice.

As an explorer in Arctic regions he would have achieved world-wide fame. Less courage than he each winter displayed amid the mountains, has secured for hundreds the hero's crown. To ordinary men there is something terrible in the wild winter storms that often sweep through the Sierras; but the louder the howlings of the gale rose, the higher rose the courage of Show-shoe Thompson. He did not fear to beard the Storm King in his own mountain fastnesses and strongholds. Within his breast lived and burned the spirit of the old Vikings. It was this inherited spirit of his daring ancestors, that impelled him to embark in difficult and dangerous enterprises—this spirit that incited him to defy even the wildest rage of the elements. In the turmoil of the most fearful tempests that ever beat against the granite walls of the High Sierras he was undismayed. In the midst of the midnight hurricane, he danced on the rocks as though himself one of the genii of the storm.

Show-shoe Thompson, from "Show-shoe Thompson" by Dan DeQuille. *Overland Monthly,* Ocober, 1886.

Clarence King

Across the Great Divide

When Clarence King and Dick Cotter bade goodbye to William Brewer and James Gardner on a shoulder of Mount Brewer on July 4, 1864[1] one of the great adventures in Sierra history was underway. On the far side of the towering Kings-Kern Divide, the four men, members of the California State Geological Survey, had spotted a peak that they correctly guessed to be the highest in the continental United States. It lay some 15 miles away, beyond a forbidding rock-and-ice wilderness that had never been seen before, let alone traversed. With six day's provisions in their packs, King and Cotter were setting out for the virgin peak—later named Mount Whitney—to try to climb it.

Cotter had been hired as a packer for the survey. King was the self-appointed dean of American mountaineering, and truly one of the most remarkable men of the 19th Century. Fresh out of Yale he had crossed the continent in search of adventure and had signed on with the survey. Within a few years his exciting— and often highly sensationalized—articles about his climbs in the Sierra were appearing regularly in the **Atlantic Monthly.** *He was lionized in the East and praised by no less than Henry Adams as "the most many-sided genius of his day." When the U.S. Geological Survey was organized in 1879, King was appointed its first director.*

King's story of his attempt to reach the highest point in the land is taken from his book, **Mountaineering in the Sierra Nevada,** *one of the great classics of Sierra literature.*

I did not wonder that Brewer and Hoffman pronounced our under-taking impossible; but when I looked at Cotter there was such complete bravery in his eye that I asked him if he was ready to start. His old answer, "Why not?" left the initiative with me; so I told Professor

---

[1]See "William Brewer: A Scientist in the Sierra," Section I.

Brewer that we would bid him good by. Our friends helped us on with our packs in silence, and as we shook hands there was not a dry eye in the party. Before he let go of my hand Professor Brewer asked me for my plan, and I had to own that I had but one, which was to reach the highest peak in the range.

After looking in every direction I was obliged to confess that I saw as yet no practicable way. We bade them a "good by," receiving their "God bless you" in return, and started southward along the range to look for some possible cliff to descend. Brewer, Gardner, and Hoffman turned north to push upward to the summit of Mount Brewer, and complete their observations. We saw them whenever we halted, until at last, on the very summit, their microscopic forms were for the last time discernible. With very great difficulty we climbed a peak which surmounted our wall just to the south of the pass, and, looking over the eastern brink, found that the precipice was still sheer and unbroken. In one place, where the snow lay against it to the very top, we went to its edge and contemplated the slide. About three thousand feet of unbroken white, at a fearfully steep angle, lay below us. We threw a stone over and watched it bound until it was lost in the distance; after fearful leaps we could only detect it by the flashings of snow where it struck, and as these were, in some instances, three hundred feet apart, we decided not to launch our own valuable bodies, and the still more precious barometer, after it.

There seemed but one possible way to reach our goal; that was to make our way along the summit of the cross ridge which projected between the two ranges. This divide sprang out from our Mount Brewer wall, about four miles to the south of us. To reach it we must climb up and down over the indented edge of the Mount Brewer. In attempting to do this we had a rather lively time scaling a sharp granite needle, where we found our course completely stopped by precipices four and five hundred feet in height. Ahead of us the summit continued to be broken into fantastic pinnacles, leaving us no hope of making our way along it; so we sought the most broken part of the eastern descent, and began to climb down. The heavy knapsacks, beside wearing our shoulders gradually into a black-and-blue state, overbalanced us terribly, and kept us in constant danger of pitching headlong. At last, taking them off, Cotter climbed down until he had found a resting-place upon a cleft of rock, then I lowered them to him with our lasso, afterwards descending cautiously to his side, taking my turn in pioneering downward, receiving the freight of knapsacks by lasso as before. In this manner we consumed more than half the afternoon in descending a thousand feet of broken, precipitous slope; and it was almost sunset when we found ourselves upon the fields of level snow which lay white and thick over the whole interior slope of the amphitheatre. The gorge below us seemed utterly impassable. At our backs the Mount Brewer wall either rose in sheer cliffs or in broken, rugged stairway, such as had offered us our descent. From this cruel dilemma the cross divide furnished the only hope, and the sole chance of scaling that was at its junction with the Mount Brewer wall. Toward this point we directed our course, marching wearily over stretches of dense frozen snow, and regions of *débris,* reaching about sunset the last alcove of the amphitheatre, just at the foot of the Mount Brewer wall. It was evidently impossible for us to attempt to climb it that evening, and we looked about the desolate recesses for a sheltered camping-spot. A high granite wall surrounded us upon three sides, recurring to the southward in long elliptical curves; no part of the summit being less than two thousand feet above us, the higher crags not unfrequently reaching three thousand feet. A single field of snow swept around the base of the rock, and covered the whole amphitheatre, except where a few spikes and rounded masses of granite rose through it, and where two frozen lakes, with their blue ice-disks, broke the monotonous surface. Through the white snow-gate of our amphitheatre, as through a frame, we looked eastward upon the summit group; not a tree, not a vestige of vegetation in sight,—sky, snow, and granite the only elements in this wild picture.

After searching for a shelter we at last found a granite crevice near the margin of one of the frozen lakes,—a sort of shelf just large enough for Cotter and me,—where we hastened to make our bed, having first filled the canteen from a small stream that trickled over the ice, knowing that in a few moments the rapid chill would freeze it. We ate our supper of cold venison and bread, and whittled from the sides of the wooden barometer-case shavings enough to warm water for a cup of miserably tepid tea, and then, packing our provisions and instruments away at the head of the shelf, rolled ourselves in our blankets and lay down to enjoy the view. . . .

A sudden chill enveloped us. Stars in a moment crowded through the dark heaven, flashing with a frosty splendor. The snow congealed, the brooks ceased to flow, and, under the powerful sudden leverage of frost, immense blocks were dislodged all along the mountain summits and came thundering down the slopes, booming upon the ice, dashing wildly upon rocks. Under the lee of our shelf we felt quite safe, but neither Cotter nor I could help being startled, and jumping just a little, as these missiles, weighing often many tons, struck the ledge over our heads and whizzed down the gorge, their stroke resounding fainter and fainter, until at last only a confused echo reached us.

The thermometer at nine o'clock marked twenty degrees above zero. We set the "minimum" and rolled ourselves together for the night. The longer I lay the less I liked that shelf of granite; it grew hard in time, and cold also, my bones seeming to approach actual contact with the chilled rock; moreover, I found that even so vigorous a circulation as mine was not enough to warm up the ledge to anything like a comfortable temperature. A single thickness of blanket is a better mattress than none, but the larger crystals of orthoclase, protruding plentifully, punched my back and caused me to revolve on a horizontal axis with precision and frequency. How I loved Cotter! how I hugged him and got warm, while our backs gradually petrified, till we whirled over and thawed them out together! The slant of that bed was diagonal and excessive; down it we slid till the ice chilled us awake, and we crawled back and chocked ourselves up with bits of granite inserted under my ribs and shoulders. In this pleasant position we got dozing again, and there stole over me a most comfortable ease. The granite softened perceptibly. I was delightfully warm and sank into an industrious slumber which lasted with great soundness till four, when we rose and ate our breakfast of frozen venison. . . .

Picking up where they had left off, they ascended a long steep snowfield with the aid of steps cut with Cotter's bowie knife. At last they reached a narrow ledge leading diagonally toward the top of a cliff.

There was no foothold above us. Looking down over the course we had come, it seemed, and I really believe it was, an impossible descent; for one can climb upward with safety where he cannot downward. To turn back was to give up in defeat; and we sat at least half an hour, suggesting all possible routes to the summit, accepting none, and feeling disheartened. About thirty feet directly over our heads was another shelf, which, if we could reach, seemed to offer at least a temporary way upward. On its edge were two or three spikes of granite; whether firmly connected with the cliff, or merely blocks of *débris,* we could not tell from below. I said to Cotter, I thought of but one possible plan: it was to lasso one of these blocks, and to climb, sailor-fashion, hand over hand, up the rope. In the lasso I had perfect confidence, for I had seen more than one Spanish bull throw his whole weight against it without parting a strand. The shelf was so narrow that throwing the coil of rope was a very difficult undertaking. I tried three times, and Cotter spent five minutes vainly whirling the loop up at the granite spikes. At last I made a lucky throw, and it tightened upon one of the smaller protuberances. I drew the noose close, and very gradually threw my hundred and fifty pounds upon the rope; then Cotter joined me, and, for a moment, we both hung our united weight upon it. Whether the rock moved slightly or whether the lasso stretched a little we were unable to decide; but the trial must be made, and I began to climb slowly. The smooth precipice-face against which my body swung offered no foothold, and the whole climb had therefore to be done by the arms, an effort requiring all one's determination. When about half-way up I was obliged to rest, and, curling my feet in the rope, managed to relieve my arms for a moment. In this position I could not resist the fascinating temptation of a survey downward.

Straight down, nearly a thousand feet below, at the foot of the rocks, began the snow, whose steep, roof-like slope, exaggerated into an almost vertical angle, curved down in a long white field, broken far away by rocks and polished, round lakes of ice.

Cotter looked up cheerfully and asked how I was making it; to which I answered that I had plenty of wind left. At that moment, when hanging between heaven and earth, it was a deep satisfaction to look down at the wild gulf of desolation beneath, and up to unknown dangers ahead, and feel my nerves cool and unshaken.

A few pulls hand over hand brought me to the edge of the shelf, when, throwing an arm around the granite spike, I swung my body upon the shelf and lay down to rest, shouting to Cotter that I was all right, and that the prospects upward were capital. After a few moments' breathing I looked over the brink and directed my comrade to tie the barometer to the lower end of the lasso, which he did, and that precious instrument was hoisted to my station, and the lasso sent down twice for knapsacks, after which Cotter came up the rope in his very muscular way without once stopping to rest. We took our loads in our hands, swinging the barometer over my shoulder, and climbed up a shelf which led in a zigzag direction upward and to the south, bringing us out at last upon the thin blade of a ridge which connected a short distance above with the summit. It was formed of huge blocks, shattered, and ready, at a touch, to fall.

So narrow and sharp was the upper slope, that we dared not walk, but got astride, and worked slowly along with our hands, pushing the knapsacks in advance, now and then holding our breath when loose masses rocked under our weight. . . .

King and Cotter had reached the crest of the Kings-Kern Divide. To their dismay, a glance ahead revealed that the slope they now had to descend was even steeper than the one they had just come up. As for the ridge itself, it was terrifyingly narrow and unstable. Uncertain of how to proceed, the two men exercised the time-honored choice of mountaineers in difficult situations, which is to sit down and eat lunch.

I suggested that by lowering ourselves on the rope we might climb from crevice to crevice; but we saw no shelf large enough for ourselves and the knapsacks too. However, we were not going to give it up without a trial; and I made the rope fast round my breast, and, looping the noose over a firm point of rock, let myself slide gradually down to a notch forty feet below. There was only room beside me for Cotter, so I made him send down the knapsacks first. I then tied these together by the straps with my silk handkerchiefs, and hung them off as far to the left as I could reach without losing my balance, looping the handkerchiefs over a point of rock. Cotter then slid down the rope, and, with considerable difficulty, we whipped the noose off its resting-place above, and cut off our connection with the upper world.

"We're in for it now, King," remarked my comrade, as he looked aloft, and then down; but our blood was up, and danger added only an exhilarating thrill to the nerves.

The shelf was hardly more than two feet wide, and the granite so smooth that we could find no place to fasten the lasso for the next descent; so I determined to try the climb with only as little aid as possible. Tying it round my breast again, I gave the other end into Cotter's hands, and he, bracing his back against the cliff, found for himself as firm a foothold as he could, and promised to give me all the help in his power. I made up my mind to bear no weight unless it was absolutely necessary; and for the first ten feet I found cracks and protuberances enough to support me, making every square inch of surface do friction duty, and hugging myself against the rocks as tightly as I could. When within about eight feet of the next shelf, I twisted myself round upon the face, hanging by two rough blocks of protruding feldspar, and looked vainly for some further hand-hold; but the rock, beside being perfectly smooth, overhung slightly, and my legs dangled in the air. I saw that the next cleft was over three feet broad, and I thought, possibly, I might, by a quick slide, reach it in safety without endangering Cotter. I shouted to him to be very careful and let go in case I fell, loosened my hold upon the rope, and slid quickly down. My shoulder struck against the rock and threw me out of balance; for an instant I reeled over upon the verge, in danger of falling, but, in the excitement, I thrust out my hand and seized a small alpine gooseberry-bush, the first piece of vegetation we had seen. Its roots were so firmly fixed in the crevice that it held my weight and saved me.

I could no longer see Cotter, but I talked to him, and heard the two knapsacks come bumping along till they slid over the eaves above me, and swung down to my station, when I seized the lasso's end and braced myself as well as possible, intending, if he slipped, to haul in slack and help him as best I might. As he came slowly down from crack to crack, I heard his hobnailed shoes grating on the granite; presently they appeared dangling from the eaves above my head. I had gathered in the rope until it was taut, and then hurriedly told him to drop. He hesitated a moment, and let go. Before he struck the rock I had him by the shoulder, and whirled him down upon his side, thus preventing his rolling overboard, which friendly action he took quite coolly. . . .

In this manner they painstakingly descended the cliff. After three hours they finally reached a frozen lake at the base of the divide. Now on easy terrain, King and Cotter walked delightedly through an alpine meadow abounding in grass and wildflowers. It was a relief, noted King, "to find ourselves again in the region of life." They camped beside a stream near timberline, then arose at 3 a.m. to begin the struggle anew.

We climbed alternately up smooth faces of granite, clinging simply by the cracks and protruding crystals of feldspar, and then hewed steps up fearfully steep slopes of ice, zigzagging to the right and left to avoid the flying boulders. When midway up this slope we reached a place where the granite rose in perfectly smooth bluffs on either side of a gorge,—a narrow cut, or walled way, leading up to the flat summit of the cliff. This we scaled by cutting ice steps, only to find ourselves fronted again by a still higher wall. Ice sloped from its front at too steep an angle for us to follow, but had melted in contact with it, leaving a space three feet wide between the ice and the rock. We entered this crevice and climbed along its bottom, with a wall of rock rising a hundred feet above us on one side, and a thirty-foot face of ice on the other, through which light of an intense cobalt-blue penetrated.

Reaching the upper end, we had to cut our footsteps upon the ice again, and, having braced our backs against the granite, climb up to the surface. We were now in a dangerous position: to fall into the crevice upon one side was to be wedged to death between rock and ice; to make a slip was to be shot down five hundred feet, and then hurled over the brink of a precipice. In the friendly seat which this wedge gave me, I stopped to take wet and dry observations with the thermometer,—this being an absolute preventive of a scare,—and to enjoy the view.

The wall of our mountain sank abruptly to the left, opening for the first time an outlook to the eastward. Deep—it seemed almost vertically—beneath us we could see the blue water of Owen's Lake, ten thousand feet down. The summit peaks to the north were piled in titanic confusion, their ridges overhanging the eastern slope with terrible abruptness. Clustered upon the shelves and plateaus below were several frozen lakes, and in all directions swept magnificent fields of snow. The summit was now not over five hundred feet distant, and we started on again with the exhilarating hope of success. But if Nature had intended to secure the summit from all assailants, she could not have planned her defences better; for the smooth granite wall which rose above the snow-slope continued, apparently, quite round the peak, and we looked in great anxiety to see if there was not one place where it might be climbed. It was all blank except in one place; quite near us the snow bridged across the crevice, and rose in a long point to the summit of the wall,—a great icicle-column frozen in a niche of the bluff,—its base about ten feet wide, narrowing to two feet at the top. We climbed to the base of this spire of ice, and, with the utmost care, began to cut our stairway. The material was an exceedingly compacted snow, passing into clear ice as it neared the rock. We climbed the first half of it with comparative ease; after that it was almost vertical, and so thin that we did not dare to cut the footsteps deep enough to make them absolutely safe. There was a constant dread lest our ladder should break off, and we be thrown either down the snow-slope or into the bottom of the crevasse. At last, in order to prevent myself from falling over backwards, I was obliged to thrust my hand into the crack between the ice and the wall, and the spire became so narrow that I could do this on both sides; so that the climb was made as upon a tree, cutting mere toe-holes and embracing the whole column of ice in my arms. At last I reached the top, and, with the greatest caution, wormed my body over the brink, and, rolling out upon the smooth surface of the granite,looked over and watched Cotter make his climb. He came steadily up, with no sense of nervousness, until he got to the narrow part of the ice, and here he stopped and looked up with a forlorn face to me; but as he climbed up over the edge the broad smile came back to his face, and he asked me if it had occurred to me that we had, by and by, to go down again.

We had now an easy slope to the summit, and hurried up over rocks and ice, reaching the crest at exactly twelve o'clock. I rang my hammer upon the topmost rock; we grasped hands, and I reverently named the grand peak MOUNT TYNDALL.

That King and Cotter were not atop the highest peak in the land was clear to them immediately.

"To our surprise, upon sweeping the horizon with my levell, there appeared two

peaks equal in height with us, and two rising even higher."

Reaching the highest point unfortunately was now out of the question. With supplies running short the two men were forced to return to their camp near Mount Brewer. King's account of the journey back is as thrilling, and undoubtedly as greatly exaggerated, as the story of his climb of Mount Tyndall. There is no slighting his accomplishment, however; despite the false bravado, his round trip with Cotter through this virgin wilderness was clearly an extraordinary achievement.

Later that year King made a second attempt on Mount Whitney. This time he chose a route too difficult to climb and was stopped several hundred feet short of the summit. In 1871 he tried again and once again, incredibly, climbed the wrong mountain.

On his final attempt in 1873, he finally met success—after nine years of trying. Regrettably, all of his efforts failed to secure the prize he had so long sought. Three fishermen from Lone Pine, California—Charley Begole, Johnny Lucas and Al Johnson—made the first ascent of Mount Whitney, the highest peak in the continental United States, on August 18, 1873, beating King to the summit by 32 days.

Across the Great Divide, from *Mountaineering in the Sierra Nevada* by Clarence King. James Osgood & Co., 1872.

Bolton Coit Brown

At Grips With
Mount Clarence King

Clarence King's experience to the contrary, Mount Whitney, the peak that defeated him three times, is in fact an easy mountain to climb. Thousands of hikers make it to the top every summer.

But mountains harder to ascend than Whitney do exist in the Sierra, and as the 19th Century progressed, a few mountaineers began seeking them out. In 1869 John Muir scaled Cathedral Peak, at the time perhaps the most difficult rock climb that had been made in America. Today it is rated class 4, meaning that the average climber is only too happy to tie a rope around his or her waist before beginning the final airy pitch to the summit.

The zenith of 19th Century Sierra mountaineering, however, was achieved by Bolton Coit Brown. Coincidentally, it involved a mountain named after the man who had made difficult climbing a way of life, Clarence King.

Brown was a professor of drawing at Stanford University. During the 1890s he climbed and explored extensively in the southern High Sierra. In July 1895, his sights set on the virgin summit of Mount Clarence King, he took off by himself into Paradise Valley in present-day Kings Canyon National Park. Traveling light, he bushwhacked up into Gardiner Basin, then bivouacked without blankets or a sleeping bag at the base of his objective.

At last stars, moon, and the night itself grew pale, and the dawn had come. A hasty toilet, some bread and peaches and a drink of water, and I set off toward a lower place in the south-eastern wall, intending, if it should prove possible, to get upon its top and follow it to the summit of Mt. King. Ledges, covered here and there with tufts and patches of sodden grass, not long free from the snow, then masses of fallen rock, with an occasional oasis of hard-frozen snow,

266

good to walk on for a change—these formed the way. In three or four hours I reached the highest point on the ridge. But the glow of satisfaction that should attend such arrivals, in this case received instant check, for as my head rose over the last rock—behold, another deep and wide basin, even larger than the one I had just climbed out of! It contained much snow and some partially thawed-out lakes, but not a tree, nor even a single bush, in its whole lonely expanse. In this inhospitable gulf of granite and snow I must have passed the night, had I succeeded in reaching the first-attempted notch on the day before.

Seeing no alternative, I worked off diagonally down the rocky slope, then across a wide snow-field, and so, just at the lower edge of this, reached the highest of the lakes. It was still partly choked up with snow, and the surface was yet filmed with ice from last night's freeze. Sitting at its edge to sketch, I was astonished to find mosquitoes, and in the water—frogs!

I was now at the very base of the last grand peak, that rose cold and grim and glorious from its snow-encumbered base. According to my best judgment, after a careful scrutiny, the wisest way—in fact, the only way—to attack it was to try for the edge of the ridge to the left. All the rest was sheer palisades, where even the snow could not cling, but lay in broad, sweeping buttresses along their base. So, with much panting and many a pause—for the altitude began to tell,—I ascended a long snow-field, and then, with a stiff scramble, got myself upon the edge of the desired ridge. This I followed hopefully toward the summit (making the sketch at the head of this article by the way), until it became obvious that between me and the top were precipices impossible to scale. To the right, was an absolute chasm; the precipice from the summit down into it was as good as vertical, and somewhere from one to two thousand feet deep. To the left was a similar basin; but between it and the top came a flattish place, just steep enough to hold the snow, and, accordingly, having upon it a wide snow-field (seen at the left in the sketch). Beyond this rose a wall like the one I was on, except that it seemed to offer a chance to reach the summit by going up it. With some qualms, I started across the snow. It was very steep, and being without ice-ax wherewith to dig secure steps, or alpenstock to control myself with in case of a slide, I naturally kept a keen eye on certain sharp rocks protruding from the snow several hundred feet below, just about where I should go to, if I did slip. But by facing the mountain and going sidewise, kicking my toes as deep as possible into the soft surface of the snow, I got over without mishap, and breathed easier. Then, by good fortune, I found what seemed the only pass from the snow to the top of the cliff. Having safely ascended this, I began to clamber up the last few hundred feet. The wall was not wide,—to the right a reasonable precipice, with the snow-field below; but to the left, dropping sheer down from the edges of my shoes, an abyss of air, awful to look into, and requiring some nerve to keep steady on its very brink. This whole side of the ridge, sweeping forward and becoming the whole side of the main peak, seemed fairly *concave*, it was so steep. A stone dropped over took eight seconds to reach anything.

When the climbing becomes really delicate, a knapsack always worries me. It has a bad way—mine has—of scaring me by hitting or touching something, or making me think it is going to hit or touch something, just where a touch might put your center of gravity outside your base; and then—anyway, I feel better without one. So here I laid mine aside, for the work was now simply gymnastics. Soon even my pocket-flask bothered so that it also had to be put aside, that I might hug closer to the rock. Finally the thing got so narrow that I dared not crawl round to the right of each rock, for fear of falling into the right abyss, nor to the left, for fear of the still more fearful left abyss; so I had either to go back or to hoist myself accurately over the top of each successive rock; for now the way had narrowed to practically one series of big, flat rocks, set on edge at right angles to the line of travel, and with space enough between them for a man. I could just reach their sharp tops when I stood between two. Here I proceeded, by hooking my fingers over the top and drawing myself up, and bending over until I balanced upon the pit of my stomach, then making a half-turn on that pivot, like a compass-needle, and slowly letting myself down the other side.

A person who does not climb often imagines that one who does is a reckless mortal, whose life luck alone preserves. In his mind's eye he sees him prancing gaily along giddy heights, with a straw in his teeth, skipping freely from cliff to cliff, with two chances to one to miss his footing and tumble over a frightful precipice at almost any time. As a matter of fact, however, it is probable that really serious climbing makes one more unceasingly and acutely careful than any occupation you can easily think of. When every foothold and handhold must be separately found and judged, while in the depths below certain and instant death awaits the first slip—no! average human nature is not careless then. I, at any rate, grow quite ecstatically careful—the intense nervous stimulus and tension, combined with the absolute steadiness and poise required, being exactly one of the chief delights of the sport. I am sure several men with pike-poles could not have got me off that ridge.

But it was all in vain. Presently loomed above me a vertical cliff fifty feet high—smooth as the side of a house. Only wings could go up there. From that moment my case was hopeless. I could see all of two of the three sides of the mountain, and they seemed to be both alike inaccessible. My only possible chance lay in the third, and as yet unseen, side of the mighty pyramid, on one edge of which I was perched. But that could only be reached by going far back down the mountain and circling half round it—a good day's work in itself, and therefore quite out of the question with the time at my disposal. Even then it was well along in the afternoon, and I had climbed, without eating, since the early morning lunch. Food was low, and by to-morrow night I must be at the camp in King's River Cañon. The summit was only one or two hundred feet above me; so the view was nearly as good where I was. So, considering everything, I ceased further effort, and gave myself up to the wonders of the mighty panorama beneath and around me.

The whole drainage system of the South Fork spread out like a map, and all the splendid mountains away off north and east of Paradise Valley, where the map shows nothing, were beautiful exceedingly, as the shadows of vast fields of floating clouds slid over them, bringing out now this one and now that, and revealing far more fully their real forms than sunshine or shadow alone ever can. Far to the north-east I could see a fine group of shining lakes that seemed to be the head-waters of the South Fork. One seemed very large, even from my great distance. I dreamed of great expeditions throughout all that new region; and, strange to say, a few weeks later one of them actually came to pass.

With a longing look at the granite spire towering so still there in the deep blue, yet seeming almost to reel as I gazed, I put my back to it, retraced my way, secured my abandoned property, and hit off down the crest.

Like Clarence King himself, Brown was not one to give up easily. The following summer he was back in Paradise Valley, this time in the company of his wife Lucy.

But we had not been there very long when I began to hanker for another try at Mt. King, which I had tried last year, but had not succeeded in climbing. One evening I suggested to Lucy that I rise very early the next day and endeavor to get to the summit of Mt. King, and return before night. She replied, "I wish you would; and I hope you will get to the top. I would a great deal rather that you should do it than anybody else." After that, what could I do but go?

So in the morning, about an hour after sunrise,—which was at least two hours later than it should have been,—I took a lunch and a forty-foot rope and started out. Lucy came with me to the river bank, and the old mare ferried me over. Realizing that there was not a second to waste, I at once put on full steam and hustled through tangles of bushes, and trees, and jumbles of fallen rocks at a great rate. All the raspberry bushes had been recently pawed over, and the ripe berries had been eaten, so I fully expected to see a bear, but none appeared. However, in a way, I had a bear as guide; for I followed the tracks of one up the gulley of the second tributary from the east, gaining thus the wider cañon above. The first section of this cañon is painfully long, and its floor is exceedingly rough. At its head I ascended a steep slope, two or three hundred feet high, alongside of a series of cascades. From the top of this rise, exactly centering the picture between the cañon walls, there appeared a sharp, hard peak, which I knew must be the edgewise view of Mt. King. It looked very far away, and seemed as though it would take at least the rest of the day to reach its base, let alone climbing it. However, I kept on going, and tore through the exasperating jungle of interlocked manzanita bushes and crooked poplars, "regardless." Finally I got above this, and hurrying up grassy slopes and rocky knolls, at last left the timber altogether, and ran a couple of miles to the head of a long couloir that terminates against a southern spur of Mt. King. At about half after eleven I sat a few minutes and lunched by the very last green spot. Then I went directly up the steep southern face of the peak, until, some five hundred feet below the summit, I could look over its eastern shoulder—a look which quite gave me a qualm—it being absolutely sheer for more than a thousand feet beneath. Working across to the western edge, I looked over that precipice, and it was deeper still. These two walls approached each other, and where they met is the summit. Near the top the rocks got steeper and became more like vertical cliffs. At last I could climb no higher unaided.

Poised on a narrow ledge, I noosed the rope and lassoed a horn of rock projecting over the edge of the smooth-faced precipice overhead. But a pull on the rope toppled the rock bodily over, nearly hitting me, who could not dodge. So I took out the noose, and having tied a big knot in the rope-end, threw it repeatedly until this caught in a crack, when I climbed the rope. I did not dally with the job either, for every second I was afraid the knot would pull through the crack. A few yards above, the operation had to be repeated, and before the summit was reached, it was repeated several times. The ugliest place of all was exactly at the last rock, only a few feet below the top. With great caution, and as much deliberation as I had used speed below, I finally looped the rope over an all-too-slight projection, along the upper edge of the side face of the topmost block, and compelled myself to put one foot in it and lift myself, and so stand, dangling in that precarious sling, until I could get my arms on the top and squirm over.

This summit is more like that of the spire of Strassburg Cathedral (550 feet) where I once stood, than any other peak I ever climbed. It is a true spire of rock, an uptossed corner at the meeting of three great mountain walls. It is about thirteen thousand two hundred feet high, stands somewhat isolated, and commands a glorious view. It is accessible only at the place where I went up, and only with a rope at that. The top of the summit-block slopes northwest, is about fifteen feet across, and as smooth as a cobblestone. If you fall off one side, you will be killed in the vicinity; if you fall off any of the other sides, you will be pulverized in the remote nadir beneath.

About half-past one I roped myself down again, spider-wise, from this airy pedestal; and having left a row of monuments as far as the green spot where I had lunched, scampered away down the long couloir, jumping bowlders, pools, and streams in the highest spirits. I continued to run wherever the surface did not make it absolutely impossible, hurried in the tail of the afternoon across what seemed like miles and miles of chaotic masses of big talus blocks, then, in the deepening shadows, down the throat of the narrow gorge where the stream dashes, in the twilight over massive bowlders in titanic heaps along the base of the Paradise Valley walls; then, in the dark, across the rushing river I went, foolhardily, mid-thigh deep; and then, rustling through the fallen white oak leaves, I sighted the gleam of Lucy's fire, and in a moment more,—was home.

In one day, the professor of drawing had climbed and then descended nearly 7,000 vertical feet, hiked ten miles cross-country, and completed the first ascent—solo—of a mountain still regarded as one of the most difficult to climb in all the Sierra.

At Grips With Mount Clarence King, from "Three Days with Mt. King" by Professor Bolton Coit Brown. *Sierra Club Bulletin,* January, 1896; and "Wanderings in the High Sierra, between Mt. King and Mt. Williamson, Part II," by Professor Bolton Coit Brown. *Sierra Club Bulletin,* May 1897. Reprinted by permission of The Sierra Club.

James S. Hutchinson

A Climb for Bachelors

Through the early years of the 20th Century, Joseph LeConte, Jr. and James S. Hutchinson were the leading luminaries among Sierra mountaineers. LeConte was the son of Professor Joseph LeConte, whose "University Excursion Party" had rambled through Yosemite in 1870.[1] The younger LeConte climbed in the Sierra for more than 40 years, toting along his Kodak at a time when cameras were anything but standard equipment for mountaineers. More than a fine climber, "Little Joe" LeConte earned a well-deserved reputation as the first great photographer of the Sierra.

LeConte's most important climbs were made in the company of his friend James S. Hutchinson. In 1903 they teamed up for the first ascents of North Palisade and Mount Sill, the third and fourth highest mountains in the Sierra. Five years later with Duncan McDuffie, they completed the first continuous pack trip from Yosemite to Kings Canyon, thereby forming an important link between Theodore Solomons's dream of a high mountain route[2] and its realization in the construction of the John Muir Trail.

In the company of other climbers, Hutchinson bagged first ascents of several of the Sierra's most notable peaks, including Black Kaweah, Mount Abbot, Matterhorn Peak and Mount Humphreys. Joe LeConte himself had attempted Mount Humphreys in 1898 and failed. From the summit of North Palisade in 1903, he pointed the mountain out to his friend Hutchinson and described his earlier attempt. Hutchinson decided then and there to take a crack at Humphreys himself. A year later, with two friends and his brother E. C. Hutchinson, he found himself scrambling up a steep, narrow couloir on the west side of the peak.

---

[1]See "Joseph LeConte: Rambling Through the High Sierra," Section III.
[2]See "Theodore Solomons: The Enchanted Gorge," Section I.

The whole mountain—at least the cap of it for a thousand feet down—is composed of terra-cotta-colored granite, cracked and broken into huge blocks by the frost and ice. As we looked up the gorge we saw that the cleavage-planes all ran parallel and dipped down toward the east at an angle of sixty or seventy degrees. On the cliff to our right were the places from which the huge cubes and parallelograms of granite had broken off, and in the bottom of the gorge were the fallen masses. The loosened blocks on the western wall, which was somewhat inclined, although cracked, broken, and misplaced, still remained approximately in their original positions.

After crossing a snow-field, which was frozen hard, a small shelf was reached, the last level place on the mountain, and from here commenced the final ascent of the gorge. Almost immediately we came upon the same large smooth, polished granite slope which had baffled Messrs. LeConte and Cory. It formed the bottom of the gorge, and sloped upward for a distance of thirty feet as steep as a cathedral roof. To add to its difficulties, it was completely covered with a thin layer of ice, about a quarter of an inch thick. A single trial of walking on it was enough, for we immediately went tobogganing to its foot. We tried it on all fours, but this was impossible. Finally, to the right was found a tiny rocky chute between this icy granite slope and the eastern wall of the gorge. Up this for ten or fifteen feet I climbed, and here, being blocked by a large boulder, it terminated; but from this point, running off diagonally to the left, there was a tiny cleavage-joint in the granite slab. The nails in my shoes would cling to this as I reclined on my hands, face downward, against the frozen surface. In this way I worked crosswise over the slope and up to the broken cliffs above. Once there, it was an easy matter to reach the top of the boulder which had blocked the tiny chimney. Soon all of us were over this difficulty. Upward we went, clambering over boulders, hands and feet both in constant use. The chute was frequently blocked by the huge slabs and cubes of granite fallen from the cliffs above. In places the blocks had fallen in such a manner as to make caves, the floor of the cave being the bottom of the gorge, the ceiling the under portion of the boulder itself. From the ceiling of one of these caves we found suspended many long icicles the size of broomsticks or larger. These we found to be delightfully refreshing, and quenched our thirst by nibbling on them or else by catching tiny drops of water which were trickling from their ends. Our altitude was now about 13,500 feet, and I dare say that these icicles in this cave form the highest source of any of the branches of the San Joaquin River. The huge boulders, dropped as they were in this narrow gorge, were a constant source of trial and menace to us. Some of them were unstable, and must be avoided on that account; others were so lodged that they formed little precipices which we must circumvent.

A hundred feet more of climbing and crawling on hands and knees, and the gorge opened up a little. All knew that shortly our fate would be sealed and the worst must be known. At this moment I happened to be ahead. Suddenly, and almost unawares, I came upon the knife-edge of the Sierra crest and looked over into a yawning abyss, down two thousand feet, to a wide-spreading snow-field held in a granite-walled amphitheater. I turned toward the summit above us, but could not see the extreme top, for it was hidden by the wall to our left, which arose two hundred feet above us, still inclined at an angle of seventy degrees. The lower part of the wall to a height of perhaps fifty feet was smooth and unbroken, except for a few crevices and projecting ridges caused by the cleavage of the rock. To ascend this seemed possible, and I called to the others, "I think we can make it." It appeared to be the only way. Without realizing how precipitous the slope was, I started up it, getting here a toehold and there a fingerhold, all the while pressing my body closely against the cliff. In this way I ascended for thirty feet, and then the wall seemed absolutely smooth and unbroken. I gazed to the right and to the left and up above me. All was apparently as smooth as glass. In an unguarded moment I looked downward to see if I could retrace my steps. My first view was through the cleft where the gorge broke through the crest knife-edge almost directly below me and down and down the cliffs and on to the snow. I looked for the tiny ridges in the wall by which I had ascended, but could not see them, so closely was I pressed against the wall to avoid going over backwards. A cold chill crept down my back. My knees began to shake. The alarm, however, was only momentary. I saw the uselessness of fear, turned my face to the wall, and then looked on things above, determined not again to look downward. When I had fairly gathered myself together, I noticed above me about ten feet, and somewhat to the left, that a couple of blocks of granite had been split out, leaving a little pinnacle. If this place could be reached I would have accomplished something, and would have a vantage-ground from which to look for better things. If not to go up higher, I at least could have the rope thrown to me and, with a hitch about the pinnacle, could descend to the gorge again. Finally, off to the left I found a little foothold which had been over-looked before, and somewhat above it a fingerhold. By the use of these and a few others which appeared, and by hugging the rock very closely, the pinnacle was finally reached. Above this the inclination of the wall was not so great, and to the left there ran up a number of little parallel chimneys caused by the breaking out of the blocks along the clevage-planes; but each chimney at some point was blocked with a large cube which had not yet been fully dislodged. It was possible, however, to work from one chimney to another, and thus avoid the obstructions in each move from chimney to chimney, gaining ten or twenty feet in altitude. Presently, after a climb of about two hundred feet from where I had left the others, I reached the knife-edge of the buttress of which I have already spoken. The summit of the mountain was only about twenty feet above this and the way was clear. I then searched around for a better way of ascent. The western wall of the buttress was a sheer drop over five hundred feet to a shelf, and from the shelf there was still another drop to the talus slope. The south side of the buttress was a mere knife-edge, notched throughout with sharp pinnacles. I returned to the eastern side and examined all the little chimneys running down there. All of them before reaching the bottom of the gorge ended, leaving a smooth cliff thirty or forty feet in height.

I returned through the little chimneys by which I had ascended as far down as I could, reaching a point where the wall below the chimney was more inclined then below the other chimneys, and where it was also more broken. At this point the rope was thrown up to me. I made it fast around a projecting rock, and with its aid my brother hauled himself up to my position. We then lowered the rope again for the others to follow, but they—the married men of the party—had been deliberating and holding a council in the interim, and had decided that they had no right to take the risks which appeared necessary to complete the climb. Instead of attempting to follow us, they climbed a prominence which formed the summit of the eastern wall of the gorge. This they said was "Married Men's Peak," and joking called themselves "moral heroes."

Finally, at 11 o'clock, my brother and I scrambled on the summit (14,055 feet[1]), and no longer looked on things above, but rather on things beneath—and far beneath. Circling all about us, three thousand feet below us, west of the main crest, lay the great granite amphitheater four miles in diameter, covered with large patches of snow and lakes of various sizes and shapes. Lake Desolation was just below us. This amphitheater is bounded on the south and southwest by the snow-tongue ridge over which we had passed, on the west by the Pinnacles, and on the northwest by a range midway between us and the Abbott group. These form an inner semicircle, beyond which is another concentric one, inclosed by the Evolution Group, the Goddard Divide, the divide between the South Fork of the San Joaquin and the King's River, the Seven Gables, and the Abbott Group, commencing on the south and extending far around to the north. Beyond the Abbott Group lay Red Slate and Red-and-White peaks. To the eastward the mountain dropped off a sheer precipice for two thousand feet or more into a huge snow amphitheater. From there the snow slopes at a steep angle several thousand feet further, and then a rolling volcanic country completes the balance of the distance down to the town of Bishop, more than ten thousand feet below us and about sixteen miles distant. Owen's Valley is laid out in square farms like a checkerboard, and for miles and miles the green alfalfa-fields gave life to what would otherwise have been an almost lifeless scene. To the southward we could see the rugged line of the Palisades. Far below us, both north and south, forming part of the main crest, were several mesas, or tablelands, probably remnants of the old base-level through which the knife-edge and saw-teeth of Humphreys had cut their way.

The sumit of Humphreys is not more than eight feet square and contains the same parallel lines of cleavage which I have referred to as existing in the gorge. It is one mass of cracked and broken blocks, thrown loosely together in such a way as to warn one to move

---

[1]Now given as 13,989 feet.

cautiously lest the whole top should break off and fall into the great abyss to the eastward. While my brother built a cairn as a last resting-place for our Sierra Club register, I examined very carefully all about the summit for a possible way of ascent other than that by which we had come. The north side was almost sheer for five hundred feet down to the peak on which LeConte and Cory had climbed. The whole western side was a series of precipices and shelves down to the talus slope, and then on down at a gradual angle to the granite basin. The southern wall, as I have already said, dropped at least a thousand feet to the knife-edge of the main ridge, which then extended on downwards until it connected with Mt. Emerson, near Piute Pass. The drop on the east was the worst of all.

There were no signs of any one having been on the summit of the peak before. Probably no one had ever stood where we then were, unless perhaps during the early Jurassic period, before the mountain was fully sculptured. Then the mariners of that age (if there were any) might have sailed upon the waters of the Pacific close to the base of the mountain, and, there landing, have climbed up its then gently sloping sides. The mountain is very different from most peaks of the Sierra. It stands absolutely remote and alone. The nearest peaks are those of the inner semicircle of which I have spoken, but they do not reach much over 12,500 feet, and from our position appeared low. The nearest peak which approached us in height was Mt. Darwin, eight miles distant.

After an hour spent in viewing the landscape, we signaled to the others, and finally all met at the gorge where we had parted company. The process of descent to this gorge was about the reverse of our upward trip. The rope was in constant use, and we both heaved a sigh of relief when we were safely down. From there on the descent was practically over the same course by which we had ascended. It was much easier, for in many places where in ascending we had climbed on hands and knees now we could make a toboggan-slide of fifteen or twenty feet over a smooth surface or down a gravel chute. It was somewhat hard on portions of our clothing, but we "got there," and that, for the time being, was the main object. The rope was again used several times. The rocks in the steep chute lay so loosely that great care had to be used lest we should start an avalanche. Whitney and

Noble went on ahead down one of these chimneys, and were several hundred feet below us. My brother and I moved with the utmost care to avoid setting any stones in motion, but suddenly a number started; these started others, and in a moment a deluge of them was tearing down the chute directly toward those below us. We shouted like mad for Nobel and Whitney to get out of the way. They looked back and saw the torrent coming. This chute was bounded on its eastern side by a precipitous wall, in which, near where they were standing, was a deep vertical niche. They rushed for this, and had no sooner concealed themselves than the avalanche went shooting past them. This was a warning, and thenceforth in similar places we all remained close together. In an hour we had reached the top of the talus. Here, by making a slight detour, we reached a snow-field which gave us a toboggan-slide of several hundred feet down to the granite basin. It seemed like an easy matter to cut across this basin directly to our camp, but the similarity of the snow-fields, lakes, and the granite bosses made it like a maze, and even when we were within a short distance of our camp it took us many long minutes of searching to locate it. Soon a drink of some newly brewed tea refreshed us.

We were unanimous that we ought not to remain another night in this exposed place, and so at once shouldered our bundles and descended five hundred feet to the thickest of the several clumps of trees which we had passed the day before. Here, beside an old sheep-corral, we made a more comfortable camp, protected on all sides by the mountain pines, and having here a bountiful supply of wood. Below us was a fine brook, and a plunge in this had the magical effect of making us whole again and putting new life into every fiber, vein, and muscle. What a glorious camp-fire we had that night!

A Climb for Bachelors, from "First Ascent: Mt. Humphreys" by J.S. Hutchinson, Jr. *Sierra Club Bulletin,* January, 1905. Reprinted by permission of The Sierra Club.

Norman Clyde

The Search for Walter Starr

Summarizing the mountaineering career of Norman Clyde in a few sentences is like summarizing the military career of Napoleon: it can't be done. This greatest of all Sierra mountaineers made his first trip into the Sierra in 1914 and his last in 1970 at the age of 85. Between the two he chalked up more than 200 first ascents among the thousand or so peaks that he climbed. At the time of his death in 1972 Thomas H. Jukes observed in the American Alpine Journal: *"He had lived as every alpinist wants to live, but as none of them dare to do, and so he had a unique life. . . . He was the only man I know who gave himself up completely to a passionate love of the mountains."*

Clyde lived, roamed and climbed in the Sierra year-round, usually by himself. He ascended Mount Whitney 50 times and scores of remote, nameless peaks at least once, peaks that other climbers didn't discover for decades. He was happiest when climbing alone and unroped up an unexplored ridge or face. Backpackers and climbing partners he tolerated grumpily, preferring to have the Sierra to himself. He treated the range as a resident treats his home, which for Clyde it was.

As if his climbing prowess were not enough to create the Clyde legend, there was a second factor as well: the size of his pack. David Brower called Norman Clyde "the pack that walks like a man." Cast-iron skillet, four pair of boots, Hudson Bay axe, five cameras, a pistol, several fishing rods, spare reels, a library of hardcover classics that he read in the original Latin, Greek, German, French, Spanish and Italian: this was a portion of his kit. Honest men swear that it is true. "If I want to carry a rock in my pack to keep me steady down the trail," said Clyde, "that's my business."

At no time were Clyde's climbing skills and his knowledge of the mountains revealed more dramatically than in his search for Walter A. Starr, Jr. Starr, a fine solo climber in his own right, failed to return from one of his climbs in August 1933. He was more than a week overdue when his deserted camp was found at Lake Ediza. Clyde heard the news and quickly rushed to the scene to join the search party.

Norman Clyde

Upon reaching it, I found that a party of about twenty had already assembled, including volunteer friends from San Francisco and Los Angeles, representatives of the Forest Service and the California State Highway Patrol, together with Walter A. Starr, Sr. Among them were a half-dozen trained mountain climbers.

A plan of procedure was quickly formed. In the vicinity stand two high mountains, Mt. Ritter and Banner Peak, with summits averaging slightly over 13,000 feet. South of them a short distance stand a long crescent-like line of jagged spires averaging some 12,000 feet in elevation, and several miles in length from the northwest to the southeast. These are very appropriately called The Minarets.

Almost undoubtedly Walter Starr had met with mishap somewhere in this group of mountains, the Ritter Range, and was either somewhere on them or in the country lying between them and his camp. If killed or seriously injured he was probably in the mountains, but if he were only crippled he might have attempted to reach camp and, being unable to do so, would be in the lower country. A man with a sprained ankle or broken leg may spend days in going a short distance. The plan of campaign was based on these facts. Those without special mountaineering experience were to comb the area lying between his camp and the base of the Ritter Range. The mountaineers were to search the peaks and spires, a difficult, arduous, and somewhat hazardous undertaking.

Early the next morning four climbing parties were on their way. Three excellent young climbers, Jules Eichorn, of San Francisco, together with Glen Dawson and Richard Jones of Los Angeles, proceeded to search one portion of the Minarets, especially the second-highest—Michael's Minaret—while Oliver Kehrlein of Oakland and I were to direct our efforts to another section of the great spires, focusing upon the highest of them, known as Clyde's Minaret.

Past a number of groves of mountain hemlocks, and through gradually rising alpine meadows we filed along to the glaciated bluffs immediately below the Minarets. Along these cliffs Kehrlein and I proceeded, carefully inspecting every foot of the way until we were abreast of the highest of the Minarets. Aside from a few footprints which might have been those of a party other than the one for whom we were searching, we discovered nothing. Unfortunately we did not know the pattern of the soles of the basketball shoes generally worn by the missing man when rock climbing.

Leaving the bluffs, we crossed a small but rather steeply pitching glacier to the base of Clyde's Minaret and continued up its precipitous north face. More tracks were observed in the decomposed granite on the ledges, but these also were in all likelihood those of another party. Upon reaching the jagged top of the great spire, the signature of Walter Starr was not in the register in the cairn. However, we knew that he did not always sign his name on the top of a mountain, and furthermore there was no pencil in the register can and he might have failed to bring one with him. No evidence of his having been there was discovered.

As we looked out over the mountains an inky mass of clouds was seen advancing from the southwest and another from the northeast. As the top of a pinnacle more than 12,000 feet above the sea is not the most desirable place to encounter an electric storm, we left the summit before we had searched it to our entire satisfaction. On our way down we zigzagged back and forth, minutely observing every square yard for clues, but none were found.

When we reached the glacier, I swung around a promontory and found a long ledge running across the northeast face of the peak. Knowing the adventurous character of the lost man, I had a strong suspicion that he would attempt this apparently sheer, and so far as we knew, hitherto unscaled front of the mountain. About midway across the latter I came upon a "duck"—a small heap of rocks, usually pyramidal in form, erected as a marker to indicate a route followed. Presently I saw another and then a whole line of them leading to the head of a steep chimney on the southeast shoulder of the mountain. The ducks had evidently been constructed no great while before, as some of them were so unstable that they would have toppled over under the first heavy wind. However, it did not seem very likely that Starr would have approached this face from the southeast, and we knew that another party, of whose movements we had not been informed, had also been in this vicinity. Later we learned that such a party had recently made an unsuccessful attempt to scale the Minaret by this route.

As it was now late afternoon we were obliged to return. While doing so we paused and reconnoitered on the margin of Upper Iceberg Lake, lying on Minaret Pass a short distance northeast of Clyde's Minaret at an elevation of some 10,000 feet. We thought Starr might have passed this lake on his way to the mountain. While looking about, I noticed a strip of handkerchief with blood marks on it.

"Someone has lost his footing and cut his finger on a sharp rock as he came up the steep slope to the north of the pass," I thought as I stowed it away in my rucksack.

Upon our return to camp we found that the large party had come upon no certain evidence of any kind in the lower country. During the day an aeroplane carrying Francis P. Farquhar, President of the Sierra Club, as observer, had circled the peaks of the Ritter Range several times, evidently without result.

Walter A. Starr, Sr. and his son Allan had climbed Banner Peak and searched the North Glacier in descending, but found no record on the summit. Two, however, who had climbed Mt. Ritter, Douglas Robinson, Jr., and Lilburn Norris, discovered that Starr had written a note in the register on its summit. Among several statements was one to the effect that he had his ice axe with him. The latter having been found at his camp was proof of his safe return from Mt. Ritter. The other Minaret party which had climbed Michael's Minaret from the west, saw a line of ducks similar to those encountered by us. The markers crossed the upper end of a chute and led to "The Portal" on the north side of Michael's Minaret. There were also several footprints and a portion of a cigarette, which was said to be the brand usually smoked by the missing man. Eichorn and Dawson had climbed from "The Portal" to the summit of the Minaret but found no evidence of Starr having been there, and were forced to make a hurried descent by the same storm that drove me from Clyde's Minaret. By its brown marking the fragment of the handkerchief which I had brought in was identified as similar to those generally carried by Starr.

Haunted by the ducks on the northeast face of Clyde's Minaret, Kehrlein and I returned on the following morning to Upper Iceberg Lake. Swinging around to the slope east of it, we selected a vantage point from which the entire northeast face could be readily surveyed with binoculars. An object about a third of the way up the mountain puzzled me. The fact that it was brown indicated that it might be a khaki-clad person, but as the light falling upon it seemed to be diffused through it rather than reflected from it, this inference seemed to be precluded.

Having come to the decision that this face of the peak should be thoroughly investigated, we proceeded to climb it. In about half an hour we reached the long ledge. After examining several ducks, I carefully removed the rocks of one of them. Beneath was a tuft of grass the color of which had not faded in the least. This was certain proof that the ducks had been made very recently. As we began to advance up the peak we presently came upon more ducks. Then there was a gap. Evidently the climber was in the habit of putting markers only when he thought that there might be special occasion for them on his return. A little later we reached the object which had aroused our curiosity. It was a bed of oxalis, or miner's lettuce, a few feet in length on a ledge, with a profusion of brown seed vessels; both the color and the diffusion of light were therefore explained.

The ducks appeared to lead into a large alcove-like recess in a chute or couloir, with almost vertical walls of perhaps a hundred feet above it. Then they were lost again. Working my way upward along narrow shelves, I succeeded in getting within a few yards of the rim of the wall, but the remainder being very hazardous, I desisted from the attempt to scale it. While traversing to the right along ledges toward the rib of rock separating this couloir from another adjoining it to the north, I again came upon ducks. There was one on the very crest of the rib and others in the next chute. I called down to Kehrlein. In a few minutes he joined me.

Together we proceeded up the couloir. Although the line of ducks was not continuous, there were sufficient to indicate clearly the route taken by the climber. As we neared the head of the couloir, an approaching mass of dense black cloud, together with thunder in the distance, warned us that we had better get off the precipitous face. The rocks were difficult enough to scale when dry, and furthermore, a storm striking the pinnacle would be likely to precipitate loose ones down upon us. (Starr's name was found the following year by Jules Eichorn on the summit of the Minaret, faintly marked on a piece of cardboard. Starr's diary subsequently proved that the ducks we followed marked his route.)

When we reached the foot of the peak, several hours of daylight still remaining, we proceeded southward around the base. We had not gone far before we observed Eichorn and his party coming from the opposite direction, making their way down a steep couloir. Confronted by a vertical drop of perhaps fifty feet, capped by a great stone, they spent some little time in looking about for a rock to which a rope might be safely attached. Eventually finding one, they were presently seen gliding in turn down the double rope, which the last man pulled down after him. A short time later they joined us. They had found ducks leading up the second chute north of Michael's chimney which eventually connected with the ducks seen by them before, leading along the arête to the pinnacle of Michael's Minaret. The ducks had been recently placed by an experienced route-finder as

Banner Peak and Mt. Ritter (behind)

indicated by the excellence of the route chosen. Having climbed to the summit of Michael's Minaret from this position the day before, they had climbed the third-highest, Eichorn's Minaret, on which they hoped some evidence would be discovered. Disappointed in this, they had descended and had gone around Michael's Minaret and climbed a considerable distance up the southwest face of Clyde's Minaret and then passed through a notch to the side on which we were.

When we reached camp late in the evening we found that the large party had come to the conclusion that there was little or no possibility of finding Starr in the territory which they had carefully searched, and had, therefore, left the mountains. At a round table of the mountaineering parties, after considerable discussion, it was decided that it would be well to investigate the east face of Banner Peak, as there is a dangerous and only once-traveled route up it, which, it was thought, might have enticed the missing man to attempt it.

On the ensuing morning, therefore, we walked several miles northwestward to the east base of Banner Peak. After going slowly and carefully along this without finding any evidence, the party divided, Eichorn and his two companions proceeding up the lower portion of the route in question, while Kehrlein and I swung around a rock promontory onto a glacier, from which we could command the northeast face immediately below the route. Several hours of searching by both parties indicated that Starr had not attempted to scale this face of Banner Peak. We therefore returned to camp.

At another round table that evening, after an animated debate, it was decided that further search would almost undoubtedly prove futile, and it would be best to give it up. To find a person in such a maze of pinnacles, only a few of which had been scaled, was like finding a needle in a haystack, it was thought. Not yet ready to abandon the quest, however, I declined to accompany the remainder of the party.

On the following morning I set forth on my lone quest. There is another Minaret—Leonard's—climbed but once prior to that year, which it seemed possible that Starr might have attempted to scale. It might be well, therefore, to ascend this, and incidentally to ascertain whether the missing man had gone north of Michael's Notch. In a word, my plan was to be one of gradual elimination. As now there was no further hope of finding Starr alive, there was no special occasion for hurry.

Through the alpine meadows, already beginning to show signs of the approach of autumn, and over the bluffs I picked my way to a glacier beneath the north face of the spire which I wished to scale. After examining it carefully, I crossed the glacier and climbed a short distance to a wide notch. From this I followed a narrow knife edge, involving some rather difficult and dangerous climbing, to the top of the spire. However, no one had recently been there. While carefully sweeping the Minarets with my binoculars—as I did a score of times daily—I trained them on the northwest face of Michael's Minaret.

"A capital place for a fall," I reflected, as I thrust my glasses into a pocket of my rucksack.

Upon reaching the wide notch again, I decided to go down to the west base and follow it until abreast of Michael's Notch, a cleft about a third of the way southward along the sweeping crescent described by the Minarets. I carefully examined every foot of terrain over which I passed, without, however, finding a single indication of anyone having gone that way. Passing through the notch to the opposite side of the Minarets, I returned to camp. Starr, I felt certain, had not been north of Michael's Notch. This was step number one in my plan of elimination.

I was not yet entirely satisfied as to Clyde's Minaret. Almost without doubt Walter Starr had climbed it, or at least had attempted to do so. This was indicated both by the line of ducks on the peak and by the fragment of handkerchief found on the margin of Upper Iceberg Lake. He was also reported as having said that he contemplated bivouacing at this lake the night preceding a proposed ascent of Clyde's Minaret.

With these things in mind, I therefore went again to the lake. Despite careful search, however, nothing further was observed until the south end of the lake was reached. There I found footprints, and recent ones at that, in the granite sand. The imprints indicated a shoe larger than that worn by the missing man and of a type not used by him when on rock climbs. As the person who made them seemed to have come up Minaret Creek from the South, I went down over cliffs to Minaret Lake. There horse tracks were found. Evidently a forest ranger or a sheep man had come up the stream. This day's search therefore added nothing to my stock of information.

As human muscles have a habit of eventually clamoring for rest, after climbing and searching for an average of at least ten hours daily for five days, I thought it might be well to accede to their demand by spending a day in camp. On the following day, the twenty-first of August, I decided to settle, if possible, the matter of Clyde's Minaret. Returning to the northeast face, I again followed the line of ducks up its precipitous front. They ceased entirely at the head of the couloir up which Kehrlein and I had followed them on the previous climb. Continuing to the summit, I inspected cairn and rocks very carefully without finding any certain evidence. Barring the possibility of his having been forced back by a storm, however, I felt convinced that Starr had been there.

In the descent I swung in long zigzags back and forth across the northeast and north faces. At the base of the latter lies a glacier, and along its upper margin runs a deep bergschrund. One of the theories of the disappearance of Starr was to the effect that he had fallen into this crevasse. As I rounded the glacier the light happened to fall at such an angle that I could inspect the bottom of the bergschrund through almost the entire length. The fact that nothing was seen did not, however, prove that Starr had not fallen into it, for snow cornices were frequently collapsing into it, and rocks, including small slides, often rattled down the face of the mountain, for the most part plunging into it.

Several other considerations, however, were almost conclusive that he had not gone into the crevasse. In the first place, Starr was a climber of such skill that he would not be likely to suffer a fall on this face, a considerably easier one than the northeastern which he had evidently scaled. Secondly, a person would not, in all likelihood, have been precipitated any great distance down the face of the mountain without leaving some evidence in the form of clothing, rucksack, or other personal belongings on the ledges with which it is seamed. I had so carefully scrutinized these that even a chipmunk exposed on them could scarcely have escaped my detection. In the third place, had a person fallen down the face of the mountain, there was a fair likelihood that either he or some of his effects would have jumped the crevasse and remained lying on the surface of the glacier. Assessing the evidence, both positive and negative, I returned to camp convinced that Walter Starr had climbed Clyde's Minaret, or had attempted to do so and had been driven back by storm, but that in either case he had returned to camp without mishap. The Minaret was therefore eliminated from further consideration.

On the ensuing day the search was primarily a binocular one. Beyond Minaret Pass I continued southward, eventually traversing a glacier and crossing a pass to the southwestern side of the Minarets. From various vantage points I carefully and repeatedly swept the entire reach of cliffs, including the east front of Michael's Minaret, which thrusts out about midway along the crescent formed by this line of great spires, without, however, detecting a single bit of evidence of any kind. On my return I scaled an outlying Minaret and repeated the procedure, with a like result.

After returning to camp, I summed up the evidence as follows: In the limited time at his disposal, Starr would in all probability not have attempted to scale more than Clyde's and Michael's Minarets. There was no indication of his having been any distance southeast of the former, or of his having been north of Michael's Notch. He had obviously climbed, or attempted to climb, Clyde's Minaret, but after most careful search, there was no reason to believe that he had not returned safely to camp. There remained Michael's Minaret. I decided to rest a day in camp and then attempt it.

Early in the morning of the twenty-fifth I again traversed the alpine meadows, again clambered up on the glaciated bluffs and then continued up a long slanting ledge ending in a short chimney, out of the upper end of which I climbed into Michael's Notch. From it an easy descent brought me to the west base of the Minarets. I then went southward about a mile to the west side of Michael's Minaret and continued around its southwestern shoulder. Noting a shelf running along the precipitous—almost sheer—west face, I decided to follow it for some distance and then climb above it in order to get a vantage point suitable for using my binoculars.

While reconnoitering, I came to the conclusion that higher up probably a ledge would be found leading around this shoulder and into the upper portion of a deep chute to "The Portal", from which the final spire of the Minaret is usually scaled. While I advanced upward the climbing became rather delicate, as the holds grew progressively smaller. They were firm and sharp angled, however, and there was no occasion to worry about loose rocks—the face was too steep for rocks to find lodgement.

As anticipated, a ledge did lead into the couloir. After going some distance up the latter, I examined the northwestern face of the spire. Evidently it was scalable, but the ledges tended to slope downward at a precarious angle, and there was a predominance of rounded corners. Knowing Starr's reliance on rubber-soled shoes, I made a mental comment to the effect that this reliance was perhaps a little too great. After climbing it for some distance I suddenly made the decision:

"This can be climbed, but I am not going to do it."

Having returned to the couloir, I continued up it to the notch ("The Portal") at its head. The ascent of perhaps five hundred feet from it to the narrow, blade-like summit of the spire involved a good deal of aerial and some rather hazardous climbing. Seated on the topmost rock, several feet in diameter, for upwards of a half hour, I swept the Minaret with my binoculars. Gathering clouds then warned me that I had better be gone.

As I carefully and deliberately made my way down toward the notch, I scanned and re-scanned the northwestern face. Much of it was concealed by irregularities. Suddenly a fly droned past, then another, and another.

"The quest is nearing an end," I reflected.

Upon reaching "The Portal" I began to follow a ledge running in a northwesterly direction. When I had gone along it but a few yards, turning about, I looked upward and across the chute to the northwestern face. There, lying on a ledge not more than fifty yards distant, were the earthly remains of Walter A. Starr, Jr. He had obviously fallen perhaps several hundred feet, to instantaneous death. The quest had been long, arduous, and hazardous, but the mystery of the vanishing of Walter Starr, Jr. was at last solved. The life of the daring young climber had come to a sudden and tragic end.

A few days later a party of four was again scaling Michael's Minaret. We followed the route which Starr had marked with ducks while making his climb three weeks before. Several hundred feet below the remains, two stopped, but Jules Eichorn and I continued up the perilous face. We interred the body of Walter A. Starr, Jr. on the narrow ledge where it lay, while his father looked up from below. Such an aerie would have been chosen as his final resting place by this departed lover of the mountains.

The Search for Walter Starr, from *Norman Clyde of the Sierra Nevada* by Norman Clyde. © 1971 by Scrimshaw Press. Reprinted by permission of Dave Bohn and Mary Millman.

Robert Underhill

The East Face
of Mount Whitney

Through the 1920s, the techniques of modern mountaineering developed by European climbers remained almost unknown among their counterparts in the Sierra. New systems of rope management, the use of pitons to secure ropes and climbers to mountains, the technique of "belaying," whereby one climber advances while protected by a second climber firmly anchored to the peak—these methods enabled the Europeans to climb at a far higher standard than mountaineers in the Sierra.

Some controversy surrounds the question of when these techniques were introduced into the Sierra. Mountaineering writer Steve Roper has pointed out that John Mendenhall and James Van Patten belayed each other up Laurel Mountain in 1930; Norman Clyde claimed to have learned the European system from Swiss guides in the Canadian Rockies even earlier.

Whatever the facts, it is clear that it was not until 1931 that a concerted effort was made to teach modern climbing techniques to Sierra mountaineers. In the summer of that year, Francis Farquhar demonstrated the fundamentals to a group of Sierra Club climbers, who then used them during an ascent of Unicorn Peak. Shortly thereafter, Robert Underhill joined the group to teach what he had learned during several seasons of mountaineering in the Alps.

Underhill, an Easterner, was one of America's top mountaineers. Earlier in 1931 he and Fritiof Fryxell had made the first ascent of the north ridge of Wyoming's Grand Teton, probably the most difficult climb that had yet been done in the United States. In the Sierra he found some talented and ambitious pupils. After leading training seminars in the Ritter Range and the Palisades, Underhill headed south with Farquhar, Norman Clyde, and two gifted young climbers— Jules Eichorn and Glen Dawson—to tackle what they considered the Sierra's greatest challenge: the east face of Mount Whitney.

293

At Farquhar's invitation and under his expert arrangement of program, I was enjoying a first climbing season in the High Sierra. The unclimbed east face of Mount Whitney had been in both our minds from the start. True, whenever the subject came up for express discussion Farquhar was wont to observe with a chuckle that the face was pretty much of a precipice; but this seemed to diminish in nowise his estimate of the value of paying it a visit, and I eventually became highly stimulated by his view that sleek verticality was merely the normal terrain for rock-climbing activities. Clyde, when he joined the party, gave a guarded confirmation of the topographic point, by judging, from his more intimate acquaintance with the mountain, that the face was "pretty sheer." However, he showed himself completely indulgent to the enterprise, and gave us the immense benefit of his practical knowledge, without which we should have lost much time in coming to grips with our problem. The other two members of the group—Jules Eichorn, of San Francisco, and Glen Dawson, of Los Angeles, young natural-born rock-climbers of the first water—had never seen the mountain; but neither had they seen any up and down the Sierra that they could not climb, and they were all enthusiasm.

On August 15th, then, we started up the Mount Whitney trail from Lone Pine. Here I discovered that the best way to obtain a pure enjoyment of mountain scenery is by all odds to entrust the con-comitant task of making elevation to a mule. However, we had to reassume operating responsibilities ourselves, and thereby give up all but a practical interest in the scenery, at a point somewhat short of the usual base camp, and strike up the North Fork of Lone Pine Creek. Relieving the pack train of its load, we here shouldered outrageously heavy knapsacks (Clyde's being an especially picturesque enormity of skyscraper architecture), and worked up the side cañon via a high southerly shelf discovered by Clyde upon a previous occasion. Ripe currants, or at least the opportunity to delay while eating them, seemed to be a great attraction to some along here. The shelf at length debouched upon a knoll, on the farther slope of which, above the stream, we found the most beautiful camp-ground I had yet seen in the Sierra. It lay at an altitude of about 10,500 feet, with the eastern escarpment of the whole Whitney group high and clear before it. In recognition of the fact that Clyde had discovered the spot, at least for mountaineers, and had hitherto been the only climber to use it, we hailed with one accord Farquhar's suggestion that it be christened "Clyde Meadow."

As we contemplated our mountain, in the evening light, I felt that it would be a mighty hard nut to crack. Certain vertical black lines, indicating gullies or chimneys, were indeed visible, but the questions remained whether they were individually climbable and susceptible of linkage together into a route. Every rock-climber knows, however, that such questions as these can be answered only at very close quarters; in particular, the broadside view of a peak, at any distance, is wholly non-committal or misleading. One feature, indeed, impressed us greatly. The northerly section of the east face stands forward from the remainder in a great square abutment, terminating above in a shoulder that lies some hundreds of feet below the actual summit. The object was clearly to gain this shoulder, and Clyde informed us of his own experience (for he had once descended thus far from the top) that the ascent from it to the summit was easy.

Somewhat before seven o'clock the next morning, August 16th, we left camp. After the prolonged bad weather, we were treated to something more than what is considered, in the Sierra, an ordinary good day, and would rate as a perfect one elsewhere; even the Californians did not succeed in remaining impeccably *blasé* about it. (I observed that they took to exclaiming, later on, over the hundreds of miles of clear visibility into Nevada and southern California.) Clyde led us down across the brook meadows and up along an "apron" of granite on the other (north) side to the floor of the next higher basin, thus neatly avoiding a long talus-slope in the line of more direct ascent. Crossing the brook again to the south, we now mounted the heel of a ridge which ran directly west into the mountain. This ridge rose in several steps, and at the top of each we paused a few moments to scrutinize, from ever higher and nearer, the problematic face. And it continued to look, I must confess, downright unclimbable. We had rather grown into the feeling, in the Palisades, that every Sierra mountain-wall could be climbed if only one tackled it properly; but at the present juncture I personally found myself becoming shaken in this conviction and wondering whether we weren't at last up against the so-called exception that proves the rule. I took to mapping out a route up the couloir to the south of the mountain in lieu of one up the face proper.

Our ridge now ran level for a bit, then sank slightly, preparatory to joining Mount Whitney itself, up which it swung for a distance in the shape of a steep but broken rib. At its low point it formed the barrier of a subsidiary cirque to the north (i.e., to the northeast of Whitney) that contained a little lake. On the shore of this lake, just under the peak, we gathered for a final intensive bit of observation. Suddenly I saw what seemed a just possible route, and simultaneously Dawson and Eichorn exclaimed to the same effect. It turned out that we all had exactly the same thing in mind. Through the field-glasses we now examined it in detail as well as we could, noting that much of it seemed possible, but that there were several very critical places. Rating our chances of success about fifty-fifty, we were eager to go ahead with the attempt.

To our extreme regret, Farquhar now decided to leave us. Not having had as long a period of training as the rest of us, he felt that his presence might delay the party at critical points, and for the general good he renounced a share in the climb. After watching us for a while he set out alone, at his own pace, by way of the gully to the north, with which he was familiar through having descended it with Clyde in 1930.

Leaving at the lake everything we could spare, we left it at 9:30 and proceeded up the rib already mentioned about five hundred feet over loose rock, past one small tower on the left and to the foot of another, where the rock steepened and became firm. Here we roped up (10:00), Dawson and I together, and Eichorn and Clyde. (I might remark at once that the whole climb was a thoroughly coöperative enterprise. At times one rope would go ahead, then the other; and each rope shifted leaders several times.) The first problem was to get from our position in the outjutting rib back to the true face of the mountain, to the left (south) of it. A direct rising traverse along the left flank of the rib looked inviting at first, but when I had climbed up here some distance I didn't like the looks of the remainder and suggested that Eichorn and Clyde try around to the right instead. This latter proved to be the preferable way: climbing some seventy-five feet diagonally to the right up the tower before us, we then traversed along its right flank to a little col; here we recrossed the rib to the left (south),

descended to a little gully some forty feet, and moved a few steps
farther to the south on a good ledge to the face of the mountain, just at
the level where its lower precipice breaks back in some rising tiers of
slabs.

These slabs were climbed easily for some three hundred feet up
into a little recess, bounded on the right by the rib we had left, on the
left by a low rock wall, and in back, or straight ahead of us, by a new
uplift of sheer cliff. We now surmounted the wall to our left, and
found ourselves on the southerly edge of the huge rectangular abutment previously mentioned (it was the face of this abutment which
we had hitherto been climbing), and looking into the deep reëntrant
right-angle where it joined the southern half of the general east face, or
the main body of the mountain. Descending slightly we traversed
right (west) along the side of the abutment into this corner.

It was clear that the hardest part of the climb now lay before us.
The right wall of the corner—the wall of the abutment leading to the
shoulder—was out of the question. The left wall—that of the mountain
proper—sloped back promisingly after a couple of hundred feet, but
that initial section looked like trouble. We attacked it at first close to
the corner. After climbing up perhaps fifty feet here, however, we were
confronted by a bad crack. It looked climbable at a pinch—in fact,
Dawson and Eichorn were both confident of being able to do it and
eager to have a try—but before such a *tour de force* was undertaken
Clyde and I urged that a traverse, which we had all already noticed
out to the left, be investigated. For this we descended part way again
and then moved out to the south around a minor protruding rib
which had obscured the farther view. Encouraged by what we saw
we continued the traverse, which now led us out in a very exposed
position directly over the tremendous precipice that falls a thousand
feet to the snow-fields and talus-fields at the foot of the mountain.
Some loose rocks which we here pried off fell without a sound for
an uncanny number of seconds before crashing once for all at the head
of the glacier. The hazard, however, was only illusory, as the holds
were good and the climbing not difficult, though involving more
delicate problems of balance than had any hitherto.

The traverse, perhaps a hundred feet in total length, turned
diagonally upward into the foot of a small chimney containing much

loose rock. Half-way up this chimney we moved out of it again on the right and climbed directly up over a couple of shelves. The last of these was spacious enough to accommodate the whole party, and here, in a very airy situation, fronting the magnificent drop to the glacier, we paused twenty minutes for lunch.

We had now practically passed the band of difficult rock. A short movement to the left, across the head of the little chimney, a straightforward pitch or two upward, and a longer easy traverse back again to the right returned us into the corner formed by the great abutment, at a point where its left flank (upon which we were) took the shape of a large gully sloping back at a pleasant angle. Up this we scrambled, at first easily for a hundred feet over scree, then with increasing difficulty for seventy-five feet more over a series of huge granite steps. The last of these steps was surmounted, in its left-hand (southwest) corner, by means of a pretty little chimney, the secret of which—discovered by Dawson, leading, for the whole party—was to step out, near the top, upon the south wall of the great gully. Here we observed that a route from our lunching-place, directly up the south ridge of the gully to the point where we now stood, would probably have been easier than the one we had taken up the other granite steps in the base of the gully itself.

Our difficulties were now over. Moving around the head of the gully to the right (north), we found ourselves upon the shoulder that caps the great abutment, with nothing but easy broken rock, as Clyde had foretold, between us and the summit. The monument hove in view, unexpectedly close above, and was greeted with a cheer. Taking off the ropes, which were no longer necessary, we made our way individually up the final stretch by various routes (the easiest seemed to be around to the left near the top), and at 12:45 were shaking hands with Farquhar on the summit.

The route we had followed was exactly that which we had mapped out originally while standing by the little lake. Much of the fascination of our climb lay, in fact, in seeing the sections which we had marked out for ourselves as critical successively opening up to permit us a way. The rock work was not really difficult. There is, I should say, less than a thousand feet of it from the roping up to the unroping place, and I believe a good climbing party that knew the route could ascend the lake to the summit in something like half the time we required upon this first occasion. The beauty of the climb in general lies chiefly in its unexpected possibility, up the apparent precipice, and in the intimate contact it affords with the features that lend Mount Whitney its real impressiveness.

The East Face of Mount Whitney, from "Mount Whitney by the East Face" by Robert L.M. Underhill. *Sierra Club Bulletin.* February, 1932. Reprinted by permission of The Sierra Club.

Yvon Chouinard

Muir Wall—El Capitan

Robert Underhill's introduction of modern climbing techniques to the Sierra in 1931 opened up a whole new world of possibilities for Sierra climbers. Within two years they were ready to attack the great unclimbed—and previously uncontemplated—walls of Yosemite Valley. As the decade progressed, routes were put up on scores of high-angle faces, including the Cathedral Spires, Royal Arches, Washington Column, and Lower and Middle Brothers.

During the Forties the use of expansion bolts and pitons for direct aid (that is, for standing on by means of attached stirrups) enlarged the possibilities even further. John Salathé climbed the Lost Arrow chimney and the southwest face of Half Dome with Anton Nelson, and the north face of Sentinel Rock with Allen Steck. A new generation of daring, imaginative and richly talented climbers arrived in the Fifties, ushering in the era during which Yosemite Valley has risen to prominence as the greatest center for rock climbing in the world.

Perhaps unavoidably, much of the writing from this period is as technical as the climbing itself; the story of a modern Yosemite ascent often gets buried beneath an avalanche of jargon and inscrutable technical details.

Several of the finest climbers, however—Royal Robbins, Chuck Pratt, Galen Rowell and Yvon Chouinard among them—have risen above this level of writing, turning out wonderfully evocative and insightful accounts of their days and nights on the towering walls of the valley. In the following article, Yvon Chouinard tells the story of the first ascent of the Muir Wall, an enormously intimidating route on El Capitan's 3,000-foot vertical face. During their eight days alone on the wall, Chouinard and climbing partner TM Herbert found themselves growing more and more in tune with their vertical environment, and with the stunning natural world that surrounded them as they pushed on through rain and cold toward the summit.

Just beyond this glorious flood the El Capitan Rock, regarded by many as the most sublime feature of the valley, is seen through the pine groves, standing forward beyond the general line of the wall in most imposing grandeur, a type of permanence. It is 3300 feet high, a plain, severely simple, glacier-sculptured face of granite, the end of one of the most compact and enduring of the mountain ridges, unrivaled in height and breadth and flawless strength.

—JOHN MUIR, *The Yosemite*

More than any other mountain or formation, El Capitan has been responsible for the changing philosophy and rising standard of American climbing. I speak not only of rock climbing but of ice as well, for new standards of ice climbing are being established by Yosemite-trained "rock specialists."

The new philosophy is characterized by small expeditions going into remote areas and trying new and extremely difficult routes with a minimum of equipment, no support parties nor fixed ropes to the ground; living for days and weeks at a time on the climb and leaving no signs of their presence behind. This purer form of climbing takes more of a complete effort, more personal adjustment, and involves more risk, but being more idealistic, the rewards are greater.

Probably the basis for this type of climbing was established by the naturalist John Muir. He used to roam the Sierras for weeks, eating only bread and whatever he could pick off the land, sleeping under boulders in only his old army overcoat, and rejoicing with the summer storms. He chose to accept nature as it was without trying to force himself onto the mountains but rather to live *with* them, to adjust *himself* to the rigors of this sort of life.

It was a vigorous life indeed, but his writings tell us of his communion with nature and his profound mystical experiences. Scientists will explain that when the body is weakened by fasting the senses become more acute and receptive. This partly explains Muir's mysticism but does not explain how, even though he was essentially fasting, he still managed to keep his prodigious strength. The answer to this is simple; he was fully adjusted to his environment and to eating less food.

This same attitude was later accepted by John Salathé and "Axe" Nelson, who trained their bodies to do with very little water in anticipation of their 1947 Lost Arrow climb. Their five-day ascent with only one pint of water per man per day is still the most remarkable achievement in American climbing.

The nine-day first ascent of the North American Wall in 1964 (*A.A.J.,* 1965, 14:2, pp. 331-338.) not only was the first one-push first ascent of an El Capitan climb, but a major breakthrough in other ways. We learned that our minds and bodies never stopped adjusting to the situation. We were able to live and work and sleep in comparative comfort in a vertical environment. When the food and water ran low, we found that we could obtain an enormous amount of energy from eating just ten raisins. We reached the summit feeling as if we could go on for another ten days. No longer would we ever be afraid of spending so many days on a climb, whether it was a Yosemite wall or a long Alaskan ridge.

After this climb we asked ourselves the inevitable question, "What next?" The answer was obvious . . . another first ascent on "El Cap" in one push with two men instead of four. This would not only double the work load and responsibility, but would also considerably decrease the safety factor.

It is the unknown that frightens brave men and there are plenty of unknown factors in trying a new route on this great wall. In the spring of 1965, after studying our proposed route for two years, calculating our equipment down to the last piton and cup of water, and weighing the consequences of a failure high up on the face, TM Herbert and I felt at last ready for the big push.

Our proposed line started to the left of the Salathé-Wall route, ascended some inside corners and arches, crossed the Mammoth terraces and continued more or less up, keeping to the left of the south face or "Nose" route,

June 14: In the cool early morning we walked to where we had left our duffel bags and equipment the day before. The climb begins at the "Moby Dick" slab, a popular two-pitch climb of F9 severity. From the ledge at the top we dropped down *en rappel* for twenty feet to the left and began nailing up. The pitons held well but they were awkward to place in the inside corner that leaned left. There was gardening of dirt and grass before a piton could be placed and as usual, belays in slings. We had to place two bolts in order to reach a

EL CAPITAN.

sixty-foot-long horizontal flake and from these we hung our hammocks and had a secure, restful sleep.

June 15: I completed the traverse placing the pitons very carefully so that the flake would not expand. Then TM continued on, alternating pitons and bolts in a dangerous-looking loose arch. After reaching a trough-like groove, the climbing became easier and we rapidly gained height. Towards sundown TM pendulumed to a large ledge where we were to spend the night. Somehow our hauling system got fouled and many a terse word was exchanged and much needed water spent in perspiration before we were able to lift our two 50-pound bags onto the ledge. The strain of the climbing, the terrible California sun and that ever-present fear and uncertainty were all working away, and were reflected in us.

We had a fine ledge where we could lie out at full length and use our hauling bags for extra warmth. Besides, in the morning there would be no problem in having to repack the bags while hanging from pitons. The single fact that we had a ledge put us back into an elated mood and we joked and talked until we fell asleep.

June 16: As we had expected, the third day turned out to be mostly moderate free climbing up the right side of the "Heart." In the late afternoon we reached another fine ledge a pitch above the enormous "Mammoth terraces." The last lead was done in the rain as the weather had quickly turned from oppressive heat to a fine drizzle. When it began to pour in earnest we crouched in our *cagoules* and waited. In a brief break TM started nailing the next day's lead, while I belayed and collected water that was running down the rock. But the water had a bright green color and tasted so foul that we decided to keep it only as a reserve for the last day.

June 17: For the first half of the day we followed a single crack and then switched to another which we followed until we were forced to quit climbing early when the intermittent rain settled into a downpour. Since we were obviously in for a nasty bivouac, we prepared for it as best we could. We even tried to hang our hammocks above us as a shield against the torrents of rain. It never stopped all night and the cold was intense, as in a high mountain storm. Soaked through, we huddled together to keep warm. TM had a particularly bad night, shivering so violently that he could hardly speak. When he did, he sounded almost delirious. We were despondent and for the moment had lost the vision and our courage. Yet we kept any thoughts of retreat to ourselves.

June 18: The returning light restored our courage. A perfect crack in an overhanging corner allowed us to gain height rapidly while the overhanging wall shielded us from the rain. At the top of the corner Herbert began placing bolts across a blank area, doing a fantastic job of stretching out the distance between them. This traverse we hoped would lead us to the "Grey Bands" from where we would reach the beginning of the upper part of our route. After resting from the exhausting work of placing eleven bolts, all horizontally, he dropped down, went around a corner and began to layback up vertical flakes. Losing voice-contact with me, he painstakingly backed down until he could belay from the top of a very shaky flake. It was a tremendous effort and certainly saved the day. I just had time to finish the next pitch and to reach the "Grey Bands" before dark. We rappelled down to a good ledge and fumbled around in the dark to set up our bivouac. My down jacket was hopelessly soaked from the constant rain and so TM gave me his sweater, which had to do for the rest of the climb.

June 19: The cold grey dawn revealed an appalling sight. Barring us from the summit were 1000 feet of wild, overhanging wall capped by a 30-foot ceiling. A quick inventory showed two days' worth of food and water and only nine expansion bolts. There was no going down from here. The only practical retreat would be to traverse the "Grey Bands" for 400 feet to the "Nose Route", up which we knew we could make the top in two or two-and-a-half days. Aside from the uncertainty of the way ahead and our short supplies, we were physically and mentally exhausted from the strain of the climbing and the cold, wet bivouacs. Should we retreat or go on? Here was that line that has to be crossed of which Herzog speaks so eloquently in *Annapurna.* The cost of a failure can be dear, but the values to be gained from a success can be so marvelous as often to change a person's whole life.

After all, why were we here but to gain these personal values? Down below there were only ten people who even knew we were up here. Even if we were successful, there would be no crowds of hero worshippers, no newspaper reports. Thank goodness American climbing has not yet progressed to that sorry state.

Our decision made, TM led upwards. At this point the route becomes vague in my mind. The artificial climbing blends into the free. The corners, dihedrals, jam-cracks, bulges, are all indistinguishable parts of the great, overhanging wall. The pitches never end, and one day merges into another. I recall only bits and pieces. A horrible flaring chimney sticks in my mind, and the most difficult pendulum in my life. Always the overhangs and bulges keep us from knowing exactly where to go. And I remember a wonderful Peregrine falcon eyrie deep back in a chimney; soft white pieces of down stuck on to the crystals of grey granite.

June 20: The view below our hammocks was terrific—2500 feet between us and the ground. But that was another life and we began to discover our own world. We now felt at home. Bivouacking in hammocks was completely natural. Nothing felt strange about our vertical world. With the more receptive senses we now appreciated everything around us. Each individual crystal in the granite stood out in bold relief. The varied shapes of the clouds never ceased to attract our attention. For the first time we noticed tiny bugs that were all over the walls, so tiny they were barely noticeable. While belaying, I stared at one for 15 minutes, watching him move and admiring his brilliant red color.

How could one ever be bored with so many good things to see and feel! This unity with our joyous surroundings, this ultra-penetrating perception gave us a feeling of contentment that we had not had for years. It reminded TM of his childhood days when the family all came together on the porch of his home to sit and watch the setting sun.

The climbing continued to be extreme and in our now very weakened state strenuous pitches took us hours to lead. TM is normally a fairly conservative climber, but now he was climbing brilliantly. He attacked the most difficult pitch of the climb, an overhanging series of loose flakes, with absolute confidence; he placed pitons behind the gigantic loose blocks that could break off at any moment, never hesitating and never doubting his ability.

June 21: Awakening on the eighth day, we promptly devoured the last few bites of food and the last of our water. Four bolts were left; 400

feet to go, and always that summit overhang weighing on our minds. It was going to be close. When the cracks were good, they were all one size; we had constantly to drop down and clean our own pitches in order to use the same pitons higher up. Often the cracks were bottoming, which meant having to put pitons back to back and tying them off with only the tips holding. The slow progress was extremely frustrating. The rain continued to fall in a silvery curtain that stayed a good 25 feet away from us. Hanging from pitons under an overhang we placed our last bolt, hung by a "cliff hanger" on a tiny flake and barely reached a good crack to our left.

Our friends on top urged us on with promises of champagne, roast chicken, beer and fresh fruit. But the summit overhang still barred us and we almost insanely tried one blind crack after another. Finally, with the help of a light from above, we placed the last piton. We took a few halting steps on the horizontal and abandoned ourselves to a gastronomic orgy.

Looking back up at our route late one afternoon when a bluish haze covered the west side of El Capitan, it seemed to have lost a bit of its frightfulness but appeared even more aloof and mysterious than before. It is far too deep-rooted to be affected by the mere presence of man. But we had been changed. We had absorbed some of its strength and serenity.

John Muir in Yosemite Valley

SECTION VI: THE CONSERVATIONISTS

In May 1832, George Catlin, the great painter of the American Indian, arrived in Fort Pierre, South Dakota. The westward migration had scarcely begun and the country lying west of Fort Pierre was still a vast wilderness, abounding in game, virgin mountain peaks, and wild, free-flowing rivers. Displaying a remarkably prescient eye, Catlin foresaw the taming of it all. In a letter to the New York *Daily Commercial Advertiser,* he offered the imaginative suggestion that the western wild lands "might in future be seen (by some great protecting policy of government) preserved in their pristine beauty and wildness, in a *magnificent park,* where the world could see for ages to come, the native Indian in his classic attire, galloping his wild horse . . . amid the fleeting herds of elks and buffaloes."

The idea of a national park cannot be said to have originated with Catlin, but he was the first to put it quite so clearly. Within thirty years, one didn't need a discerning eye to see that unless his suggestion was adopted immediately, the wild West would certainly fall prey to the plow and the axe of the civilizers.

That a few Americans resisted such an outcome was a remarkable and fortuitous turn of events. It was a national imperative, many believed, to tame the untamed; yet by the 1860s, there was a full-blown movement in the United States to do just the opposite—to preserve a part of the American wilderness exactly as it had been found. The contribution of such writers as Henry David Thoreau, Ralph Waldo

Emerson and George Perkins Marsh, and such painters as Thomas Cole and Frederic Church to the growth of this movement was enormous. So too, curiously, was the founding during the 1830s of scenic cemeteries near many eastern cities. Established as alternatives to barren and unhygienic urban cemeteries, these landscaped rural burial grounds unexpectedly proved hugely popular as outing sites for non-mourners.

Additionally, many people were both horrified and indignant at a practice commonly seen during the westward movement, the wanton destroying of lands and wildlife by commercial interests motivated only by profits. Americans were beginning to understand that in the natural wonders of the West, they possessed something unique and priceless. Wilderness gave the nation an edge on Europe, whose traditions and culture were the envy of many Americans. Here was an antidote for that envy. The Old World had kings and cathedrals, but nothing of the wild and the primitive. In the splendors of the West, Americans discovered a ready-made source of national pride.

These factors, plus the rather more practical one that there appeared to be no great economic value in a remote tract in California called Yosemite Valley, combined in 1864 to bring about a momentous event. Congress passed almost without opposition a bill granting the valley and the Mariposa sequoia grove to the state of California "for public use, resort, and recreation . . . inalienable for all time." Here was the first instance of a governmental body setting aside land for scenic preservation, and the legislative beginning of the nation's—and the world's—national park system.

Today California's good fortune at hosting the birth of the preservation movement is evident to anyone who visits the Sierra Nevada. Thousands of square miles of mountainous terrain are set aside in three national parks and a network of federal wilderness areas, placing much of this land off limits to highways, logging, off-road vehicles, and hamburger stands. The pristine character of the protected portions of the Sierra makes the adulteration of much of the remainder all the easier to see and deplore: overdeveloped Lake Tahoe, clearcut national forests, shrinking Mono Lake.

Paradoxically, it is a tribute to the protected status of much of the High Sierra that American vacationers think of Colorado, not

California, as the Mountain State. The reason is simple. Magnificent views of Colorado's peaks are available to anyone with an automobile. Mining roads approach all the peaks, and highways lead to the very summits of some.

The grand panoramas of the far more spectacular Sierra, on the other hand, are hidden from the casual tourist. Views of the alpine Sierra open up only after a hard day's hike from the nearest road; visits to the high summits lie a day or two beyond. In the protected High Sierra, one finds trails and campsites, not roads and motels.

"For all the losses since John Muir's time," David Brower has written, "an invaluable resource still lives. Much of the Sierra wilderness is essentially what it was half a century ago, altered only by natural succession. The favorite, untouched high places are a constant that can reassure a man."

Why some of the high places are untouched, and others touched beyond repair, are the subjects of the selections that follow.

Anonymous

The Alarm is Sounded

Midway through the 19th Century, the nation knew little about the California mountains beyond their value as a gold producer. Yosemite Valley had not yet acquired a reputation as a tourist attraction, while the Sierra Nevada was known solely as a bad idea to be done with by travelers as quickly as possible.

The discovery of the Calaveras Grove of sequoia trees in 1852 changed this almost overnight.[1] Suddenly worldwide attention was focused on the Sierra. In short order, private enterprise stepped in to capitalize on the public's curiosity about sequoias. Several giants were cut down and their bark shells shipped to New York for public display.[2] The desecration went unlamented by most observers, but for a few it touched a raw nerve. In all seriousness, poet James Russell Lowell wrote an article entitled "Humanity to Trees," and proposed the establishment of a society for the prevention of cruelty to trees. When an illustration of a downed sequoia reached London's influential Gleason's Pictorial *in 1853, the editors published the picture, together with some irate remarks from a California reader.*

To our mind it seems a cruel idea, a perfect desecration, to cut down such a splendid tree. But this has been done, not, however, without a vast deal of labor. It was accomplished by first boring holes through the body with long augers, worked by machinery, and afterwards sawing from one to the other. Of course, as the sawing drew to a close, the workmen were on the alert to notice the first sign of toppling, but none came; the tree was so straight and evenly balanced on all sides, that it retained its upright position after it had been sawed through. Wedges were then forced in, and a breeze happening to spring up, over went the monster with a crash which was heard for miles around. The bark was stripped from it for the length of fifty feet

---

[1]See "James M. Hutchings: A Curiously Delusive Dream," Section IV.
[2]See "Anonymous: A Carpeted Saloon," Section IV.

from the base, and is from one to two feet in thickness. It was taken off in sections, so that it can be placed, relatively, in its original position, and thus give the beholder a just idea of the gigantic dimensions of the tree. So placed it will occupy a space of about thirty feet in diameter or ninety feet in circumference and about fifty feet in height. . . . At last accounts the tree was at Stockton, on the way to San Francisco, where it was to be exhibited, previous to its shipment to the Atlantic States. Probably it will not be very long, therefore, before our readers will be able to get a view of this monster of the California woods for a trifling admission fee. In Europe, such a natural production would have been cherished and protected, if necessary, by law; but in this money-making, go-ahead community, thirty or forty thousand dollars are paid for it, and the purchaser chops it down, and ships it off for a show! We hope that no one will conceive the idea of purchasing Niagara Falls with the same purpose! The Mammoth Cave of Kentucky, is comparatively safe, being *underground*; and then it would be impossible to get it all away through the limited size of the entrance. So, for the present, at least, we need not expect the cave [to be carried off] this way. But, seriously, what in the world could have possessed any mortal to embark in such a speculation with this mountain of wood? In its natural condition, rearing its majestic head towards heaven, and waving in all its native vigor, strength and verdure, it was a sight worth a pilgrimmage to see.

The Alarm is Sounded, from *Gleason's Pictorial Drawing-Room Companion,* October 1, 1853.

Israel Ward Raymond

If We Can Obtain
This Grant . . .

By the early 1860s, Yosemite Valley was known throughout the nation. Few tourists had yet visited the valley, but its splendors had been well publicized in the eastern press. Horace Greeley called Yosemite the "greatest marvel on the continent" in his 1860 account of his trip west. Even more influential was a widely circulated series of articles by Thomas Starr King describing the sublime scenery of the valley.

Before long, actual views of Yosemite by such artists as Thomas A. Ayres and Albert Bierstadt and photographer Carleton E. Watkins were making their way east. When in 1864 a group of citizens concerned about the private exploitation of the valley and its trees decided to petition Congress for help, they were raising an issue of national importance.

Among the members of the group was Israel Ward Raymond, the California representative of the Central American Steamship Transit Company of New York. Raymond wrote to California Senator John Conness, asking him to urge Congress to grant Yosemite Valley to the state of California "to prevent occupation and especially to preserve the trees in the valley from destruction." Leaving nothing to chance, Raymond enclosed a selection of Carleton E. Watkins photographs with his letter.

88 Wall Street
New York, 20th February, 1864.

Hon. John Conness
Washington
Dear Sir:

I send by Express some views of the Yosemite Valley to give you some idea of its character. No. 1 is taken from a point on the Mariposa trail and gives a view of about seven miles of the Valley, and the principal part of it. You can

314

BIG TUOLUMNE MEADOWS WITH MOUNT DANA AND MOUNT GIBBS, FROM NEAR THE SODA SPRINGS.

see that its sides are abrupt precipices ranging from 2500 feet to 5000 feet high. Indeed there is no access to it but by trails over the debris deposited by the crumbling of the walls.

The summits are mostly bare Granite Rocks in some parts the surface is covered only by pine trees and can never be of much value.

It will be many years before it is worth while for the government to survey these mountains. But I think it important to obtain the proprietorship soon, to prevent occupation and especially to preserve the trees in the valley from destruction and that it may be accepted by the legislation at its present session and laws passed to give the Commissioners power to take control and begin to consider and lay out their plans for the gradual improvement of the properties.

May not this be a sufficient description:

"That cleft or Gorge in the granite peak of the Sierra Nevada Mountains situated in the County of Mariposa, State of California, on the head waters of the Merced River and known as the Yo Semite Valley with its branches or spurs in length fifteen miles and in width one mile back from the main edge of the precipice on each side of the valley the lines to be defined on Sectional lines when surveyed, by the Surveyor General of the United States and in the spirit of this act."

I take this length and width to secure the approaches from any annoyance. The south end is narrow and filled by the Merced River. The North end leads to Mono, is narrow and filled with rocks, and impassable to a mule.

"Also all those quarter sections in Mariposa County on which stands the grove of Gigantic trees known as the 'Mariposa Big Trees' not exceeding in all Four Sections of one mile square each, the lines to be defined in the spirit of this act by the Surveyor General of the United States when surveying the said County of Mariposa."

I say "quarter" section because the trees are too scattered to be covered by four square miles in compact.

If thought best to have a compact tract it should require six or eight sections.

"The above are granted for public use, resort and recreation and are inalienable forever but leases may be granted for portions not to exceed ten years. All income derived from leases or privileges are to be expended in the preservation and improvement of the prospectus or the roads leading thereto."

The properties shall be managed by (5.7.9) commissioners who shall not receive any payment for said services. Vacancies for death, removal, or resignation shall be filled by the others subject to confirmation by the State Senate. The first Coms. to be:

The Governor of the State of California, Ex. off.
The Collector of the Port of San Francisco.
Prof. Whitney—State Geologist.
Fred Law Olmsted of Mariposa.
George W. Coulter of Coultersville.

[Added by Conness in space left by writer:]
The Mayor of the City of San Francisco.
Prof. John F. Morse   do.
I. W. Raymond   do.

Full reports to be made annually to the Senate of the State.

If we can obtain this grant, I believe we can get Subscriptions in California to make improvements. Submitting the above,

I am very truly yours,
(Sgd.) I. W. RAYMOND.

If We Can Obtain This Grant . . . , from "Yosemite: The Story of an Idea" by Hans Huth. *Sierra Club Bulletin,* March, 1948. Reprinted by permission of The Sierra Club.

The Yosemite Grant

On March 28, 1864, California Senator John Conness introduced the Yosemite Act of 1864 *in Congress. Based largely on the letter he had received from Israel Ward Raymond,*[1] *Conness's bill moved through both houses of Congress with ease.*

The photographs of Yosemite Valley that Raymond had had the foresight to include with his letter apparently made their way to President Abraham Lincoln. Favorably impressed, and with more urgent problems on his mind, Lincoln signed the bill into law on June 30, 1864. Whether he recognized the significance of the bill is uncertain, but it was by any measure a precedent-setting law—the first ever to set aside public lands for the express purpose of preserving their scenic and recreational values, "inalienable for all time."

An Act authorizing a Grant to the State of California of the "Yo-Semite Valley," and of the Land embracing the "Mariposa Big Tree Grove."

Be it enacted by the Senate and House of Representatives of the United States of America in Congress assembled, That there shall be, and is hereby, granted to the State of California the "Cleft" or "Gorge" in the granite peak of the Sierra Nevada mountains, situated in the county of Mariposa, in the State aforesaid, and the headwaters of the Merced River, and known as the Yo-Semite valley, with its branches or spurs, in estimated length fifteen miles, and in average width one mile back from the main edge of the precipice, on each side of the valley, with the stipulation, nevertheless, that the said State shall accept this grant upon the express conditions that the premises shall be held for public use, resort, and recreation; shall be inalienable for all time; but leases not exceeding ten years may be granted for portions of said premises. All incomes derived from

---

[1]See previous selection.

leases of privileges to be expended in the preservation and improvement of the property, or the roads leading thereto; the boundaries to be established at the cost of said State by the United States surveyor-general of California, whose official plat, when affirmed by the commissioner of the general land-office, shall constitute the evidence of the locus, extent, and limits of the said cleft or Gorge; the premises to be managed by the governor of the State with eight other commissioners, to be appointed by the executive of California, and who shall receive no compensation for their services.

SEC. 2. *And be it further enacted,* That there shall likewise be, and there is hereby, granted to the said State of California the tracts embracing what is known as the "Mariposa Big Tree Grove," not to exceed the area of four sections, and to be taken in legal sub-divisions of one quarter section each, with the like stipulation as expressed in the first section of this act as to the State's acceptance, with like conditions as in the first section of this act as to inalienability, yet with same lease privilege; the income to be expended in preservation, improvement, and protection of the property; the premises to be managed by commissioners as stipulated in the first section of this act, and to be taken in legal sub-divisions as aforesaid; and the official plat of the United States surveyor-general, when affirmed by the commissioner of the general land-office, to be the evidence of the locus of the said Mariposa Big Tree Grove.

APPROVED, June 30, 1864.

The Yosemite Grant, from *Yosemite Grant,* U.S. Congress: Act of June 30, 1864 (13 STAT., 325). An Act Authorizing a grant to the State of California of the "Yo-Semite Valley," and of the land embracing the "Mariposa Big Tree Grove."

The Carcass of a Horse

The Yosemite Act did not make a national park of Yosemite. Rather it ceded the valley and the Mariposa Grove—federal lands—to the state of California for preservation and public use.

However prudent this action may have seemed at the time, it soon proved disastrous. The California legislature refused to appropriate funds adequate for the park's upkeep. Yosemite commissioners were political appointees with no overriding interest in the park's preservation. Indifferent to their responsibilities as overseers, most were easy targets for private interests bent on exploiting the park's natural features. By 1890 the beauty of Yosemite Valley was literally threatened with destruction.

If a lesson was learned from all of this, it was forgotten periodically during the years ahead. Private interests attempted to wrest public-interest lands away from the federal government during the Land Grab of the 1940s and the Sagebrush Rebellion of the 1980s. Supporters of the takeovers put forward the specious argument that local people should control local lands, ignoring the fact that this is not an argument at all but a mandate for exploitation. However plodding and impersonal federal management of national-interest lands may be, Washington has the interests of the nation at heart, while local managers have only their own. As a February 1890 editorial in The Nation *pointed out, under California management Yosemite Valley had deteriorated shockingly, and it was time for something to be done.*

It is being gradually recognized that a mistake was made by Congress in 1864 when it reserved merely the Yosemite Valley and its immediate surroundings as a public park, and placed it under the protection of the State of California. Perhaps it would have been better had it remained national property, like the Yellowstone Park. But one thing is certain—the grant should have included a much larger territory. Those who have visited the Yosemite, and have had time to inspect not only the valley itself, with its precipitous surrounding peaks, but also the neighboring cañons, cliffs, and lakes, or who have read a description of them in Prof. Whitney's admirable manual (now unfortunately out of print), are aware that the Yosemite valley is merely the grand climax of a series of cumulative natural wonders which make the heart of the Sierra Nevada Mountains the most romantic and sublime region in the world. It needs no argumentation that these neighboring wonders also should be reserved for all time as national property, for the benefit of the thousands who in future generations will spend their summers here in pursuit of health and pleasure.

At a meeting of the Yosemite Commissioners last June, it was suggested that the National Government should enlarge the Yosemite grant, making it include about fifty square miles instead of eight. Unless this is done, the lumber-men will ere long despoil these wonderful mountain-sides of their superb forests, as they have the shores of that gem of mountain lakes, Tahoe, for the purpose of supplying Carson City with fuel and Virginia City with planks for the mining shafts. It is expected that Senator Stanford will introduce a bill during the present session of Congress in accordance with the suggestion of the Yosemite Commissioners, and if this is done it should enlist the active support of the entire press of the country, for it must be borne in mind that the disappearance of forests in the vicinity of the Yosemite would cause the snow to melt much sooner, and thus dry up very early in the season the many waterfalls which are the chief glory of the valley.

The laudable action of the Yosemite Commissioners in urging an additional grant cannot, however, disguise the fact that the past management of the valley has been open to serious reproaches. The sensational attacks on the management printed last winter in a San Francisco newspaper were too obviously prejudiced and exaggerated to do any good. But the January number of the *Century* contains an editorial article and letters by Mr. R. U. Johnson, G. G. Mackenzie, and Lucius P. Deming, which give a starling picture of errors of commission and omission in the treatment of the valley. What takes the matter entirely out of the field of controversy, and shows that the allegations are bare facts, is the circumstance that Mr. Johnson is in possession of about a hundred photographs on which the sins committed in the valley are recorded indelibly. We have seen these photographs, and can testify from them and from personal observation last May that the strictures in the *Century* are not exaggerated or fanciful. Notwithstanding the Congressional enactment that "the premises shall be held for public use, resort, and recreation," a portion of the floor of the valley has been fenced in and the ground made to bear, instead of the beautiful flowers and grasses which naturally clothe it, hay for the horses of the transportation company, although it has been proved that the hay could have been more cheaply brought in on wagons. Horses and cattle have also been turned loose and allowed to trample down the wild azaleas and other flowers that constitute one of the special attractions of a trip to the Yosemite. Some of the finest trees have been needlessly destroyed, and Mr. Mackenzie writes that "there are places in the valley where one is forced to wonder

Sheep in Whitney Meadow

why the axes themselves did not turn and smite the men who were putting them to such base uses." Mr. Johnson writes that "near the Yosemite Falls an unnecessary swath has been cut through the forest, to the sacrifice of some of the noblest oaks in the valley, the boles of which lie where they were felled. The object of this is represented to have been to open a vista from the bar-room of Barnard's Hotel, to rival the natural view of the same fall from the Stoneman House."

Among the artificial attractions of the valley last spring were the carcass of a horse, and several huge piles of cans, one of them just behind the chapel, where all tourists pass on their way to Glacier Point. The State hotel was so badly constructed that it has been condemned as unsafe. One of its outhouses is a pigsty, which is sometimes so offensive that tourists are obliged to leave the piazza. The hotel is surrounded by a field of blackened stumps, and its location is as inconvenient as possible to all the chief sights, obviously to compel tourists to hire carriages of horses. The roads and bridges are laid on the principle of convenience, without reference to specially artistic view-points; nor are there any foot-paths or benches. It is said, however, that the poetic Governor who is at the head of the Commission, has suggested the introduction of horse-cars for the convenience of those who are too poor to hire horses; and an active member of the Board has threatened to cut down all the trees under thirty years old, because "underwood" is dangerous in case of fire; in reply to which it may be stated that dead logs and heaps of dry bushes, which are much more liable to spread a fire than green underbush, are lying about everywhere. Some of the grossest nuisances in the valley will doubtless be remedied now that the venerable pioneer, Mr. Galen Clark, has been appointed guardian; but after all he is only an executive officer subject to the orders of the Commissioners. These Commissioners receive no salary, and meet only twice a year, and cannot be expected to give to the valley the attention it needs. It is therefore imperatively necessary that a salaried landscape expert be appointed to superintend the valley, and a provision for his salary should be included in the proposed new grant.

The Carcass of a Horse, from "Preservation of the Yosemite Valley." *The Nation,* February 6, 1890.

John Muir

The Tuolumne Yosemite

As state-managed Yosemite Valley continued to deteriorate, conservationists adopted a two-point agenda: management of the valley must be turned over to the federal government; and a huge national park encompassing the entire watersheds of the Merced and Tuolumne rivers must be created.

Robert Underwood Johnson, associate editor of The Century Magazine, *was an enthusiastic supporter of both imperatives. It was he who suggested the idea of a Yosemite National Park to John Muir during a camping trip the two made to Tuolumne Meadows in 1889. Muir agreed to open a national park campaign by writing a series of descriptive articles for the* Century. *Johnson rallied public support in the pages of his magazine, and used his considerable influence in Washington to help push a park bill through Congress.*

Muir's first article, "The Treasures of Yosemite," appeared in August 1890. "Features of the Proposed Yosemite National Park" ran the following month. In the second article, Muir issued a plea for the preservation of Hetch Hetchy Valley. It was a plea that, without Muir's knowledge, brimmed with irony; in 1890 he could hardly have guessed the fate that awaited Hetch Hetchy a quarter of a century later.

MOST people who visit Yosemite are apt to regard it as an exceptional creation, the only valley of its kind in the world. But nothing in Nature stands alone. She is not so poor as to have only one of anything. The explorer in the Sierra and elsewhere finds many Yosemites, that differ not more than one tree differs from another of the same species. They occupy the same relative positions on the mountain flanks, were formed by the same forces in the same kind of granite, and have similar sculpture, waterfalls, and vegetation. The Hetch Hetchy Valley has long been known as the Tuolumne Yosemite. It is said to have been discovered by Joseph Screech, a hunter, in 1850,

KOLÁNA ROCK, HETCH HETCHY VALLEY.

a year before the discovery of the great Merced Yosemite. It lies in a northwesterly direction from Yosemite, at a distance of about twenty miles, and is easily accessible to mounted travelers by a trail that leaves the Big Oak Flat road at Bronson's Meadows, a few miles below Crane Flat. But by far the best way to it for those who have useful limbs is across the divide direct from Yosemite. Leaving the valley by Indian Cañon or Fall Cañon, you cross the dome-paved basin of Yosemite Creek, then bear to the left around the head fountains of the South Fork of the Tuolumne to the summit of the Big Tuolumne Cañon, a few miles above the head of Hetch Hetchy. Here you will find a glorious view. Immediately beneath you, at a depth of more than 4000 feet, you see a beautiful ribbon of level ground, with a silver thread in the middle of it, and green or yellow according to the time of year. That ribbon is a strip of meadow, and the silver thread is the main Tuolumne River. The opposite wall of the cañon rises in precipices, steep and angular, or with rounded brows like those of Yosemite, and from this wall as a base extends a fine wilderness of mountains, rising dome above dome, ridge above ridge, to a group of snowy peaks on the summit of the range. Of all this sublime congregation of mountains Castle Peak is king: robed with snow and light, dipping unnumbered points and spires into the thin blue sky, it maintains amid noble companions a perfect and commanding individuality.

You will not encounter much difficulty in getting down into the cañon, for bear trails may readily be found leading from the upper feeding-grounds to the berry gardens and acorn orchards of Hetch Hetchy, and when you reach the river you have only to saunter by its side a mile to two down the cañon before you find yourself in the open valley. Looking about you, you cannot fail to discover that you are in a Yosemite valley. As the Merced flows through Yosemite, so does the Tuolumne through Hetch Hetchy. The bottom of Yosemite is about 4000 feet above sea level, the bottom of Hetch Hetchy is about 3800 feet, and in both the walls are of gray granite and rise abruptly in precipices from a level bottom, with but little debris along their bases. Furthermore it was a home and stronghold of the Tuolumne Indians, as Ahwahne was of the grizzlies. Standing boldly forward from the south wall near the lower end of the valley is the rock Kolána, the outermost of a picturesque group corresponding to the Cathedral Rocks of Yosemite, and about the same height. Facing Kolána on the north side of the valley is a rock about 1800 feet in height, which presents a bare, sheer front like El Capitan, and over its massive brow flows a stream that makes the most graceful fall I have ever seen. Its Indian name is Tu-ee-u-la-la, and no other, so far as I have heard, has yet been given it. From the brow of the cliff it makes a free descent of a thousand feet and then breaks up into a ragged, foaming web of cascades among the boulders of an earthquake talus. Towards the end of summer it vanishes, because its head streams do not reach back to the lasting snows of the summits of the range, but in May and June it is indescribably lovely. The only fall that I know with which it may fairly be compared is the Bridal Veil, but it excels even that fall in peaceful, floating, swaying gracefulness. For when we attentively observe the Bridal Veil, even towards the middle of summer when its waters begin to fail, we may discover, when the winds blow aside the outer folds of spray, dense comet-shaped masses shooting through the air with terrible energy; but from the top of the cliff, where the Hetch Hetchy veil first floats free, all the way to the bottom it is in perfect repose. Again, the Bridal Veil is in a shadow-haunted nook inaccessible to the main wind currents of the valley, and has to depend for many of its gestures on irregular, teasing side currents and whirls, while Tu-ee-u-la-la, being fully exposed on the open cliff, is sun drenched all day, and is ever ready to yield graceful compliance to every wind that blows. Most people unacquainted with the behavior of mountain streams fancy that when they escape the bounds of their rocky channels and launch into the air they at once lose all self-control and tumble in confusion. On the contrary, on no part of their travels do they manifest more calm self-possession. Imagine yourself in Hetch Hetchy. It is a sunny day in June, the pines sway dreamily, and you are shoulder-deep in grass and flowers. Looking across the valley through beautiful open groves you see a bare granite wall 1800 feet high rising abruptly out of the green and yellow vegetation and glowing with sunshine, and in front of it the fall, waving like a downy scarf, silver bright, burning with white sun-fire in every fiber. In coming forward to the edge of the tremendous precipice and taking flight a little hasty eagerness appears, but this is speedily hushed in divine repose. Now observe the marvelous distinctness and delicacy of the various kinds of sun-filled tissue into which the waters are woven. They fly and float and drowse down the face of that grand gray rock in so leisurely and unconfused a manner that you may examine their texture and patterns as you would a piece of embroidery held in the hand. It is a flood of singing air, water, and sunlight woven into cloth that spirits might wear.

The great Hetch Hetchy Fall, called Wa-páma by the Tuolumnes, is on the same side of the valley as the Veil, and so near it that both may be seen in one view. It is about 1800 feet in height, and seems to be nearly vertical when one is standing in front of it, though it is considerably inclined. Its location is similar to that of the Yosemite Fall, but the volume of water is much greater. No two falls could be more unlike than Wa-páma and Tu-ee-u-la-la, the one thundering and beating in a shadowy gorge, the other chanting in deep, low tones, and with no other shadows about it than those of its own waters, pale-gray mostly, and violet and pink delicately graded. One whispers, "He dwells in peace," the other is the thunder of his chariot wheels in power. This noble pair are the main falls of the valley, though there are many small ones essential to the perfection of the general harmony.

The wall above Wa páma corresponds, both in outlines and in details of sculpture, with the same relative portion of the Yosemite wall. Near the Yosemite Fall the cliff has two conspicuous benches extending in a horizontal direction 500 and 1500 feet above the valley. Two benches similarly situated, and timbered in the same way, occur on the same relative position on the Hetch Hetchy wall, and on no other portion. The upper end of Yosemite is closed by the great Half Dome, and the upper end of Hetch Hetchy is closed in the same way by a mountain rock. Both occupy angles formed by the confluence of two large glaciers that have long since vanished. In front of this head rock the river forks like the Merced in Yosemite. The right fork as you ascend is the main Tuolumne, which takes its rise in a glacier on the north side of Mount Lyell and flows through the Big Cañon. I have not traced the left fork to its highest source, but, judging from the general trend of the ridges, it must be near Castle Peak. Upon this left or North Fork there is a remarkably interesting series of cascades, five in number, ranged along a picturesque gorge, on the edges of which we may saunter safely and gain fine views of the dancing spray below. The first is a wide-spreading fan of white, crystal-covered water, half leaping half sliding over a steep polished pavement, at the foot of which it rests and sets forth clear and shining on its final flow to the main river. A short distance above the head of this cascade you discover the second, which is as impressively wild and beautiful as the first, and makes you sing with it as though you were a part of it. It is framed in deep rock walls that are colored yellow and red with lichens, and fringed on the jagged edges by live-oaks and sabine pines, and at the bottom in damp nooks you may see ferns, lilies, and azaleas.

Three or four hundred yards higher you come to the third of the choir, the largest of the five. It is formed of three smaller ones inseparably combined, which sing divinely, and make spray of the best quality for rainbows. A short distance beyond this the gorge comes to an end, and the bare stream, without any definite channel, spreads out in a thin, silvery sheet about 150 feet wide. Its waters are, throughout almost its whole extent, drawn out in overlapping folds of lace, thick sown with diamond jets and sparks that give an exceedingly rich appearance. Still advancing, you hear a deep muffled booming, and you push eagerly on through flowery thickets until the last of the five appears through the foliage. The precipice down which it thunders is fretted with projecting knobs, forming polished keys upon which the wild waters play. . . .

I have thus briefly touched upon a number of the chief features of a region which it is proposed to reserve out of the public domain for the use and recreation of the people. A bill has already been introduced in Congress by Mr. Vandever creating a national park about the reservation which the State now holds in trust for the people. . . . Unless reserved or protected the whole region will soon or late be devastated by lumbermen and sheepmen, and so of course be made unfit for use as a pleasure ground. Already it is with great difficulty that campers, even in the most remote parts of the proposed reservation and in those difficult of access, can find grass enough to keep their animals from starving; the ground is already being gnawed and trampled into a desert condition, and when the region shall be stripped of its forests the ruin will be complete. Even the Yosemite will then suffer in the disturbance effected on the water-shed, the clear streams becoming muddy and much less regular in their flow. It is also devoutly to be hoped that the Hetch Hetchy will escape such ravages of man as one sees in Yosemite. Ax and plow, hogs and horses, have long been and are still busy in Yosemite's gardens and groves. All that is accessible and destructible is being rapidly destroyed—more rapidly than in any other Yosemite in the Sierra, though this is the only one that is under the special protection of the Government. And by far the greater part of this destruction of the fineness of wildness is of a kind that can claim no right relationship with that which necessarily follows use.

The Tuolumne Yosemite, from "Features of the Proposed Yosemite National Park" by John Muir. *The Century Magazine,* September, 1890. Reprinted by permission of *Current History.*

Warren Olney

To Explore, Enjoy, and Render Accessible

The campaign for a Yosemite National Park succeeded. Unfortunately, there was a gaping hole in the bill that President Benjamin Harrison signed into law on October 1, 1890: a huge national park taking in the watersheds of the Tuolumne and Merced rivers was indeed created, but the management of Yosemite Valley was left in the hands of the state of California.

Conditions in the valley worsened during the years that followed. To compound the problem, the newly formed national park created its own headaches. State and federal administrators clashed over management plans. Questions of who had responsibility for what went unanswered. In the high country, sheep owners refused to abide by the new national park regulations. The summer after sheep were barred from the park, 90,000 of them were brought in to graze (and overgraze) Yosemite's meadows.

Many now saw the urgent need for a committee of concerned citizens to be formed to fight for the preservation and wise use not only of Yosemite Valley but of the entire Sierra Nevada. John Muir threw his support behind the idea. University of California professor J. H. Senger agreed to bring the interested parties together. On May 28, 1892, 27 Bay Area residents gathered in the office of San Francisco attorney Warren Olney for an organizational meeting. A week later the 27 signed Articles of Incorporation drawn up by Olney. They elected John Muir first president of the organization, which they decided to call the Sierra Club.

Know all men by these presents:

That we, the undersigned, a majority of whom are citizens and residents of the State of California, have this day voluntarily associated ourselves together for the purpose of forming a Corporation under the laws of the State of California. *And we hereby certify as follows, to wit:*

I.

That the name of said Corporation shall be the Sierra Club.

II.

That the said Association is made, and the said Corporation is formed, not for pecuniary profit.

III.

That the purposes for which this Corporation is formed are as follows, to wit: To explore, enjoy and render accessible the mountain regions of the Pacific Coast; to publish authentic information concerning them; to enlist the support and co-operation of the people and the government in preserving the forests and other natural features of the Sierra Nevada Mountains; to take, acquire, purchase, hold, sell and convey real and personal property, and to mortgage or pledge the same for the purpose of securing any indebtedness which the Corporation may incur, and to make and enter into any and all obligations, contracts, and agreements concerning or relating to the business or affairs of the Corporation, or the management of its property.

IV.

That the place where the principal business of said Corporation is to be transacted is the City and County of San Francisco, State of California.

V.

That the term for which said Corporation is to exist is fifty years from and after the date of its incorporation.

VI.

That the number of Directors or Trustees of said Corporation shall be nine (9), and that the names and residences of the Directors or Trustees who are appointed for the first year, to serve until the election and qualification of their successors, are as follows, to wit:

John Muir, Martinez, Cal.

Warren Olney, Oakland, Cal.

J. H. Senger, San Francisco, Cal.

Wm. D. Armes, Oakland, Cal.

David S. Jordan, Palo Alto, Cal.

R. M. Price, Berkeley, Cal.

Mark Brickell Kerr, Golden Gate, Alameda Co., Cal.

Willard D. Johnson, Berkeley, Cal.

John C. Branner, Palo Alto, Cal.

VII.

That the said Corporation has, and shall have, no capital stock. *And we further certify and declare:*

That the above-named Directors of the Corporation were duly elected Directors thereof by the members of said Corporation, at an election for Directors held at 101 Sansome Street, in the City and County of San Francisco, State of California, at eleven A.M., on this 4th day of June, 1892, and that a majority of the members of said Association and Corporation were present and voted at said election, and that at such election each of the said Directors received the votes of a majority of the members of the Corporation present at such election;

Sierra Club 1902 Outing

as more fully appears from the certificate of the two Tellers of Election hereunto annexed and hereby referred to and made a part hereof.

In witness thereof, we have hereunto set our hands and seals this 4th day of June, A.D. 1892.

W. H. Beatty,
Ralph C. Harrison,
George C. Perkins,
G. B. Bayley,
John C. Branner,
James O. Griffin,
Willard D. Johnson,
Josiah Keep,
Hermann Kower,
Hubert P. Dyer,
W. H. Henry,
L. deF. Bartlett,
W. L. Jepson, Jr.,
Warren Olney,
John Muir,
J. H. Senger,
William D. Armes,
Mark Brickell Kerr,
Dorville Libby,
Charles A. Bailey,
C. D. Robinson,
C. B. Bradley,
Fred S. Pheby,
Charles G. Harker,
R. M. Price,
Will Denman,
Warren Gregory.

To Explore, Enjoy, and Render Accessible, from Sierra Club *Articles of Incorporation,* June 4, 1892.

Charlie Leidig

Both Men Did the Talking

In an 1895 letter to Century Magazine *editor Robert Underwood Johnson, John Muir summarized the conditions in Yosemite Valley: "It looks ten times worse now than when you saw it seven years ago."*

Three hundred horses were turned loose nightly "to feed and trample the flora out of existence." Saloons, warehouses, barns, private homes, pig pens, and chicken coops littered the once pristine valley; most of the trees had been cut down for lumber. Concluded Muir: "As long as the management is in the hands of eight politicians appointed by the ever-changing Governor of California, there is but little hope."

By contrast, the efforts of the federal government were paying off at last in the national park surrounding the valley. Back-country rangers were succeeding in their attempts to expel recalcitrant sheep herders, and Muir was delighted to report that the meadows were recovering from decades of overgrazing. Clearly, it was crucial that management of Yosemite Valley be taken over by the federal government.

In the years that followed, Muir devoted himself to this goal, arguing his case with whoever would listen. When he was invited to accompany President Theodore Roosevelt on a Yosemite camping trip in 1903, Muir jumped at the chance: never was he likely to gain the ear of a more influential listener.

Yosemite ranger Charlie Leidig accompanied Muir and Roosevelt on this adventure, and later wrote a third-person account of the trip. The first night the three men, together with ranger Archie Leonard and Army packer Jacher Alder, made camp beside the Grizzly Giant sequoia tree in the Mariposa Grove.

The President said to Charlie Leidig, "Leidig, please do not let anybody disturb me, because I am tired and want rest and sleep." Charlie did the cooking. He said they had fried chicken and beefsteak for supper that night. The President drank strong, black coffee and went to bed early that first night under the Grizzly Giant. The only shelter provided for the President was "shelter half" under which about forty blankets were piled to serve as a bed. The President got just as deep into these as he wanted for warmth and comfort. Four mules were used to haul this equipment.

On May 3, 1903, Leidig states they broke camp at Mariposa Grove and were on horses at 6:30 A.M. The President directed Leidig to "outskirt and keep away from civilization." Leidig led the party down the Lightning Trail. They crossed the South Fork at Greeley's and hit the Empire Meadows Trail. They especially avoided approaching the Wawona Hotel for fear the President would be brought into contact with members of his own official party which had remained for the night at Wawona. They had a cold lunch on the ridge east of Empire Meadows. There was lots of snow as they crossed towards Sentinel Dome; they took turns breaking trail through deep snow. In the Bridalveil Meadows the party plowed through 5 ft. of snow. The President mired down and Charlie had to get a log to get him out. It was snowing hard and the wind was blowing.

Muir proposed that they camp on the ridge just back of Sentinel Dome. Leidig's suggestion, however, that they travel down to the approximate location of the present campgrounds at Glacier Point where water and better camping conditions in May could be found, prevailed. It snowed 5 in. during that night and everything was frozen in the morning.

Around campfire that night Leidig stated that Roosevelt and Muir talked far into the night regarding Muir's glacial theory of the formation of Yosemite Valley. Leidig stated they talked a great deal about the conservation of forests in general and Yosemite in particular. He heard them discussing the setting aside of other areas in the United States for park purposes. Leidig stated that during the trip Muir seemed to bother the President by picking twigs for the President's buttonhole. He also said that some difficulty was encountered because both men wanted to do the talking.

On the morning of May 4, the party went down to Glacier Point for pictures that had been prearranged. . . . As they left Glacier Point, the President rode in front followed by Leidig, Leonard, Muir and the packer. They were all dressed in civilian attire. The rangers wore blue overalls, shaps and spurs. They went into Little Yosemite Valley for lunch. Here they encountered a considerable crowd of valley visitors, since it had been widely advertised in the papers that the President was visiting the park. . . .

The President requested that all people be kept at a distance in order that he could carry out his desire for a "roughing trip"; so everybody was kept at a respectful distance.

When the party reached Camp Curry at 2 P.M., they found a big crowd of women in front of the camp. They had formed a big line across the road in an attempt to stop the President. They all wanted to shake hands with him. Charlie Leidig states he was riding second in line with a Winchester rifle and six-shooter. His horse was a high spirited animal. The President said, "I am very much annoyed, couldn't you do something?" Leidig replied, "follow me." He gave spurs to his horse and as he reared, women fell apart and the President's party went through the gap. The President waved his hat to the group in the road.

At Sentinel Bridge, Muir suggested that they camp that evening near Bridalveil Fall.

As they left the bridge, the President saw Ellen Boysen standing by her mother on the ground holding a flag. He reached down, picked her up under the pits of her arms and kissing her said, "God bless you, you little angel," and put her down. He waved his party off and started down the valley. He asked Charlie Leidig where Bridalveil Meadow was, saying that Muir had suggested it, and whether it was a fitting place. They went down the south side of the river followed by a big string of people on horseback, in buggies, surries, and others on foot. Leidig stated there must have been 300 or 500, or possibly 1000 of them in the crowd, filling the Bridalveil Meadows. As they reached their camping place on a grassy slope just south of the present road through the Bridalveil Meadows, the President said to Leidig, "those people annoy me. Can you get rid of them?" Charlie said he walked out and told the crowd that the President was very tired and asked them to leave. They went—some of them even on tiptoe, so as not to annoy their President.

When Charlie returned to the camp site the President said, "Charlie I am hungry as Hell. Cook any dam thing you wish. How long will it take?"

Charlie told him it would take about 30 minutes, so the President lay on his bed of blankets and went to sleep and snored so loud that Leidig could hear him even above the crackling of the campfire.

After dinner, Muir and the President went out in the meadow until way after dark. When they returned they sat around the campfire where the President told them of his lion hunting trips, etc.

People came again in the morning. Crowds could be seen all through the brush. Leidig kept them away. The stage came down containing the President's offical party. After breakfast, the President and Muir got into the stage and as they left the President called Leidig and Leonard to him and said, "Boys, I am leaving you. Good-bye, and God bless you."

Many times during his trip in Yosemite National Park Leidig related that President Roosevelt demonstrated his great love for birds by whistling and that they would answer him. He also knew most of them.

In later years Roosevelt recalled the morning he awakened beside Muir at Glacier Point, his blankets covered with snow, as "the grandest day of my life."

In the official party with Roosevelt and Muir was California Governor George Pardee. At the end of the trip he was as impressed as Roosevelt with the idea of adding Yosemite Valley to the surrounding national park. The support of these two powerful allies helped park advocates immeasurably during the debate that followed. Many business interests as well as San Francisco's leading newspapers were fiercely opposed to the proposal to surrender Yosemite Valley to Washington. The Examiner *ran a petition for its readers to sign: "There is no legitimate reason for placing the management of this marvel of natural beauty in the hands of the Federal Government."*

Nevertheless, the California legislature approved the turnover in March 1905; the U.S. Congress followed suit on June 11, 1906, and Yosemite Valley at last became part of Yosemite National Park.

Exclaimed John Muir: "Sound the timbrel and let every Yosemite tree and stream rejoice!"

Both Men Did the Talking, from *Charlie Leidig's Report of President Roosevelt's Visit in May, 1903* by Charlie Leidig. Reprinted by permission of the Yosemite National Park Research Library.

TUOLUMNE MEADOWS, LOOKING SOUTH.   UNICORN PEAK AND CATHEDRAL PEAK.

John Muir

Dam Hetch Hetchy!

In 1903, the city of San Francisco applied for the right to dam the Tuolumne River in Yosemite's Hetch Hetchy Valley, in order to utilize the river for its municipal water supply. Thus began the first great test of the inviolability of the national park system, and one of the bitterest battles ever fought between conservationists and developers. The loss twelve years later of Hetch Hetchy to the dam was a stunning defeat for those who had believed that inclusion in a national park was a guarantee of Hetch Hetchy's protection; some say it destroyed John Muir, who died just a year after President Woodrow Wilson signed the bill authorizing construction of the dam.

Throughout the battle, conservationists argued that San Francisco could find adequate water elsewhere, and that because Hetch Hetchy was in a national park, it was imperative that the city do just that. San Francisco, it turned out, wanted Hetch Hetchy water precisely because it was in a national park; as a result, it came free and clear of prior rights, and accordingly, cheap. Thus, in an ironic turn of events, those who had worked for the creation of Yosemite National Park unwittingly had played into the hands of those who eventually opened the park to development.

In a 1907 article, John Muir catalogued the wonders of Hetch Hetchy, much as he had in his famous 1890 Century Magazine article, "Features of the Proposed Yosemite National Park."[1] This time, however, he went on angrily to condemn San Francisco's plan to dam the Tuolumne and flood Hetch Hetchy.

It appears, therefore, that Hetch Hetchy Valley, far from being a plain, common, rock-bound meadow, as many who have not seen it seem to suppose, is a grand landscape garden, one of Nature's rarest

---

[1]See "John Muir: The Tuolumne Yosemite," Section VI.

337

and most precious mountain mansions. As in Yosemite, the sublime rocks of its walls seem to the Nature-lover to glow with life, whether leaning back in repose or standing erect in thoughtful attitudes giving welcome to storms and calms alike. And how softly these mountain rocks are adorned, and how fine and reassuring the company they keep—their brows in the sky, their feet set in groves and gay emerald meadows, a thousand flowers leaning confidently against their adamantine bosses, while birds, bees, butterflies help the river and waterfalls to stir all the air into music—things frail and fleeting and types of permanence meeting here and blending, as if into this glorious mountain temple Nature had gathered her choicest treasures, whether great or small, to draw her lovers into close, confiding communion with her.

Sad to say, this most precious and sublime feature of the Yosemite National Park is in danger of being dammed and made into a reservoir to help supply San Francisco with water and light, thus flooding it from wall to wall and burying its gardens and groves one hundred and seventy-five feet deep. This destructive scheme has long been planned and prayed for, and is still being prayed for by the City Supervisors, not because water as pure and abundant cannot be got from sources outside of the Park, for it can, but only because of the comparative shortness and cheapness of the dam required.

Garden and park making goes on with civilization over all the world, for everybody needs beauty as well as bread, places to play in and pray in where Nature may heal and cheer and give strength to body and soul alike. This natural beauty hunger is made manifest in the little window-sill gardens of the poor, though only a geranium slip in a broken cup, as well as in the radiant rose and lily gardens of the rich, the thousands of spacious city parks and botanical gardens, and in our magnificent National parks—the Yellowstone, Yosemite, Sequoia, etc.—Nature's sublime wonderlands, the admiration and joy of the world. Nevertheless, from the very beginning, however well guarded, they have all been subject to attack by gain-seekers trying to despoil them, mischief-makers and robbers of every degree from Satan to Senators, city supervisors, lumbermen, cattlemen, farmers, etc., trying to make everything dollarable, oftentimes disguised in smiles and philanthropy, calling their plundering "utilization of natural beneficent resources," that man and beast may be fed and the Nation allowed to grow great. Thus the Lord's garden in Eden and the first forest reservation, including only one tree, was spoiled. And so to some extent have all our reservations and parks. Ever since the establishment of the Yosemite National Park by act of Congress, Ocober 1, 1890, constant strife has been going on around its borders, and I suppose will go on as part of the universal battle between right and wrong, however much its boundaries may be shorn.

The first application to the Government by the San Francisco Supervisors for the use of Lake Eleanor and the Hetch Hetchy Valley was made in 1903, and denied December 22 of that year by the Secretary of the Interior. In his report on this case he well says: "Presumably the Yosemite National Park was created such by law because of the natural objects of varying degrees of scenic importance located within its boundaries, inclusive alike of its beautiful small lakes, like Eleanor,

Hetch Hetchy Valley before the dam

and its majestic wonders, like Hetch Hetchy and Yosemite Valley. It is the aggregation of such natural scenic features that makes the Yosemite Park a wonderland which the Congress of the United States sought by law to preserve for all coming time as nearly as practicable in the condition fashioned by the hand of the Creator—a worthy object of National pride and a source of healthful pleasure and rest for the thousands of people who may annually sojourn there during the heated months."

Should this noble Valley be submerged as proposed, not only would it be made utterly inaccessible, but the great Tuolumne Cañon way leading to the Upper Tuolumne Meadows, the focus of pleasure travel in the High Sierra, would also be blocked. None, as far as I have learned, of all the thousands who have seen the Yosemite Park is in favor of this destructive water scheme, and the only hope of its promoters seems to be in the darkness that covers it. Public opinion is not yet awakened, but as soon as light reaches it I believe that nine-tenths or more of even the citizens of San Francisco would be opposed to Hetch Hetchy destruction. The voice of the San Francisco Board of Supervisors is not the voice of California nor of the Nation.

In 1912, Muir expanded upon this article and incorporated it into the final chapter of his book The Yosemite. *Despite the best efforts of preservationists, the plan to develop Hetch Hetchy had somehow taken on a life of its own by this time, and many of the valley's friends had begun to believe that nothing they could do would ever stop the dam.*

The old warrior Muir, however, was not ready to give up yet. In the stirring conclusion to The Yosemite, *he rose to a fever pitch and thundered the angriest and perhaps the most eloquent words of his life: "These temple destroyers," he wrote, "devotees of ravaging commercialism, seem to have a perfect contempt for Nature, and, instead of lifting their eyes to the God of the mountains, lift them to the Almighty Dollar.*

"Dam Hetch Hetchy! As well dam for water-tanks the people's cathedrals and churches, for no holier temple has ever been consecrated by the heart of man."

But to no avail. The struggle continued for one more year. Then on December 19, 1913, President Woodrow Wilson signed the bill authorizing the flooding of Hetch Hetchy Valley; the following year, construction on the O'Shaughnessy Dam across the Tuolumne River began. Today, three-quarters of a century later, the dam stands as a reminder to conservationists everywhere that in the struggle to preserve the splendors of nature there are holding actions but never permanent victories.

Dam Hetch Hetchy! from "The Tuolumne Yosemite in Danger" by John Muir. *The Outlook,* November 2, 1907.

David Brower

Gentle Wilderness

Not many who know David Brower as perhaps the most important and effective conservationist leader of the past two decades realize that during the 1930s he was one of America's premier mountain climbers. Brower began climbing in the Sierra at the time of the Underhill revolution, [1] *and soon compiled one of the most impressive first-ascent records, summer and winter, ever recorded in the range.*

Brower's intense experience with the mountains led him into the conservation movement, where he became a passionate and outspoken champion of environmental sanity. He founded Friends of the Earth in 1969, after serving for 17 years as executive director of the Sierra Club.

Among Brower's many accomplishments is that of making the large-format book of nature photographs practically a staple in American households. As editor of the Sierra Club's award-winning Exhibit Format Series, he subtly and persuasively brought the conservationist position to the attention of countless numbers of people. In the foreword to Gentle Wilderness: The Sierra Nevada, *a collection of photos by Richard Kauffman and quotations of John Muir, Brower addressed the issue of use versus preservation of the Sierra wilderness.*

What John Muir had to say in *My First Summer in the Sierra* led me, forty years ago, to feel I had already been in the Yosemite High Sierra he was discovering for the first time. Nearly a century after John Muir's first summer, Richard Kauffman has come along with camera instead of notebook to recapture the sense of discovery, and the vividness of what Muir called the Range of Light. Here is the Sierra the way Muir saw it, the way others have seen their first summers

---

[1]See "Robert Underhill: The East Face of Mount Whitney," Section V.

confirmed, when they read of Muir's. A cool Sierra wind blows through the photographs, a gentle wind. It is a Sierra illumined by the light of the gentle hours, warm light on a friendly, inviting land.

Is it really gentle wilderness? There is room for argument. Certainly the gentleness of this Sierra wilderness is never soft enough to be cloying. Fear can be mixed with your exhilaration. The passes come impressively high, your breath short, and your pulse rapid. Some of the deepest snows in North America fall there and nothing is gentle about the avalanches when the slopes unload, or about winter temperatures that may drop to fifty-five below. You don't feel very pampered when you are on a half-inch ledge halfway up one of the half-mile-high sheer Yosemite cliffs, or when the March wind finds you and, even though you brace against it with ski poles, flattens you on Mount Lyell's icy shoulder, or when a driving spray drenches you if you venture within a hundred yards of the foot of Vernal Fall in flood, or when a desert sun bakes you at the foot of the Sierra's eastern escarpment, two vertical miles below the summit of Mount Whitney.

Still there is always enough gentleness in the Sierra, or soon will be, when the storm clears or the rough climb ends. No other of the world's great ranges that Mr. Kauffman knows, or that I know, or that so far as we know Muir knew, is as gentle as the Sierra.

If there is to be objection, it is that the Sierra is too gentle—too gentle to counter man's assaults against it. John Muir saw this in his first summer and in the later summers and winters when the Sierra was his address. He dedicated his life to a counterassault on man's misuse of wilderness and wildlife. He helped establish national parks, enlisted support of national leaders in a preservation movement, battled Gifford Pinchot's predominantly utilitarian interest in conservation, wrote and talked and led with exuberant energy—with the same energy that took him through his favorite forests, among the alpine gardens he loved, and on up so many of the Sierra peaks. He also founded the Sierra Club "to explore, enjoy, and render accessible" the mountain range it was named after. In 1911 he dedicated *First Summer* to the members of the club for their good work.

One of his ideas for rendering the Sierra accessible was a program of summer wilderness outings which he and William E. Colby initiated in 1901. Too many of the places he loved were being lost

A Sierra Club campfire, 1940s

because too few people knew about them. There would be no hope of sparing Sierra meadows from being overgrazed and devastated by domestic sheep, for instance, unless people saw the damage firsthand and also saw unspoiled meadows so as to evaluate the loss. The giant sequoias were being logged for grape stakes. Hetch Hetchy Valley itself was to be dammed—in the last analysis to produce hydro-electric power for San Francisco. It was not enough to write about the beauty of these places and the tragedy of losing them. People must see for themselves, appraise the danger to the spot on the spot. Informed, devoted defense would ensue.

For sixty-three years since then the concept has worked, modified only slightly. Early in the game Muir had felt that accessibility should include a fairly formidable road net through the High Sierra. Late in the 'twenties the Sierra Club directors were still advocating several trans-Sierra roads they would shudder to think about today. The words "render accessible" were being misunderstood as an argument for mechanized access and were amended out of the bylaws. The emphasis shifted to getting people to know wilderness as wilderness, to travel there by foot, to leave the fewest possible marks, to spare for another generation the opportunity to discover that which they themselves had loved.

There was not yet much concern about what the foot—a man's or a mule's—might do to wilderness. The high-country was still fairly empty. As late as 1934 I myself could still spend a month in the Kings-Kern country without seeing anyone but my knapsacking companion. Before our ten-week knapsack survey of the John Muir Trail and the Sierra crest was over, we encountered only a few independent travelers—and an entire Sierra Club High Trip of nearly two hundred people and one hundred pack animals. But even then we had only to walk a mile or two to be in empty mountains again (a summer I described in "Far from the Madding Mules," *Sierra Club Bulletin,* annual magazine number, 1935).

Today a thousand people may walk up the east-side trail to the summit of Mount Whitney over the Labor Day week end; forty thousand may hit Yosemite Valley over a Memorial Day week end. There is a new dimension in mountain use—"visitation," the National Park Service calls it. Park Service ecologists have now identified a few hot spots in the high country above Kings Canyon and Sequoia national parks, places where recreational erosion exceeds a given camping area's capability of recovering. Human erosion itself is not too noticeable, but the associated grazing, trampling, and littering by packstock is severe. What Muir had objected to in the impact of commercial sheep is now being accomplished by animals hired for pleasure. A Forest Service ranger spent a year studying what sheer numbers were doing along Bear Creek, south of Yosemite, and concluded that large groups of wilderness travelers should be eliminated: don't concentrate use in a few places, but disperse it and build primitive toilets and fireplaces in many parts of the wilderness to encourage the dispersal. Not a hundred people in one spot, but ten people in ten spots, or five in twenty. Meanwhile, back in Washington, his parent agency was arguing before Congress that there was probably already too much wilderness set aside; considering the little use it was getting, it was far more important to expedite the construction of timber-access roads and logging operations into undedicated wilderness and to make sure that dedicated wilderness was as free as possible of commercial trees. Too little use, yet so much use the land suffered; log it and end the debate!

The confusion continues. The big-trip use that Muir had advocated was the easiest target to hit, or to encourage others to hit. It also happens to be the trip that could serve the widest range of physical and financial abilities. The man too old to carry much of a pack, or the child too young to, can still walk a wilderness trail. Packstock can carry the duffel, the food, the camp equipment. Crew members (usually students who can travel fast enough to break one camp late and make the next one early) allow the wilderness visitor maximum time to enjoy the country with minimum housekeeping. If the moves aren't too far, the stock can relay loads, and half the number of stock can serve the same number of people. Four or more wilderness travelers can thus be served per head of packstock—on a moving trip, the kind that gives the visitor the feel of big, continuous wilderness.

Could wilderness be experienced in such a crowd? Could you see the mountains for the people? As a knapsacker I thought not, but changed my mind in the course of spending a year of summer days on Sierra Club High Trips, making careful notes of what happened, checking with Forest Service and National Park Service observers and ecologists, joining with trip leaders and packers in taking the dozens of steps that minimized the impact of people, whether on the wilderness itself or on other people. I was partial then, and still am eight years later, to the moving trip that can give the visitor the feel of a big, continuous wilderness—one in which you can cross pass after pass and know that on the other side you don't drop into civilization, but stay in wilderness instead. In big wilderness you learn how important size itself is to the viability of wilderness. It needs enough buffer to keep its heartland essentially free from the pervasive influences of technology. Such big wilderness is scarce, and is vanishing at the rate of about a million acres a year, chiefly to the chainsaw. People who know it can save it. No one else.

Were Muir alive today he would see the issue clearly and would keep it clear of all the conscious and unconscious confusion. He would know that the choice was not between pristine wilderness and wilderness overused in spots, but between some overuse and no wilderness at all. He would not forget irreplaceable Glen Canyon, hard-hit at some camps along the river, but still not known by enough people to be saved. The Bureau of Reclamation solved the problem of slightly overused campsites by drowning the entire length of the canyon, permanently, with an unnecessary reservoir.

Muir would see what was happening in the Sierra, and would not be fooled by the forces hostile to preservation who now point a diversionary finger at wilderness footprints. He would point out the marks far more damaging than footprints—logging roads, stumps, and trash-clogged streams—that forever killed gentle wilderness on the Kern Plateau because of too little conservationist use. He would note how the real, unbroken wilderness of the High Sierra climax, extending from the Tioga Road in Yosemite down to the Kern, is still vulnerable: a corridor for a needless trans-Sierra road is relentlessly being kept open at Mammoth Pass, and another south of Whitney Meadows. Because there had been too little use, Muir would observe, the wilderness of Vermilion Valley and of a beautiful basin in the North Fork of the Kings had been drowned by power reservoirs—in a day when hydro-electric power means less and less and unspoiled recreation places mean more and more. Muir would not have been impressed by tears about footprints in eyes that winked at mechanized scooters snorting over wilderness trails.

I am sure that John Muir would still believe that firsthand knowledge of places is vital to their survival and that their survival is vital to man. He needs places where he can be reminded that civilization is only a thin veneer over the deep evolutionary flow of things that built him. Let wilderness live, and it would always tell him truth.

For all the losses since John Muir's time, an invaluable resource still lives. Much of the Sierra wilderness is essentially what it was half a century ago, altered only by natural succession. The favorite, un-touched high places are a constant that can reassure a man. So is the roll of familiar things you pass on your way up the heights—the oak savannah, the digger pines, the orderly succession of ponderosa, incense cedar, sugar pine, the firs, then the denizens of timberline.

One trouble these days is that you have to call the roll of friends too fast. Speed and the wide highway have brought a deprivation, for the right reason perhaps, but in the wrong places. Speed shrinks wilderness, and there wasn't really enough in Muir's day to serve all those who followed him to California or who will one day be here to look or to live.

Even as in Muir's time, the Sierra Club's purpose is still to gather together people from all over who know how important it is that there should always be some land wild and free. They are needed to counter the rationalizations of the highway builders, and dam and logging-road builders, who would slice through and dismember the wilderness. The purpose of this book is to remind everyone (to paraphrase Newton Drury) that neither California nor the rest of America is rich enough to lose any more of the Gentle Wilderness or poor enough to need to.

John McPhee

Mineral King[1]

Following the loss of Hetch Hetchy to the O'Shaughnessy Dam, the major preservation battles moved away from the Sierra. A kind of post-Hetch Hetchy peace settled over the range, and for a while the Sierra became a place to enjoy, not to contest. Mining, logging and grazing abuses decreased as relatively benign use of the mountains became the rule. Conservationists scored important victories when Sequoia National Park was substantially enlarged in 1926, and Kings Canyon National Park was established in 1940. A bid by the city of Los Angeles to create its own Hetch Hetchy legacy in Kings Canyon was squelched before it had a chance to gain momentum. Perhaps most important of all, passage of the Wilderness Act in 1964 fulfilled a long-held preservationist dream by establishing a system of wilderness reserves closed to logging, motor-vehicle use and commercial development. Several million acres of California wild lands today are protected under the Wilderness Act, and several million more await assignment to the wilderness system by the Congress.

Gradually it became clear, however, that all was not well in the Sierra. Overdevelopment at Lake Tahoe posed grave threats to the lake Mark Twain had called "the fairest picture the whole earth affords."[2] Water diversions from Mono Lake to Los Angeles created an ecological disaster. Lumber-company abuses in the national forests forced a 1979 citizens committee to report that the U.S. Forest Service was emphasizing timber harvesting to the detriment of other forest resources.

The issue that captured the most public attention involved a beautiful valley near the southern end of Sequoia National Park called Mineral King. In his book-length profile of Friends of the Earth Chairman David Brower, Encounters with the Archdruid, *John McPhee summarized the issue.*

---

[1]Mineral King, reprinted by permission of Farrar, Straus and Giroux, Inc. From "Encounters with the Archdruid" from *Encounters with the Archdruid* by John McPhee. Copyright © 1971 by John McPhee. This material originally appeared in *The New Yorker.*

[2]See "Mark Twain: The Fairest Picture," Section II.

I thought of Brower in the Sierra Nevada, in the Valley of the Mineral King. To conservationists, the Mineral King had become an Agincourt, a Saratoga, an El Alamein. Walt Disney Productions wanted to string the slopes with lifts and build enough hotels there to draw a million people a year. Mineral King had been mentioned as an excellent setting for the Winter Olympics of 1976, celebrating the two-hundredth anniversary of the birth of the nation. Brower and I went to Mineral King together. My impression was that—all other considerations aside—it was an extraordinarily good site for a skiing resort. A stream ran through the middle of the valley, and if you stood beside it and looked up and around you saw eleven conical peaks, the points of a granite coronet. The steep slopes of these mountains were covered with red fir, juniper, aspen, and foxtail pine. Great rising swaths were treeless and meadowed. Hannes Schneider had called it the best potential ski area in California. So much snow had been there the winter before that avalanches had sheared off many hundreds of trees twenty feet above the ground—the snow was that deep. The avalanches had been so powerful that they had not stopped at the bottom of the valley but had climbed the other side, smashing trees. In the geological history of the Sierra Nevada, Mineral King was an old valley. The Sierra Nevada had been a minor mountain range of about four thousand feet when it began the great upheaval that made it higher than the Rockies. New streams cut through the new uplift and created valleys like the Yosemite, with wide, flat floors and sheer walls. The Mineral King was lifted with the mountains and remained intact, a V-shaped valley—alpine, ancestral—and it caught snow like nothing else in a mountain range that was named for the snow that fell there. Brower had done a ski survey of Mineral King once, long ago, and had said that he favored limited development. He said now that he essentially felt the same way. Sitting under a big cottonwood with his feet in the stream, he pointed out that the valley was, for one thing, not wilderness. A road reached into it. A couple of dozen buildings were there, a sawmill, and corrals belonging to a pack station. Listening to him, a surprised conservationist might have thought that the Antichrist had come to the Mineral King disguised as David Brower. But to the Disney interests Brower would not have seemed like much of an advocate. Looking around at the Mineral King peaks,

David Brower

he decided that although he was for limited development, he was against ski lifts. He said he preferred to see people earn their ski runs by climbing with skins attached to their skis. Moreover, he was against improvement of the existing access road, an incredibly twisting cliff-hanger so narrow and serpentine that a million people trying to use it would grow old before they reached the valley. Brower said Disney Productions should build a hundred-million-dollar tunnel, or fly people in—save the approaching mountains, hang the cost. Told he was being almost poetically impractical, Brower responded that the Disney people were going to change something forever, so they could amortize the changes over a thousand years.

Mineral King, reprinted by permission of Farrar, Straus and Giroux, Inc. From "Encounters with the Archdruid" from *Encounters with the Archdruid* by John McPhee. Copyright © 1971 by John McPhee. This material originally appeared in *The New Yorker.*

William O. Douglas

The River as Plaintiff

Although the Mineral King controversy consumed nearly as much time and court costs as the Hetch Hetchy fight, the two differed in one fundamental way: the proposal to develop Mineral King was defeated.

One unexpected result of the Mineral King debate was the emergence of a new legal tool for preservationists. Law professor Christopher D. Stone had been looking for a case to test his thesis that natural objects should have legal rights just as human beings do—in other words, that natural objects should have "standing."

In 1972 the U.S. Supreme Court reviewed a lower court decision that allowed the U.S. Forest Service to grant a permit to Walt Disney Enterprises to develop Mineral King. Recognizing this as the case he had been looking for, Stone saw to it that an article he had written outlining his position was brought to the attention of Justice William O. Douglas. The Supreme Court upheld the lower court ruling—the defeat of the Disney proposal would come later—but in his dissenting opinion, Justice Douglas, a staunch conservationist in his own right, made liberal use of Stone's ideas, and brought them to national attention.

The critical question of "standing" would be simplified and also put neatly in focus if we fashioned a federal rule that allowed environmental issues to be litigated before federal agencies or federal courts in the name of the inanimate object about to be dispoiled, defaced, or invaded by roads and bulldozers and where injury is the subject of public outrage. Contemporary public concern for protecting nature's ecological equilibrium should lead to the conferral of standing upon environmental objects to sue for their own preservation. . . .

Inanimate objects are sometimes parties in litigation: A ship has a legal personality, a fiction found useful for maritime purposes. The corporation sole—a creature of ecclesiastical law—is an acceptable adversary and large fortunes ride on its cases. The ordinary corporation is a "person" for purposes of the adjudicatory processes, whether it represents proprietary, spiritual, aesthetic, or charitable causes.

So it should be as respects valleys, alpine meadows, rivers, lakes, estuaries, beaches, ridges, groves of trees, swampland, or even air that feels the destructive pressures of modern technology and modern life. The river, for example, is the living symbol of all the life it sustains or nourishes—fish, aquatic insects, water ouzels, otter, fisher, deer, elk, bear, and all other animals, including man, who are dependent on it or who enjoy it for its sight, its sound, or its life. The river as plaintiff speaks for the ecological unit of life that is part of it. Those people who have a meaningful relation to that body of water— whether it be a fisherman, a canoeist, a zoologist, or a logger—must be able to speak for the values which the river represents and which are threatened with destruction.

I do not know Mineral King. I have never seen it nor travelled it, though I have seen articles describing its proposed "development." . . . The Sierra Club in its complaint alleges that "One of the principal purposes of the Sierra Club is to protect and conserve the national resources of the Sierra Nevada Mountains." The District Court held that this uncontested allegation made the Sierra Club "sufficiently aggrieved" to have "standing" to sue on behalf of Mineral King.

Mineral King is doubtless like other wonders of the Sierra Nevada such as Tuolumne Meadows and the John Muir Trail. Those who hike it, fish it, hunt it, camp in it, or frequent it, or visit it merely to sit in solitude and wonderment are legitimate spokesmen for it, whether they may be a few or many. Those who have that intimate relation with the inanimate object about to be injured, polluted, or otherwise despoiled are its legitimate spokesmen.

The Solicitor General, whose views on this subject are in the Appendix to this opinion, takes a wholly different approach. He considers the problem in terms of "government by the Judiciary." With all respect, the problem is to make certain that the inanimate objects, which are the very core of America's beauty, have spokesmen before they are destroyed. It is, of course, true that most of them are under the control of a federal or state agency. The standards given those agencies are usually expressed in terms of the "public interest." Yet "public interest" has so many differing shades of meaning as to be quite meaningless on the environmental front. Congress accordingly has adopted ecological standards in the National Environmental Policy Act of 1969, . . . and guidelines for agency action have been provided by the Council on Environmental Quality of which Russell E. Train is Chairman. . . .

Yet the pressures on agencies for favorable action one way or the other are enormous. The suggestion that Congress can stop action which is undesirable is true in theory; yet even Congress is too remote to give meaningful direction and its machinery is too ponderous to use very often. The federal agencies of which I speak are not venal or corrupt. But they are notoriously under the control of powerful interests who manipulate them through advisory committees, or friendly working relations, or who have that natural affinity with the agency which in time develops between the regulator and the regulated. As early as 1894, Attorney General Olney predicted that regulatory agencies might become "industry-minded," as illustrated by his forecast concerning the Interstate Commerce Commission:

> "The Commission is or can be made of great use to the railroads. It satisfies the public clamor for supervision of the railroads, at the same time that supervision is almost entirely nominal. Moreover, the older the Commission gets to be, the more likely it is to take a business and railroad view of things." M. Josephson, The Politicos 526 (1938).

Years later a court of appeals observed, "the recurring question which has plagued public regulation of industry [is] whether the regulatory agency is unduly oriented toward the interests of the industry it is designed to regulate, rather than the public interest it is supposed to protect."

. . . The Forest Service—one of the federal agencies behind the scheme to despoil Mineral King—has been notorious for its alignment with lumber companies, although its mandate from Congress directs it to consider the various aspects of multiple use in its supervision of the national forests.

The voice of the inanimate object, therefore, should not be stilled. That does not mean that the judiciary takes over the managerial functions from the federal agency. It merely means that before these priceless bits of Americana (such as a valley, an alpine meadow, a river, or a lake) are forever lost or are so transformed as to be reduced to the eventual rubble of our urban environment, the voice of the existing beneficiaries of these environmental wonders should be heard.

Perhaps they will not win. Perhaps the bulldozers of "progress" will plow under all the aesthetic wonders of this beautiful land. That is not the present question. The sole question is, who has standing to be heard?

Those who hike the Appalachian Trail into Sunfish Pond, New Jersey, and camp or sleep there, or run the Allagash in Maine, or climb the Guadalupes in West Texas, or who canoe and portage the Quetico Superior in Minnesota, certainly should have standing to defend those natural wonders before courts or agencies, though they live 3,000 miles away. Those who merely are caught up in environmental news or propaganda and flock to defend these waters or areas may be treated differently. That is why these environmental issues should be tendered by the inanimate object itself. Then there will be assurances that all of the forms of life which it represents will stand before the court—the pileated woodpecker as well as the coyote and bear, the lemmings as well as the trout in the streams. Those inarticulate members of the ecological group cannot speak. But those people who have so frequented the place as to know its values and wonders will be able to speak for the entire ecological community.

Ecology reflects the land ethic; and Aldo Leopold wrote in A Sand County Almanac 204 (1949), "The land ethic simply enlarges the boundaries of the community to include soils, waters, plants, and animals, or collectively, the land."

That, as I see it, is the issue of "standing" in the present case and controversy.

The River as Plaintiff, from Supreme Court of the United States No. 70-34, "Sierra Club v. Rogers C.B. Morton, On Writ of Certiorari to the United States Court of Appeals to the Ninth Circuit," April 19,1972.

Huey D. Johnson

Mono Lake
Doesn't Need to Die

Defeat of the plan to develop Mineral King did not result in an end to the threats facing the Sierra, merely a change of scene. One of the most critical of today's unresolved problems concerns Mono Lake, a million-year-old body of water located near the eastern boundary of Yosemite National Park. Mono Lake is one of the most important bird-breeding grounds and migratory rest stops in North America. Tragically, water diversions from Mono's tributary streams to the city of Los Angeles have caused a dramatic drop in the level of the lake and brought on a series of environmental disasters. The lake's salinity has doubled. Brine-shrimp numbers in the lake have declined sharply, leading to the annual starvation of thousands of birds. Thirty square miles of former lake bottom have been exposed, creating land bridges to once-protected bird-breeding islands in the lake, and raising caustic dust clouds into the mountain air.

California Secretary for Resources Huey D. Johnson testified before a Congressional Subcommittee in May 1982, supporting a proposal to grant National Monument status to Mono Lake. In his remarks, Johnson summed up the conservationist position on Mono Lake.

Mono Lake is a national treasure whose continued survival is threatened by the diversion of four of its five input streams. The real tragedy is that Mono Lake does not need to die. A single decision, a single stroke of the pen by one political jurisdiction could reverse the Lake's fate. The Department of Water and Power of the City of Los Angeles has the opportunity—particularly in this extraordinarily wet year—to halt Mono Lake's slow death. Instead the City's response has been to redouble its lobbying against efforts to protect Mono Lake. If the City had put as much effort into protecting the Lake and its resources as they have into opposing Congressman Shumway's

VIEW OF THE MONO PLAIN FROM THE FOOT OF BLOODY CAÑON.

National Monument legislation, we would not need to be here today.

Mono Lake should be considered an indicator of our interest in survival. The recent history of Mono Lake demonstrates how over-consumption and special interest manipulation can threaten the long-term survival of unique and productive resources that are important to a wide range of species—including our own. The arrogance implicit in the City's position is manifested by its recent assertion that the public trust doctrine—a protection as old as the Magna Carta—is "irrelevant" to the Mono Lake situation. If the alternatives were costly and harsh, the Mono Lake case study would be easier to understand. But the alternatives are reasonable. An extensive inter-agency study four years ago determined that water conservation, reclamation and alternative supplies could make up for a reduction in diversions from Mono Basin sufficient to save the Lake. Mono Lake is a victim of waste and mismanagement.

The Department of Water and Power is the captive of a cornucopian philosophy which assumes that there will always be more. Rather than face the realities of limited resources and turn to modern water conservation practices which would provide reasonable and economic solutions to the City's problems, it steps up its public relations efforts.

The smog in Los Angeles, worse than usual this week, symbolizes the kinds of management problems that large urban areas face. The best solutions to these problems lie in balanced management, not single purpose decision-making. A good water conservation and management program can help the citizens of Los Angeles save water, energy, and money.

Because of the lack of cooperation on the part of the Department of Water and Power, things have reached a political stage. Some Los Angeles citizens have become convinced that institutional arrangements within the City of Los Angeles are themselves a major impediment to change. They are seriously considering a door-to-door petition drive that would overhaul the Department's approach to water and energy management.

As a scenic and recreational resource, Mono Lake has a national importance. If you have visited the Mono Basin, you will know what I am talking about; if you haven't, I would urge you to do so on your next trip to California. Mono Lake is a profound experience. Rimmed on the West by snow-covered granite peaks of Yosemite National Park, and on the east by the high desert and ranges of the Great Basin, Mono Lake offers a special sense of space and geologic transition to the thousands that visit each year. Recogizing its scenic value, John Muir and others sought to have Mono Lake included within Yosemite National Park.

Mono Lake is valuable as a seasonal and nesting habitat for over 70 species of migratory birds and waterfowl. Large proportions of the world's eared grebe and Wilson's phalarope populations stop at Mono Lake. Mono Lake supports the State's second largest inland population of snowy plover, an endangered shorebird. On many late Summer and Fall days, over a million individual birds of various species are present. They don't come for the scenery, but for the extremely productive brine shrimp and brine fly populations. They use Mono Lake as a rest and "refueling" stop en route to South America or other winter homes. For most of these birds, there is no alternative "refueling" area. The Wilson's phalarope, for example, flies directly from Mono Lake to South America—a 5,000 mile nonstop journey. The loss of the Mono Lake brine shrimp populations will mean the loss or drastic reduction in the number of these bird species.

Mono Lake is also valuable as a nesting ground for the California Gull. Mono Lake is the summer habitat for 95 percent of the California Gulls that nest in California, or 20 to 25 percent of the world's population. In 1978, more than 25,000 gulls nested on islands in Mono Lake, taking advantage of predator-free nesting areas and an abundant food supply.

Each of these values is threatened by the continued diversion of Mono Lake's tributary streams at current rates. Diversions have had three devastating impacts on Mono Lake.

First, diversions have reduced the Lake level by almost 50 feet since 1940. This lowering has exposed a broad band of former Lake bed to wind erosion. The fine alkali sediments which were formerly under the Lake are now lifted by the strong winds of the area, posing a health risk to the inhabitants of the area and to visitors.

Second, diversions have reduced nesting habitat by making peninsulas of what were once islands. Negit Island, the largest historical nesting area, supported 17,000 nests in 1978. After it became connected to the mainland in 1979, there has been no successful nesting on Negit. Although gulls have nested on smaller islands, there has been an overall decrease in nesting activity of 20 percent since 1978. Two islands that now provide about one-third of the nesting sites are threatened with loss this year at present rates of diversion.

Third, diversions are fundamentally altering the chemical and temperature characteristics of Mono Lake. Since 1940, the volume of the Lake has been cut in half. Because Mono Lake has no outlet, this has caused a dramatic increase in salinity and alkalinity. These changes stress both the bird species and the brine shrimp populations on which they depend. Last year, the early brine shrimp hatch, the first of two annual hatches at Mono Lake, was less than 10 percent of normal. This was a radical departure from past patterns. Although we may not know for sure until it's too late, the overwhelming likelihood is that salinity and temperature changes caused the poor brine shrimp hatch. Although the second shrimp hatch was near normal, the failure of the first brine shrimp hatch led to the loss of 95 percent of the gull chicks in 1981. This pattern is repeating itself in 1982. Reports from the field indicate that the early brine shrimp hatch is again only 10 percent of normal, and we can expect to lose most of the gull chicks for a second year.

These are warning signs that we should not ignore. Although scientists argue about what is happening at Mono Lake, the range of disagreement appears to be narrowing. Increasingly, observers are applying the phrase "ecological collapse" to the situation at Mono Lake. If this is indeed what we are witnessing, the loss of Mono Lake's value as habitat and as a productive ecosystem will be sudden and it will be irreversible. . . .

The loss of Mono Lake—an incredibly rich and productive ecosystem—would be a tragedy of major dimension. It was John Muir, an early Mono Lake enthusiast, who pointed out that all things in nature are interconnected. We should not casually contemplate the destruction of this resource. We have a responsibility to save Mono Lake—a responsibility to ourselves and our children and grandchildren.

Mono Lake Doesn't Need to Die, from "Mono Lake: The Developing Tragedy" by Huey D. Johnson. Testimony before Subcommitte on Public Lands and National Parks, U.S. House of Representatives, John Seiberling, Chairman, May 18, 1982. Reprinted by permission of Huey D. Johnson.

Arthur Hoppe

A National Parking Lot

In a 1972 Reader's Digest *article, Los Angeles attorney Eric Julber proposed that three or four aerial tramways be constructed to ferry tourists into the High Sierra, so that they could have easy access to the John Muir Trail. More than 100 years had passed since conservationists and developers first clashed over the issue of preservation of the Sierra Nevada, and the two sides obviously remained light years apart.*

Given the pattern of unforeseen developments which characterized that century of dissension, it is probably impossible to predict what the future holds for the Sierra. Nevertheless, the daring Arthur Hoppe, the deliciously incisive columnist for the San Francisco Chronicle, *has thrown caution to the winds and provided us with one possible scenario.*

Yosemite National Parking Lot, August, 2001. The Western Regional Wilderness Preserve, a 3.6-acre site just north of here was dedicated in appropriate ceremonies today.

The Preserve, along with a similar one in Maine, was established by an act of Congress as the successful culmination of a long fight by Ralph Nader, the Sierra Club and other conservation groups.

As the President said in his message read at today's ceremonies, "This act keeps safe for all time unspoiled wilderness areas from Maine to California where generations yet unborn may view our precious national heritage of God-given scenic beauty."

The entire 3.6 acres of the Wilderness Preserve here is surrounded by 12-foot-high electrified fence to keep out timbermen, miners, cattlemen, real estate salesmen, road builders and motel operators.

Visitors, on payment of $1 admission fee, enter through the West Gate and are formed in groups of 20 for guided tours of the whole preserve. The tour lasts an hour.

The first point of interest is the Governor Ronald Reagan Memorial Forest. This towering white pine tree is believed to be more than 70 years old, which would make it the oldest living tree in Western America.

The tour also includes a walk along the Izaak Walton Trout Stream. In keeping with the wilderness concept, the stream is not stocked and therefore contains no fish. However, it has actually been certified by pollution experts to be still safe for swimming. "And to keep it that way," as the guide carefully explains, "no bathing is permitted."

But the high point of the tour for the young ones is Crystal Pure Spring. This spring, which bubbles forth from a mossy cleft in the rocks, is probably the last spot in America where one can drink water just as it comes from the ground.

While the youngsters are impressed by the fact that once all of America's rivers and streams were drinkable, they don't care much for the water. Without chlorine or other chemicals, as one little boy put it, wrinkling his nose, "it sure is tasteless."

In addition, the Preserve offers three authorized camp sites available by reservation. So far, there have been no applicants. The modern camper, of course, vastly prefers the amenities offered by the up-to-date Yosemite National Parking Lot.

The new Yosemite campground here was created following the monumental traffic jam on the valley floor over the July 4th weekend of 1973. Unsnarling it proved impossible. So it was paved over.

This offered an excellent opportunity, however, to construct the very latest in up-to-date campgrounds. It features Astro-Turf, tiled bathrooms, waterfalls (from 9 a.m. to 5 p.m. daily), an ample supply of Presto-Logs for those who like old-fashioned campfires, and the huge "Ol' Fishing Hole" into which 10,000 trout are dumped at 11 a.m. daily for the benefit of an equal number of fishermen.

Naturally, there is a long waiting list for each of the 10-by-12-foot camp sites. And the campground has turned a nice profit every year. By contrast, experts fear the Wilderness Preserve will operate at a loss.

But as the President said in his message today, "No price is too high to pay to show our children and our children's children what America was like before their forefathers tamed the wilderness."